More Adventures of a World-Traveling Scientist

More Adventures of a World-Traveling Scientist

Stanley Randolf, M.Sc.

Tasora

Tasora Books

5120 Cedar Lake Road
Minneapolis, MN 55416
(952) 345-4488
Distributed by Itasca Books

Printed in the U.S.A.

Cover design by Debbie Johnson and John Houlgate
Original cover photo
Section separator design by Irina Zharkova, modified by Debbie Johnson

Publishers Note: These stories are either true chronologically as experienced by the author or expressed as a combination of related events in a different order from what the author experienced.

Disclaimer: Any connection to any person living or deceased is purely coincidental; the names in these stories have been changed.

Library of Congress Cataloging-in-Publication Data

Randolf, Stanley.
More Adventures of a World-Traveling Scientist/Stanley Randolf
Summary: Volume 2 of truth-based adventure tales - Fourteen short stories of adventure spanning the globe. Includes adventures in sports fishing, hunting, hiking, culture-building, native cultures, native beliefs, aliens, travel, murder, healing, and safari-adventures.
ISBN 978-1-934690-97-0 (softcover)
1. Travel - Non-Fiction   2. Adventure – Non-Fiction   3. Sportsmen Adventure – Non-Fiction

Printed in the United States of America

Dear Reader,

What a surprise! My grandkids and their friends enjoyed the journeys and adventures in my first book, *Adventures of a World-Traveling Scientist*. Now, kids of all ages and their parents are enjoying them around the world – they read well out loud! You'll know which stories the kids will like best.

I didn't realize how many stories I missed while writing the first "Adventures" book. It woke me up to a treasure trove of memories I didn't have room to share with you in that book, so here they are! Many of the experiences and hidden secrets revealed are highlighted with easy-to-understand science.

My planned business travel often results in unexpected, daring adventures. You don't need reservations to travel along with me . . . .

Happy Trails into Mysterious Worlds!

Stanley Randolf

Stanley Randolf

Dedication

To my loving wife Phyllis Jean and my many science colleagues and business partners around the world. Without them the experiences, understandings, and perspectives revealed in these stories would not have occurred or, at best, would have been substantially limited.

Table of Contents

Author on Corregidor Island

1

Ghosts of Corregidor
Serious Times in a Place forgotten

$\mathcal{P}$rologue—a brief history:

Corregidor is one of 7,100 islands that comprise the Philippines. For centuries it has guarded the entrance to Manila Bay—the most strategic deep-water bay in the country's vast archipelago. Thirty miles from Manila, the Philippine capital, and only two miles from the infamous Bataan Peninsula, Corregidor's five-square miles look like a tadpole from the air.

Prior to the Spanish-American War of 1898, the island was central to the piracy business in the Sulu Sea; a strategic outpost for thousands of Moro (Moorish) pirates to come and go as they robbed merchant ships—silver, silk, spices, cotton, wax, and young women were priority items to plunder.

Spain ruled the Philippines from 1565 to 1898—a long time for indigenous people to be disparaged and disregarded. The Spanish attempted to unite the various native cultures under one Hispanic doctrine but never succeeded and were ousted by the United States after 1898. Hence, the Philippine archipelago became a U.S Territory. The Philippine Commonwealth was created in 1935 as an interim authority to phase the archipelago into becoming an independent nation.

As a U.S. territory, Corregidor's fortifications were significantly expanded to twenty-three artillery batteries supporting forty-five coastal guns and thirteen batteries with seventy-two anti-aircraft guns.

In addition, a formidable network of bombproof tunnels was built under the island's Malinta Hill that included a one-thousand bed hospital. Military facilities aboveground supported the underground tunnel complex including what would become General Douglas MacArthur's U.S. Army headquarters.

On December 8, 1941, less than 24 hours after attacking Pearl Harbor, the Japanese Imperial Army attacked the Philippines. The move to become an Independent nation would have to wait!

Corregidor Island, December 8, 1941

The Japanese invasion began on the main Philippine island of Luzon. The twelve thousand U.S. military personnel on Corregidor escaped the initial confrontations for three weeks. That grace period ended on December 29, 1941 when the Japanese air force bombed Corregidor continuously for two hours, seriously damaging the above ground infrastructure that supplied the tunnels. Periodic bombing and artillery shelling kept on through January into April of 1942, while the battle on Luzon's Bataan Peninsula, just a few miles away, was raging. This convinced President Franklin Roosevelt to order General MacArthur to leave Corregidor. The only mode of transportation available were small Patrol Torpedo (PT) boats. Thus, MacArthur began a six-hundred-mile escape to the Philippines' southernmost island of Mindanao, in the dark of night on March 12, 1942.

On Bataan, United States and Philippine forces surrendered on April 9, 1942 after suffering over ten thousand casualties—forcing an unimaginable seventy-six thousand prisoners, including twelve thousand American soldiers, into the hands of the Japanese. The seventy-mile Bataan Death March to a barbed wire Prisoner of War camp began immediately.

Horrific atrocities started on day one of the five-day march. No water or food was provided; stragglers and dropouts were either beaten or executed. The first murder witnessed was the beheading of a U.S. Airforce Captain whose crime was having Japanese yen in his pocket. "His head jumped off his shoulders and rolled through the column of marching prisoners," a surviving prisoner had reported. The temperature reached a lethal forty degrees Celsius (104 F) during the march—thousands of American and Filipino men perished.

One day after the U.S. surrender at Bataan, with the Death March underway, the Fourteenth Japanese Imperial Army attacked Corregidor with heavy artillery from the Bataan Peninsula. Many of Corregidor's coastal defense guns were useless; seventy-five mobile Japanese artillery guns brought on ceaseless shelling for twenty-six days coupled with aerial bombardment that, alone, delivered seventeen thousand bombs containing 365 tons of explosives—a degree of hellfire never seen before. Word War II was well underway in the Pacific and the Japanese were winning. Ghosts would soon outnumber the living!

Corregidor Island, April 10, 1942

Eardrum-rupturing explosions are everywhere. Immediately following an explosion, shell fragments—steel rain—crackle like fireworks flying in all directions and slice into sandbags surrounding the men.

"Artillery incoming from Bataan!" The marine lieutenant screams into the radio from Battery Way. A fast, rushing sound, like a race car's tires on hot pavement precedes each explosion.

Colonel Howard grabs the microphone from the corporal in Lateral Tunnel Three. "Lieutenant Johnson, confirm message!" he bellows, recognizing Johnson's voice.

"Yes sir, Colonel. Japanese artillery incoming from Bataan—big guns!"

"It's their two-hundred-forty millimeter guns! The shells are supersonic when they hit from a short distance," the colonel barks. "Their one-hundred-fifty millimeters will be next!" Other alarming radio calls come into army headquarters in the Malinta-Tunnel complex as Corregidor gets pulverized.

"Tell the battery commander to rotate the four, twelve-inch mortar cannons and make ready for firing." Colonel Howard orders the lieutenant. These monster mortars could shoot 670-pound rounds up to eight miles in any direction.

"Copy that!" Johnson shouts into to a suitcase-sized walkie-talkie. It's all artillery against artillery; no invasion—yet. The percussions of exploding 240-mm shells shock every bone in a soldier's body—a feeling like hitting your elbow's crazy bone, only your entire skeleton gets shocked.

"Colonel says shoot them—I'm waiting for coordinates," the lieutenant shouts to the battery commander. Now he can hear the whining sounds of subsonic 150- mm shells flying by, then the fragment-throwing detonations.

Johnson had just earned a bachelor's degree in Mechanical Engineering from the University of California in Los Angeles before joining the marines. He'd worked his way through college as a lifeguard on Venice Beach before Pearl Harbor was attacked.

"Looks like we'll be in this tunnel for a while," a sergeant tells the headquarters staff just as a deafening explosion hits the hill above the bombproof tunnel—lights go out and the reinforced concrete arches and walls quake, jarring two thousand military personnel, including those in the one-thousand-bed underground hospital. Sirens scream.

The shelling is horrendous, day and night. From April 29—Emperor Hirohito's birthday—to daybreak on May 6, the Japanese celebrate by intensifying the shelling to an unimaginable extent: from sixteen thousand heavy rounds per day, to thirty-six hundred rounds in one five-hour period on May 5th—averaging twelve shells per minute.

While constant shelling is destroying Corregidor's defenses, Japanese landing craft are on the way to deliver the final blow. Slowed by strong sea currents in the channel between Corregidor and the Bataan Peninsula, the first eight hundred Japanese soldiers encounter lethal resistance from both the rough sea and the U.S. Marines. Many die.

The Fourth Marine Regiment is dug in near the beach between North Point and Cavalry Point close to the island's tail. The beach is irregular and rocky, not like the smooth, sand beaches on Luzon. Corregidor is not going to be a slam-dunk for the Japanese infantry!

23:30 hours, May 5, 1942

"I can see landing craft and two barges," Lieutenant Kyle Johnson shouts to Sergeant Macalby. They're in separate jeeps positioned in a bunker west of Monkey Point, just south of the Kindley Airstrip. Four marine artillery specialists operate the two 37-mm howitzers set up between the jeeps. These guns are aimed beyond the road, midway between Cavalry Point and North Point on the north shore.

Artillery is both incoming and outgoing; two 155-mm guns in Kyson Battery are firing at the barges while getting blanketed themselves with artillery from Bataan. As soon as a battery fires, the Japanese see its location and return fire. U.S. Army trucks pulling 37-mm howitzers drive by, looking for temporary spots to set up that are not taking fire. It's not possible to keep up with the Japanese shelling—they have more guns.

The lieutenant and sergeant's bunker is eight-hundred yards from the beach. They have been ordered to set up a crossfire with Denver Battery and hit the Japanese from two directions when they move west from the island's tail.

"This could be the day we die, kid." The fifty-year-old sergeant tells the twenty-five-year-old lieutenant. "Why in the hell are you out here when you could be in the tunnel with the colonel's staff?"

"I'm trained to make sure these new 37-mm guns live up to specifications. Don't want to mess with a bunch of paperwork if they don't!" Johnson answers, grinning. The new guns hadn't been fired since arriving from California a month ago. There's a pause in the shelling, the Japanese landings are imminent.

"Stay close to me," the sergeant says with a fatherly grin—"that's an order!"

"Don't fire until you see them coming onto the road!" the sergeant shouts to the four-man artillery crew. "Remember, the Fourth Regiment Marines are dug in at the Points!"

"Kyson's one-fifty-fives are hitting directly into the first barge, it's aground with its ramp down!" Lieutenant Johnson yells. Ocean water rushes onto the eight-hundred Japanese infantry as they stumble off the ramp. The barge sways back and forth in the current.

"The Fourth Regiment Marines are killing them in scores!" the lieutenant watches with binoculars as Japanese soldiers– in tan uniforms that quickly turn red— fall over each other. Heads and arms are flying off bodies. Oil on the beach from ships sunk in the past mixes with blood producing a gruesome emulsion.

"Fire both thirty-sevens!" The sergeant bellows. "Shoot any Japanese the Fourth Regiment missed." The sergeant's battery opens fire with the two new guns. A foot-long cartridge is inserted into the receiver and immediately fires a bullet the size of a beer can, producing a sharp, echoing report. The fragmenting round detonates on impact.

The second barge lands east of North Point. Many of the disembarking troops are killed in the water by other strategically entrenched marines using fifty-caliber machine guns—quite effectively until the Japanese shoot out the searchlights. The enemy spreads out and takes cover—their exploding "knee-mortar" grenades now provide the only illumination.

"Jesus help us," Sergeant Macalby murmurs. "The survivors of the first group are joining the second group! The Japs are killing us with those knee-mortars—using them like shotguns!"

"Somewhere around twelve-hundred Japanese are five-hundred yards northeast of us!" the lieutenant blurts as the 37's report and echo. They keep shooting—one round easily kills three or more enemy at once.

The Japanese divide into two groups, one on each leg of the road's loop as they head directly west for the Denver Battery.

Lieutenant Johnson drops the binoculars; he feels nauseated and tries to hold back vomiting. There is no learning curve; this is it! Bloody war. The sheer number of Japanese would soon overwhelm them as more barges land. He checks his Colt-45 side arm and the three extra clips in his arm band. Each hold eight cartridges. He spits out a mouthful of bitter bile—there's no food in him to vomit. The dry-heaves are dehydrating; he takes a fast drink, emptying his canteen.

01:00 hours May 6, 1942

Sergeant Macalby realizes if they don't move west fast, they'll get trapped behind enemy lines and get slaughtered by the next landing. Denver Battery is strategic; it's located in the middle of the bottom side of the island, between the Tadpole's head and tail end. The road runs past it. To get to the Malinta Tunnel and Topside, (the head of the Tadpole) you must to go by Denver Battery. He checks the 30-caliber machine guns mounted on each jeep.

"Leave the thirty-sevens and get in the jeeps! Now!" the lieutenant yells, back in full form. "There's no time to save them!" He slides a timed dynamite charge down the barrel of each 37-mm gun—in five minutes they'll be scrap metal.

They drive off-road as much as possible, heading west but staying south passing Ordinance Point. This takes them closer to the oncoming Japanese who are about four hundred yards east. The two jeeps rattle and throw dust; the sergeant drives the lead jeep, the lieutenant follows. The marines manning the thirty-caliber machine guns discharge five-hundred rounds per minute at the Japanese. The recoil of this much ammunition shakes the jeeps' frames in discordance with their forward motion—it's a loud, rough ride in the dark.

In a strange quirk that often occurs in war, a marine on a horse-drawn ammo cart hands them several additional belts of thirty-caliber cartridges. It happens fast, like runners passing a baton at the Olympics; nobody stops. A virtuous, critical need is satisfied.

Marines, with help from the army, navy, and Filipino soldiers, are dug-in and firing from the Denver Battery. Rubble and ruins are everywhere from the shelling earlier.

"Fight from the west end, by the water tower," a marine corporal hollers to them. They see the destroyed water tower standing on a slant, leaking water, and drive toward it. The sergeant makes a "V" with two fingers, then points down—the lieutenant understands. Both jeeps turn nose to nose and stop, forming a "V" at a forty-five-degree angle pointing east and providing cover—their machine guns keep firing. Ping. Ping. Ping. Japanese rifle fire hits the steel shield on one of the guns.

The Japanese are now fighting on the east end of the Denver complex mostly with 50-mm grenade launchers (the knee-mortars) that one man can carry and operate. They look like tubular air pumps used for bicycle tires—two feet long with a ten inch barrel, they launch a standard Japanese grenade on an angle or horizontally. Simple and more effective than a hand-thrown grenade.

"Don't kill marines by mistake!" Sergeant Macalby hollers. It's crazy and dark, almost like a poorly acted movie. The Japanese do not appear coordinated, many trip and stumble—but they outnumber the marines.

Zee-ip! A grenade from a knee mortar flies past the lieutenant's jeep before exploding five yards away. Fragments from it hit the marine on the 30-caliber machine gun—he keeps shooting while his arms and face bleed. It's black-dark except when a knee-mortar is launched, which produces a flash—a target to shoot back at. Limited rifle shots come from the Japanese, mostly zee-ips from grenades.

"They're low on ammo," a corporal hiding behind a rebar-protruding concrete slab yells.

"Ammo canisters were probably lost during the rough landings," Macalby surmises. "They'll be fighting with bayonets!"

Why didn't the U.S. Military put a couple of tanks on Corregidor? Two M4 Shermans would be very useful right now, the lieutenant thinks. Even a World War I relic!, this is getting bad! He looks like he's aged ten years since last night. His blue eyes and blonde hair are full of grit and his uniform is stained with motor oil and sweat. A picture of Lynn, his fiancée, pops up in front of him. He blinks repeatedly… she's still there. "I love you!" he says. "I'll love you forever."

01:30 hours May 6, 1942

The Japanese are thick throughout the Denver ruins. The fighting is hand-to-hand. Japanese rifles with bayonets—slicing and stabbing—are killing marines. The marines fire their M1 semiautomatic rifles point blank into the Japanese. More than a few marines are killed by friendly fire! Japanese that still have grenades fire them horizontally into the marines.

Lieutenant Johnson shoots two Japanese soldiers who are about to slice the sergeant in half. He fires eight bullets and kills them—the first two men he ever shot with a Colt-45.

The jeep's door provides shielding while he ducks and ejects the Colt's empty magazine, then quickly inserts another. Nothing beats the 1911 model 45-pistol at close range.

Sergeant Macalby takes a round below his right knee; it fragments and breaks his leg. He stumbles to the ground. Lieutenant Johnson turns and shoots the enemy soldier who shot the sergeant. There's no time to be afraid, only to react.

"Get under the jeep!" the lieutenant barks to sergeant Macalby who's trying to stand up. The sergeant shakes his head no—and reaches for his Browning Automatic Rifle (BAR).

"That's an order!" the lieutenant shouts. The sergeant nods, surprised, then crawls fast to get under the jeep. Kyle Johnson, unflappable, slides his Colt-45 and two extra magazines to the sergeant, then picks up the BAR, his blue eyes glazed but determined, and starts firing at the enemy . . .

04:30 hours May 6, 1942

Four hundred yards west of the Denver ruins, after holding back the Japanese for three hours, the surviving marines and regulars are reinforced with five-hundred marines, the last of the last, arriving from Topside—the head of the island. But due to Japanese sniper fire and another landing of over eight-hundred troops, the marines are forced to regroup near the Malinta Tunnel—and dig in!

The conditions in the tunnel are hellish: no power, no fresh air, no sanitation, very limited food and water. In the one-thousand-bed hospital, surgeons operate in handheld flashlight beams. Blood, urine, and excrement cover the floors. In the corridors and lateral tunnels that branch off the main tunnel, thousands of soldiers and local civilians desperately wait for what fate will bring forth . . .

Outside the main entrance a local Filipino man brings sandwiches out to the dug in marines. "Fresh horse meat from the cavalry! Killed in yesterday's shelling." the man declares, surmising they hadn't eaten all day. The horse cart delivering C-rations had met up with a 240-mm shell.

"Thanks, Marcus!" Sergeant Macalby, his left leg splinted and bandaged, knows the man.

10:30 a.m. May 6, 1942

The marines entrenched outside the tunnel are ready to make a last stand. "The Alamo of the Pacific," they nervously jive with each other.

But there is a new sound now, and a strange quiet comes over them except for this sound, heard for the first time on Corregidor . . .

Tanks! Japanese tanks, coming with the last landing. They arrive pointing their long guns into the entrance of the Malinta Tunnel, ready to fire. With eleven-thousand lives at stake, all hope lost, and not a believer in suicide, General Jonathan Wainwright surrenders.

But, it's not over. A grim future awaits most of them, deadlier and even more horrific: they are about to become victims of that part of humanity that is incontrovertibly evil. The Japanese do not adhere to the Geneva Convention! Anyone who surrenders is a "coward" and "deserves" a plethora of inhumane treatments—POW camps await them.

Corregidor Island, May 1989

There it was in front of me, the Rock's Malinta Tunnel. Built in the 1930s through solid rock by the U.S. Army—a bombproof tunnel complex. I remember my Uncle Stan, my namesake, recounting many of Corregidor's chilling battle stories —stories of horror and heroism that had played out before he arrived in September of 1945, after the war.

But now, Corregidor's stories are for the ages and, of course, the tourists. I was in the Philippines on business and decided a visit to Corregidor would be a good way to spend a Sunday. It's a ninety-minute boat ride from Manila to Corregidor Island.

"Hey, Number One American, do you buy something?" a young Filipino boy asks.

"Maybe. Tell me your name."

"My name is Benjamin—Benjie."

"What are you selling, Benjie?"

Excited now, he opens the cigar box he's carrying. "Authentic G.I. souvenirs!" He says and points to various objects in the box: "These are shell casings from fifty-caliber machine guns; these are buttons from G.I. uniforms. Here are two Japanese dog tags."

I look them over; I can tell they're authentic. "Where did you find these?"

"All around here!" He swings his arm in a wide arc. I'm not surprised by his clear English. Children are taught English as a second language in the Philippines, starting in the elementary grades.

I pick out several G.I. buttons. "How much?" I ask him.

"I think . . . two U.S. dollars for you," he tells me with an appraising look.

"Okay, I agree, it's a fair price for history's sake." I give him a five-dollar bill. He fumbles through his pockets looking for change. I'm already planning my strategy . . .

"I have only one U.S. dollar but can also pay you two Australia dollars. Is that okay?" he asks, hopefully.

"That's not okay," I say. He looks down at his feet, frowning.

"I want to buy something else from you, Mr. Benjamin." Instantly his smile returns, and he reopens the cigar box. His eyes, hair and skin are medium brown; yellow shorts, a Pluto tee shirt, and flip-flops complete the boy's appearance. He looks more Latino than Asian—common in the Philippines given their 333-years under Spanish rule.

I see he's confused; but seems excited too. I shake his hand and introduce myself. Then, pointing to tour groups moving around in tramvias, I tell him I don't like organized tours.

He doesn't need any more inducement. "For three dollars I'll give you special tour," he says excitedly.

"Let's go, 'Pluto.' Do a good job and you'll also earn a nice tip!" Benjamin and I are at the Malinta Tunnel in an area called the Middleside of the island which separates the head, or Topside, from the Bottomside—finally ending at the Tail End. The four-mile long "Tadpole" slants southwest with its head looking out to the South China Sea.

Topside and Middleside were centers of activity for twelve thousand military personnel before they were shelled and bombed into oblivion in April and May of 1942. All of it was destroyed, literally, except for the Malinta Tunnel.

Benjie's in charge now; I'm just following him (running). I've done this in many places around the world, it's always exciting to find smart kids who can show you around.

The largest decimated structure, the Mile-Long Barracks, stands in front of us. A concrete skeleton from the past in the company of other skeletons: a haunted hospital, a movie theatre (projection wall intact), schoolhouses, officer's quarters, service club, other barracks, and a PX. Nothing has been done to them since May of 1942; no repairs, no remodeling, no windows replaced. They are blown apart, mind-captivating war remembrances. I remember my uncle Stan explaining his shock when he first saw these ruins, explaining: "the blood stains were still fresh!"

"Only monkeys live in them now," Benjie mentions. We could see several Asian tourists feeding peanuts to Philippine ungguys (macaques).

Benjie was excited to take me behind the destroyed barracks to show me where he finds the best military buttons. "Buttons sell best—tourists like 'em," he asserts.

It's a hot day in May, like it must have been in 1942. I was thankful Uncle Stan got here when he did, after the fight, not during!

More ruins are everywhere; tropical vines and epiphytes encroach on them producing eerie effects. The Topside hospital's remains are creepy. Built in the shape of a cross, many rooms have walls intact and, except for the roofless third floor, have ceilings that create haunting darkness. Many believe they're home to hundreds of soldier-spirits who never saw their twenty-first birthday. No one is here when we arrive. I'm impressed by the stark, untouched authenticity.

"Good place. Tourist tramvias are gone," Benji declares as we walk up a broken concrete staircase to the second floor. "Look at the pink floors in this room—maybe old blood stains?"

"I don't think it's blood. After forty-nine years it would have turned brown and washed away. It might be a pink mineral called feldspar."

"Most tourists don't explain anything," Benjie says, smiling at me with his perfectly white teeth. "Feldspar," he repeats.

"Benji, this is one strong building. Rebar is still holding the concrete walls in place, keeping them surprisingly plumb. The hospital appears to have stronger construction than the Mile-Long Barracks."

"Really strong! Because those barracks could survive typhoons!" Benji claims.

"That's right, but even with some meat left on its bones, it's a stretch not to call this hospital a skeleton." I could see a tree growing through one of the walls.

We keep walking through rooms. "What's this?" I had to pull out my small flashlight to read the graffiti on the wall. Names of Philippine soldiers were clearly printed under a skull and bones. In another room, Muslim soldiers were listed under the date January 3, 1968—"the Jabidah Massacre."

"It's about the Moro problem in Mindanao; Muslim rebels fighting Filipino army—there was killing here," Benjie tries to explain. "My father can explain better."

It made me recall a political science lecture at the University of Wisconsin where two professors were debating whether the infamous Philippine President, Ferdinand Marcos, started it or was framed and became the victim of it. A third professor who had claimed the whole thing was a myth didn't show up. Their conclusion was: "It's an unsolved mystery. Only ghosts know the truth."

I stare at the names—victims of a small war twenty-three years after a big war. I remember the professor who supported the theory that Marcos ordered the training of Muslim soldiers—special forces— and sent them to Sabah, part of Malaysia on the Island of Borneo, to raise hell so he could come in, calm things down, and annex it. That professor was the best debater. The other professor argued it was the Muslims (Moro people) who wanted to take complete control of Mindanao, so they set Marcos up with the Sabah story to gain popular support.

Going further I could see more names, Muslim names, probably from the islands of Sulu or Tawi-Tawi. "A. AKBAR" (God is Greatest) was written in capital letters above the names who were, presumably, the victims of the Jabidah Massacre.

We hear shuffling feet and women's voices outside the room—then four Muslim women come in. They are as surprised to see us as we are to see them. This broken hospital is not on most organized tours. My flashlight is off when they come in, so the only light is from the doorway.

"Kamusta," Benjamin greets them in Filipino. Only one of the four responds with a brief wave, the other three go over to the names on the wall which are hard to see in the low light. So, I turn the flashlight on for them. Immediately, they all cover their eyes with their hands; I quickly turn the flashlight off.

"Bukun!" one of them shouts pointing at the flashlight. I knew it meant No.

"Tabiya. Lumabay pa ako," Benjamin tells them in Tausug as we leave. Those women had to be roasting in those burkas—it was at least 37 Celsius (98.6 F) and humid. Enough to put anyone on edge.

"Excuse us, we're just passing by," I tell them, hopefully supporting whatever Benji said.

"Strange to see them without a man along!" I say, when out of the room.

"Maybe the ghosts of the men killed in this room are with the women." Benji whispers. A deep thought coming from a twelve-year-old!

We continue exploring the old hospital and go into one of the larger rooms on the first floor. From what I had read, this is where the wounded were triaged during World War II. Those unlikely to survive surgery were put last in line. Nurses would give them shots of morphine, then dispose of the syringes in waste drums filled with arms and legs and Lysol. Nurses interviewed after the war said the odor of decaying flesh mixed with the phenolic disinfectant was overwhelming.

We're in a big, dark room. Several bats flew out when we entered. I should have packed a larger flashlight but the small Mag-light is better than nothing.

"Be careful walking; don't trip!" Benjie advises. There is debris on the floor, old insulation that had fallen off the ceiling and scattered metal parts from a bent and rusted gurney. How many GIs were brought in on it? How many died on it? I wondered.

Benjie moves the crumpled gurney out from the wall and scares out a gray snake that slithers away.

"It's not poisonous," he assures me.

"There are thirty species of venomous snakes on the island," I remind him, having to trust his judgement.

"I saw a pink Cobra here once—over there." He points across the room. "He didn't coil so I left him alone."

"Good decision!"

"You can hear ghosts talking at night in here," Benjie says. "They whisper."

"Really? What do they say?"

"They're not happy they were killed so young."

"Can you have a conversation with them?"

"Not with all of them; many just keep repeating the same things."

"Give me an example." This is right up my alley; I'm very curious!

"One keeps saying, 'my arms are gone; my arms are gone.' Another whispers, 'I'm dead; I'm dead,' over and over. Another pleads, 'I'm lost. Where am I?'"

"Those are not the sounds of conscious souls but are random energy patterns (REPs) that sometimes separate from an individual's consciousness after a violent death—that's according to students of the paranormal and a Stanford University physicist friend of mine."

"Yeh, I think I understand; strange science stuff." Benji acknowledges.

"How many ghosts can you actually have a conversation with?" I ask him.

"Not many, only two right now. One is a young marine lieutenant who died in the war."

"How did he die?"

"He only remembers he died fast. He thinks his body exploded."

"He sounds like a real ghost—a complete soul that has crossed over but is still around for some reason. What does he say?" I ask Benjie. Part of me can't believe I'm having this conversation with a twelve year-old.

"He wants me to tell his mother he's okay—she lives in Los Angeles. My father has tried to find her, but he can't. And, he also tells about a girlfriend he planned to marry and how much he loves her."

"Does the lieutenant know the war ended almost fifty years ago?"

"I don't know. I don't think time changes where he is."

Hmm, that agrees with what my physicist friend calls simultaneity. "Anything more from the lieutenant?"

"He says his soul is strong; his mission is to help other dead solders find their way. Help them find the light!"

"Do they all eventually find it?"

"I think so. It's easy for some but difficult for others. The lieutenant says it can be as bright as a thousand suns or as dim as the spark from a firefly miles away."

"And everyone needs to find it—and go to it—to get out of the dark!" I say.

"Yes, Mr. Stan. The lieutenant says that too."

"What about the second ghost you converse with?"

"He's mad that he hasn't seen God yet. He's a Muslim soldier who's alone with nobody around—just darkness. The lieutenant is trying to help him."

"Do you come here alone?"

"Mostly. My father comes sometimes."

"How do you get these ghosts to start talking?"

"I don't do anything. Nights with thunder and lightning are best. I just come and sit here and wait. It usually starts with the lieutenant asking me if I'm okay."

"How does his voice sound?"

"Like he has a bad cold and is talking into a paper bag. He was hard to understand at first, but I'm used to him now." I shine the flashlight at Benjie. He shrugs his shoulders and stares at me with his big brown eyes. "God can be hard to find," he says matter-of-factly.

Suddenly, something tells me we need to move on, that we're at a unique juncture. It's my soul voice. I think Benji senses this too . . .

"Let's go see some big guns!" he suggests.

"Good Idea!"

"You're the trail boss," I tell him.

On the way to several artillery batteries we stop and buy lemonade from a small stand organized by two young Filipino girls.

"Hi, Benjamin," they say to him with not-so-shy smiles.

"Hi," he responds. "They're in my class at school." We walk on—a twelve-year-old boy doesn't need to converse very long with girls his age. Saying "Hi" is adequate.

The first gun battery we come to is called Battery Way. It houses four, twelve-inch, green-painted, mortar cannons—each could fire, in any direction, a 670-pound round over eight miles. A young Japanese couple is studying one of them. The boy has his head in the bore of the gun while the girl sits cowboy style on the barrel photographing him. It was interesting to see this; in fact, from what I'd seen so far, there were more Japanese tourists than Americans. I wonder what uncle Stan would think if he were here?

Then Benjamin takes me to see more guns. The biggest of all are the M1895 Coastal Defense Guns: 11.24 meters long, twelve-inch bore (305mm), muzzle velocity 2,250 feet per second, 16.8-mile range— there are eight of them Topside on Corregidor! Crockett, Cheney, Hern, Wheeler Point, and Smith batteries all had M1895s—too bad the Japanese didn't attack from the open sea!

It doesn't take long for me to get "gunned-out." I look on my map to see where we are. "Right here!" Benjie points, reaching over my arm.

"Do you live on Corregidor?" I ask him as we move south on Topside past the ruins of the Officers Club and a long line of deceased barracks that surround the rebuilt Spanish Lighthouse. I can see a man driving a tractor, mowing grass.

"Yes, I live with my father and older sister—not far from here. Do you want to meet my father?"

"Absolutely!"

"He's mowing the lawn around the lighthouse. Look, you can see him. Follow me!" This means we will be running again. "Good exercise!" I shout, sweating profusely.

The Spanish Lighthouse is starkly juxtaposed to the ruins of the barracks nearby. The original was built in 1836, destroyed during World War II, then rebuilt in the 1950s using some of the original stones. The red and white, sixty-foot tower can shine its beacon thirty miles across the South China Sea.

17

"Father, you can meet Mr. Stan!" The boy says excitedly. Benjamin introduces me to his father, Mr. Marcus Mendoza. "He bought buttons from me and now I'm taking him on a tour—he's a scientist."

"Good afternoon Stan, it's a fine pleasure to meet you!" the elderly man says shaking my hand. "You have met my twelve-year-old—I call him Energy Boy!"

I laughed. "Good nickname for him, we run everywhere on his tour."

Marcus laughed. "That's Benji! I'd be honored to have a chat with you. I'll be done mowing in twenty minutes. Can you wait?"

"Sure! Meanwhile, I'll keep an eye on Energy Boy." I'm hoping Marcus has a high tolerance for tropical sweat, I'm drenched in it.

"My father was a cook in the Malinta Tunnel," Benji remarks. "When the food ran out he made sandwiches from dead horses. The war killed horses too."

"That's very interesting! I'm looking forward to talking with him. Are you hot and sweating like me?"

"Not so much, but there's a lawn sprinkler over there; see it? Let's run through it!" Benji insists.

"Great idea, but let's walk."

The sprinkler's cool water is delightful, at least fifteen degrees cooler than the air which is still thirty-seven degrees. Punctuating the cool is the sweet petrichor of fresh cut grass. A feeling of joy comes over me for some moments, but then my mind tunes again to the gruesome carnage that occurred here five decades ago. How could my mind hold such opposing thoughts at the same time? I wonder.

"Let's climb up the lighthouse and look out," Benji exclaims. I can see Marcus still has some grass to cut. Energy Boy, of course, gets to the top ahead of me. The mild breeze coming off the ocean feels good on my wet shorts and tee shirt.

Postscript:

For the first part of the story, I researched published testimonies from both American and Filipino soldiers who had been on Corregidor during April and May in 1942, then used them to compose the war descriptions. FYI: the island was retaken by the U.S. Military in April 1945.

The second part of the story (Benji and I) is true to the word except for people's names. I've been to Pearl Harbor, Guam, Northern Australia, China, Singapore, Taiwan, Korea, Thailand, Malaysia, Japan, and other Asian World War II memorial sites. Far and away, Corregidor moved me the most!

*Most of the numerical data regarding the war was taken from Wikipedia but has been published by many separate sources.

Meet Sobo

2

The Boy and the Elephant
An African Friendship

Prologue:

More than a million Maasai live in Kenya and Tanzania. They're exemplified by tall, slender natives dressed in red shukas and equipped with walking sticks. They are the nomadic "cattle people" of East Africa whose extraordinary culture has survived in the modern world. Most live in circular villages (manyattas) in primitive houses made of mud, wood and elephant dung; but some live a more modern lifestyle away from the manyattas. Whether primitive or modern, I have observed that they continue to maintain family ties, respecting and valuing each other.

Maasai have remarkable respect for elephants, recognizing their intelligence and spirituality. It's an intricate relationship. Some of the elephants understand Maa, the Maasai language, and often unspoken thoughts! There are many elephant stories in the lore of the Maasai. I had a most compelling experience listening to some of them one rainy night in Tanzania while sitting in a kudu blind with a Maasai guide—particularly the following story.

Tanzania, May 1979

After twenty-three months in the womb, he was ready to be born. It was 2:00 a.m. on a moonless night when he arrived—a healthy baby, three-feet tall weighing two-hundred-forty pounds. His sisters, aunts, and cousins witnessed his birth under an acacia tree—helping his mother, the matriarch, with obligatory sniffing and licking before she pulled him close.

It took him four hours to learn how to stand and then only a few minutes to find his mother's milk supply. By sunrise, still surrounded by protective relatives, he was able to march next to his mother who kept him moving with gentle nudges—reinforcing her touching with low-frequency grunts. "Stay close," was her message to him. Adult elephants were not hunted by lions, but their babies were.

The youngster nursed for two years, then stayed with his mother's herd for another ten years before leaving to roam the bush and savannas alone. In those first years away, he would revisit the herd often and was always welcomed by his mother. She was his pillar of strength and wisdom.

The day he left was bright and clear on the savannah, and as the herd moved on, he crossed a muddy road going in the opposite direction. A simple sign on the dirt road that led to Serengeti National Park and its expansive wildness, bore the inscription: "As it was in the beginning."

Twenty-five years later, Tanzania, May 2004

The boy rolled a watermelon down the hill and followed it; the hill was long but not steep, so it rolled slowly. He used the butt end of his spear to control it when necessary. When the slope went flat, and the grass became green, he picked the melon up and carried it.

The forest came before the lake and at its edge several large boulders sprawled out next to a baobab tree just before the acacias thickened. This massive tree, three-thousand-years young, resonated wisdom from the plant kingdom. The boy knew this.

He sat down next to the ageless tree with the watermelon—an outstandingly large watermelon that his uncle had bought in Arusha.

It was ripe, emanating that magic aroma only a watermelon can create. He knew he'd arrived early at the tree and he made himself comfortable while keeping his spear close.

The boy's name, Leboo, meant "born in the bush" in Maa. He was delivered by his mother when she was out milking cattle. Her labor pains came fast—later, she would claim he wiggled his way out while she knelt in high grass. Now, at age fifteen, he was almost six feet tall. He didn't paint his face and arms like the tribal warriors did and was not fond of jump-dancing. Leboo was atypical for a Maasai boy. He preferred to be alone in the bush whenever he could and was teaching himself to communicate with animals telepathically—he called it "thought-talking." Elephants were particularly receptive.

I hope Enkai (god of the Maasai) will keep the fisi (hyenas) away, he thought as he sat by the tree. He knew they ate everything: dead animals, dung beetles, lion excrement, vomit, and each other—then laughed about it. The only animals he hated were the fisi.

Leboo remembered a time in the bush with his uncle Sironka ("the pure one") when they came upon an elephant carcass left by poachers, mutilated and putrid, but its belly was moving! Sironka, who had left the tribe to become a park ranger, knew what this meant.

"Step back, boy," his uncle had commanded.

"How can it still be alive?" the boy recalled asking this naive question.

"The elephant is dead! Get behind me!" Sironka shouted. With its tusks sawed off and taken away, it was certainly dead, but its stomach was expanding and contracting within a massive envelope of thick hide. Leboo would never forget the cadaverous stench coming from the huge bull elephant. He remembered strange noises coming from inside the dead elephant—wild, manic cackling and squabbling sounds—and the look of fear on his uncle's face.

The boy could still picture Sironka raising his rungu club—a wooden club with a long handle and a bulbous head—just as the animal appeared; the ugliest, blood covered, wretched, spotted fisi the boy had ever seen. The animal whooped and youped and laughed hysterically when it saw them, then coughed and growled.

"Don't run! Get down—behind me!" The boy would never forget his uncle's intensity at that moment.

Teeth dripping with putrefied elephant blood, the ferocious fisi, snarling and growling, lunged at Leboo's uncle. In a blur came the muffled thud of a fast-moving hardwood object connecting with flesh and bone—then a second thud. His uncle's rungu club had destroyed the animal's head! Sironka grabbed the boy and backed away from the dead fisi.

A few moments of silence passed as they kept backing away. That was when two more blood-soaked hyenas appeared.

Moving around the baobab tree to stay in the shade, Leboo kept his recollection going. With these clear memories from four years earlier, he closed his eyes when the elephant came into focus in his mind.

The bull elephant that had saved them from the other two hyenas was sent by Enkai. At least that was what he had concluded while lying flat on the ground behind his uncle. It was astonishing to see the elephant impale both hyenas on its mammoth tusks. It had to be god-sent—appearing exactly at the right time!

The two fisi ran straight at the elephant's head, their jaws snapping. And then, with perfect timing, the monster pachyderm powerfully jerked his head high—impaling both. The devil creatures made piercingly high-pitched screams, squirming and clawing at each other while being impaled—then vomiting and defecating as they died.

Leboo remembered all of it as he dozed comfortably in the shade cast by the baobab.

A requirement for a boy growing up in a Massai village was to learn the many dangers inherent to living in East Africa and understand the defenses required to protect the tribe from them. An unknown but significant number of Maasai women and children were killed each year by lions at night; their mud houses could be penetrated by hungry lions. Hyenas would often follow the lions as they dragged a victim away from the village, competing with each other for disregarded scraps of human flesh.

Warriors, men between sixteen and twenty-five years old, were the tribe's main defense. As boys, they trained to hunt lions with spears and clubs; older brothers helped train younger brothers. They slept with their weapons.

Leboo had three brothers, plus five half-brothers from his father's other wives; the Maasai were polygamous. He knew he had just one more year as a boy, then he'd become a man, a warrior, who would be taken on a lion hunt. It bothered him to think about that obligation.

Leboo woke when the earth had relocated the sun to its mid-morning position. It was the right time. He touched his spear confirming it was still by his side. Then scratched his head, still not fully awake—it was common for him to awaken slowly from a deep nap. A common characteristic of fifteen-year-old boys.

"When you sleep in the bush, always be close to a tree that's easy to climb," his brother Koinet ("the tall one") frequently instructed. Maasai warriors often slept out in the open when away from their villages.

The boy knew fisi couldn't climb trees, but leopards and even lions could. Koinet was always short on detail with his instructions. He should have added that it was necessary to develop the skill to climb high in a tree, well into the thin branches where big cats couldn't go!

Leboo then remembered something more about the fisi that he hated to admit, something his uncle had stressed: "Despicable scavengers like fisi help realign the disorder in nature, clean up the dead, and reduce entropy." His uncle got smart during ranger training. So, here were two opposing thoughts in Leboo's head—hating versus helping.

It was time to whistle for Sobo.

Leboo climbed the baobab tree to the first branch, stood up, and whistled loudly through his teeth, changing the pitch several times. It was a sound his friend Sobo could recognize from several miles away. He repeated whistling at the different frequencies. After five minutes, he switched to his "thought-talking" technique. His uncle, Sironka was aware of what Leboo was learning about telepathic communication with animals. He himself had been successful doing it with a troop of baboons, but they could read his mind better than he could read theirs. It was a work in progress for Sironka.

"Sobo, I'm here by the baobab tree." Silently Leboo thought the words first, then stared at the baobab tree and sent out a mental picture of it, blinking his eyes rapidly like a camera shutter in multiple-frame mode. He kept staring at the tree. His uncle had told him it was important to not think about anything else when sending an image, only how it looked. All baobabs were huge, and each one was unique—this one had some branches tangled in an unusual knot coming off the main trunk. He kept sending the mental picture a few minutes more.

Success came quickly. Sobo, the boy's name for the elephant, responded from within the forest with loud, multi-frequency trumpeting. When he arrived at the baobab tree, dwarfing it, he stood up on his two back feet and greeted Leboo as if performing at a circus, then lifted him onto his back with his trunk. Sobo knew the boy was on safely when he could feel his big ears being grabbed as handles. This was the elephant that had saved Leboo and his uncle from the hyenas.

"Jambo (hello), Sobo. I'm very excited to be riding you again!" The boy exclaimed, patting him hard on the head so he could feel it. The magnificent bush elephant was twelve feet tall and weighed eleven tons! Leboo had to spread his legs wide to fit into the concave depression in the elephant's back. Then, trunk high and trumpeting, Sobo circled the baobab tree with the boy on his back. It was an astonishing sight!

"Let's go to Lake Manyara and see your family." The elephant understood every word. "But not yet, I have a surprise for you!" The elephant stopped next to the tree allowing Leboo to climb onto a branch, then down to the ground. Leboo checked his spear to be sure it was hidden well, then bent down next to the tree's sprawling roots and picked up the watermelon. Seeing it excited the elephant—he could catch its aroma. He blinked his eyes and snorted, then gently encircled Leboo with his trunk, an elephant kiss.

Sobo loved watermelon. The last time they were together, the boy had brought him a sack of fresh maize—unpeeled cobs—which he loved almost as much! On a normal day, Sobo ate six-hundred pounds of grasses, leaves, and bark, and chased them down with fifty-gallons of water. Sweet acacia leaves were his favorite, but nothing in the world could beat a watermelon.

I brought it for you, I know you love them! Eat it now for energy—for our trip to Lake Manyara. Leboo thought the words in his head; he did not say them out loud. But his thoughts were loud, he shouted them in his head! Sobo's huge ears perked; the volume of Leboo's thoughts surprised him. He understood! Then he lifted the watermelon with his trunk, enervated by its aroma, and bit it in half. Its juice exploded in his mouth and covered his tongue. He ate the entire watermelon in two bites.

The boy and the elephant set out for Lake Manyara. Nothing but man would assault an elephant the size of Sobo, not even a sixteen-foot crocodile or a two-ton hippopotamus. Leboo could ride Sobo safely through wild Africa; just keep man away. He settled into the rhythm of the bounce produced by Sobo's eight-foot strides and sang him a song in Maa as they marched along the ecotone between forest and savannah through carpets of purple Ipomoea flowers. It was a fine day to ride an elephant.

When wild mango and sycamore fig trees appeared intermixed with yellow acacias and whistling thorn trees, Sobo turned into the forest. Leboo knew to watch for thorny branches—he was twelve feet off the ground in a forest that was prolific with thorns!

Sobo preferred to eat taller acacia trees with big leaves, providing there were no ant swarms on them! He could eat through thorns and twigs to get to the sweet leaves, but ants were a game changer; they would crawl up his trunk and bite into sensitive nerve-rich tissues! Since ants were hard for the elephant to see before chomping into a branch, Leboo spotted them for Sobo. On the way to Lake Manyara and his family herd, Sobo would need a periodic hundred-pound snack. Sironka had told Leboo to look for the Acacia mellifera tree—a favorite for elephants that was usually ant-free.

Leboo began a thought conversation with Sobo; he visualized his uncle Sironka and blinked his eyes fast. Sobo responded with low frequency grunts that signaled he liked Sironka. The grunts were below 12-Hertz (vibrations-per-second)—too low for humans to hear. But Leboo could hear them loud and clear in his head; they were like Morse code. This made him think about all the poaching investigations his uncle was involved with—something that worried him!

Sobo's tusks were worth big money! Poachers killed thousands of elephants for their ivory tusks each year. Poaching was a serious problem in Tanzania and throughout Sub-Saharan Africa. Expansive national parks were understaffed with rangers and were popular destinations for poachers because of their high game densities.

Sironka lived in Arusha and worked for the Tanzanian park service; he had left the Maasai village when he was Leboo's age and learned Swahili and English, which allowed him to westernize and advance himself. He would visit the village and often go into the bush with Leboo and talk with him about doing the same thing—becoming a ranger. It was an open question for Leboo. He could visualize being a ranger and joining the fight against poaching, he needed to learn more from his uncle—like how to speak English and work with different personalities. But not yet; this was the time to enjoy being with his best friend while he was still a boy.

The elephant and the boy came into Lake Manyara from the high hills above the lake. When the view opened, looking back in the distance to the southeast, they could see the wide, white, flat top of Africa's highest mountain.

"Kilimanjaro always has snow, Sobo." Leboo pointed back. The elephant had learned it was high and cold from older elephants that had walked in the frozen white, but he had never been to it.

When they looked straight ahead, views of Eden-green mountains behind an expanse of yellow-flowered savannah provided contrast for the "shine of Lake Manyara," as Ernest Hemingway put it in his book The Green Hills of Africa. From this distance, large grazing animals like zebra and wildebeest looked like brown and black flies on an immense yellow carpet, and the elephants, doubled for mice. From Lake Manyara north to the Ngorongoro Crater and northwest to the Serengeti plains was, arguably, the most stunningly scenic and biodiverse region on the African continent.

The boy and the elephant crossed a couple of roads leading to safari camps, which made Leboo nervous. Sobo understood this and quickly found trails through the forest that didn't compromise their secret friendship. Finding the widest spacing between trees was a challenging task for an eleven-ton bull elephant. Leboo, sitting up, legs spread wide, was able to hold onto creases in Sobo's hide. This worked fine at a slow pace; leaning forward and ear-holding was necessary if they moved fast. From where they were on the south end of the lake, it was a three-hour elephant walk to Sobo's family herd.

Leboo could feel the elephant's energy and appreciate the many pounds of grass and leaves it took to provide enough calories for Sobo to move them a kilometer. There was a different rhythm to the elephant's footsteps when the trail got rocky, requiring Leboo to rock and roll in the groove between Sobo's head and upper back. African bush elephants have concave backs while Asian elephants are convex. Though much larger and impossible to straddle, the African elephant was easier to ride bareback, at least for a tall, strapping fifteen-year-old.

The lake covered over two-hundred square kilometers, and on their way to Sobo's family herd, a zoological encyclopedia of African wildlife unfolded. From their distance and elevation, the giraffes along the lake shore looked like elephant eyelashes—tall, thin and black in the shadows. Beyond them in the lake were three million flamingoes. Mostly dominated by the pink, Lesser variety, a pastel carmine blur. Their fulltime occupation was to feed on algae that thrived on flamingo excrement. A perfect cycle.

Above the giraffes and flamingoes, squadrons of white pelicans glided over the lake's thermals. And farther beyond, but before

Sobo's elephant herd, a sizable tonnage of Cape buffalo, hippopotamus, and black rhinoceros roamed free. Had his uncle not previously explained the uniqueness of this diversity, Leboo would still be thinking that all of Africa was this way.

The trail got steeper and the forest thickened as they approached the flats and temporarily lost view of the lake. Sobo stopped at a freshwater stream and took a long drink, probably twenty gallons. Leboo slid down his trunk, kneeled, and took a somewhat smaller drink—the water was cool and clean-tasting. Lake Manyara was an alkaline, soda lake encircled by a beach of white dust—sodium carbonate. It was drinkable for animals but bitter tasting—and inoculated daily with however much fecal matter three million flamingoes produced. Sobo had grown up drinking it, his digestive tract was thick-walled and resistant, but he had grown fond of drinking cleaner water from highland streams after he left the herd. And he knew his human friend, back in the saddle now, had to drink clear stream water.

"Thank you, Sobo, for finding the Good water! Leboo thought the words, turning the volume down somewhat. He thought them with less force. Sobo appeared to nod his head and made several subtle grunts while he kept walking. Leboo realized the elephant had just said: *You're welcome.*

It was getting dark when they approached the elephant herd. To their surprise they could see a government Land Rover parked close by. Sobo was alarmed and snorted loudly with his trunk up, searching for odors. Fresh elephant dung mixed with cool air coming off the hills was not strange; the smell of two park rangers and diesel fuel was.

"It's okay, Sobo, the rangers won't harm you!" Leboo said out loud. Sobo stammered some low volume groans. The boy could see two men dressed in green-camouflage ranger uniforms.

"My uncle is one of the rangers!" Leboo was excited but nervous too. Sobo had his trunk up and could now recognize Sironka's scent. He snorted in approval.

Twenty elephant steps later, everything changed. The rangers were examining two dead elephants. Sobo lifted his trunk and trumpeted, recognizing his mother's scent. Leboo grabbed hold of his ears just in time as both rangers looked over to see him riding the huge bull elephant. Sironka immediately explained to his partner that Leboo was his nephew and Sobo, the elephant, was his friend. His partner, not Maasai but a Sukuma, had been raised in metropolitan Dar es Salaam. He seemed puzzled by Sironka's matter-of-fact explanation of such an exceptional sight.

"Jambo, Nephew!" Sironka said sadly. "Poachers did this!" Of the ten elephants left in the herd, all were females. Both Sobo's mother and aunt had their tusks sawed off—small tusks, one-third the size of Sobo's! And their ears were gone too. Elephant-ear purses were popular in parts of Europe.

"Jambo, Uncle!" Leboo said, wiping tears with his forearm. Sobo could now clearly see his mother and oldest aunt lying dead. He took several big steps to reach her corpse, then softly stroked her forehead with his trunk. Leboo slid off Sobo's substantial hindquarters—using his fingernails to slow the decent. He wanted to do something to console Sobo, but what?

Leboo knelt and straightened the skin on the mother's forehead, then smoothed the long eyelashes over her eyes. He picked some violet flowers nearby and used them to cover the bloody wounds where her ears had been attached. Then he looked up at Sobo and could see his giant eyes were wet.

Leboo and the rangers moved back as the other elephants approached the two corpses, using their trunks to touch them. They, with Sobo, would do this all night. It was dark now and the stars were out—the Big Dipper peeking over the horizon in the far north, Orion in the far west, and the Southern Cross almost overhead. Everything seemed disconnected from any concept of immortality.

Leboo stayed with the elephants most of the night, sleeping on Sobo in the concave depression in his back. Sobo didn't move except for massaging his mother's head with his trunk. Sironka and the other ranger slept in the Land Rover, not uncommon when investigating a poaching incident.

Sironka woke up first and made tea using a 12-volt electric tea kettle plugged into the Land Rover—extra strong, black Tanzanian tea.

"Let this wake you up!" He said, handing a cup to his nephew who was now in the back seat of the Rover. The boy sat up and scratched his head, itching his short stubby hair. He grabbed the tea and drank it down—ignoring its steaming temperature.

"He's gone!" Leboo felt terrible—his soul was crying.

"Didn't you expect that?" his uncle replied.

"Yes."

"Where do you think he went?"

"He's going to the secret place he goes to after an elephant dies."

"Very far?"

"Somewhat far. It's a cave where there are elephant spirits."

"I think I know that cave. If it's the one near Lake Ndutu, he'll be gone awhile."

"I know. I'm thinking with him right now. He's angry and knocking down trees!"

There were two sets of clues left by the poachers: several dozen AK47 shell casings and footprints from maybe six different individuals.

"Those boots were made in Mogadishu." Sironka pointed at the muddy prints. This suggested an organized group of Somalis had come into Tanzania through Kenya. Poaching elephant ivory was profitable and helped fund their terrorist activities. This was nothing new, but enforcement in Tanzania was often clouded by politics.

"The Kenyans missed blowing them up," Sironka's partner said in disgust. The Kenyan military, always short on soldiers, tried to stop the invading Somali terrorists by dropping hand grenades on them from helicopters when they crossed into Kenya from Somalia. The effectiveness of grenades allowed for less accuracy compared to shooting rifles from the air. Guided safaris to Tsavo National Park in Kenya, the closest park to Somalia, were often accompanied by the Kenyan military for protection. No protection, no tourists. Tanzania did not provide such service.

But there were local poachers not associated with terrorists that killed elephants too; they often worked in pairs and used shotguns (slug ammo). And vigilante groups hunted poachers—shooting suspects on sight. It was a serious quagmire. Tanzanian park rangers like Sironka and his Sukuma partner were caught in the middle between a rock and a hard place—trying to sort out who was who. Meanwhile, hundreds of elephants were killed daily in East Africa and left to rot.

"The poachers mowed them down with assault rifles! They prefer big tusker males but settle for helpless females with small tusks. Sickening!" Sironka's partner elaborated in Swahili as they drove to Leboo's village.

Leboo was in the back seat not listening. He was trying to telepathically contact Sobo, but not getting any mental pictures like he had earlier. Maybe he was too far away. Was it possible to be too far away from a thought message?

When they dropped Leboo off at his village near Karatu town, his mother was happy to see him. He was her youngest son and always respectful and willing to help with the women's work. Besides, she loved hearing his stories and secrets.

"Did poachers kill your elephant?" She asked Leboo in Maa. While he explained she fed Sironka, her oldest brother, and the Sukuma ranger—goat leg stew with carrots and yams. She put a bowl in front of Leboo, but she knew he wouldn't eat until he was through explaining. When things were complicated he had to use both Maa and Swahili.

One year later, May 2005

A year passed and Leboo turned sixteen. His tallest brother Koinet was ready to take him lion hunting and make him a warrior. His uncle Sironka wanted him to become a ranger for the park service. The conflicting advice made for many dog fights in his head— but in the end his soul-voice usually became the judge.

"We'll go to Ngorongoro Crater and kill a tree lion; it will be easy," Koinet declared in Maa. "All seven of our brothers will go along with clubs and spears."

"I'll go but I won't kill one!" Leboo replied.

"I knew you would say that. I'll teach you to be fierce and courageous! You'll change your mind!"

The lions in Ngorongoro Crater, unlike lions elsewhere, had learned to climb trees like leopards. And there would often be several in the same tree. A day-pride on the flat savannah could transform into a tree-pride at night—explaining the disappearance of many monkeys.

Leboo informed Sobo of his plans to join the hunt but that he wouldn't kill a lion. It was the most complicated message he had sent so far. It took several sessions using just words—thinking them loudly in his head—to get through to Sobo. He had tried to image the message but couldn't figure out how to do it. He stayed with words in Maa.

Sobo, understanding, replied with an image of himself petting two lion cubs with his trunk. He could walk right into a pride of lions—all eleven tons of him—and the adults would scatter but not the cubs. He enjoyed playing with them.

Four months later, September 2005

Leboo recalled the hunt. All nine brothers, faces painted red except for Leboo's, set out for the Ngorongoro Crater on foot—a massive 260-square kilometers of wild Africa sequestered by six-hundred-meter walls that defined the caldera of an ancient super volcano. Except for giraffes that couldn't navigate the steep trails down, all major African wildlife species were present. In less than two hours, an organized safari could see the Big Five (lion, leopard, rhino, elephant, and Cape buffalo). There were at least six lion prides in Ngorongoro, the largest density of lions in Africa.

The brothers in their scarlet-red shukas—believing lions feared red—advanced in a determined rhythmical stride that heralded their age-old history. They stopped to drink from streams, eat wild fruit, and gaze up at martial eagles that were hoping for scraps from an expected hunt, all while absorbing the equatorial rays. The nine of them put forth a formidable front as they strode into dusk.

The first three lions were in the forest in a fever tree: a lioness with two cubs. Nothing to hunt, just observe. Maasai warriors only hunted male lions. There was no fear of her attacking, provided they stayed back from the tree and away from the cubs. All three cats glowed in the moonlight. It would take a rare set of circumstances for her to attack the strange red beings.

Next, a two-year-old male, mane just developing, showed up on the trail. The nine warriors stood tall, blocking the trail and thumping the butts of their spears on the ground. He was too young to kill. The lion growled, turned, and went back to where he came from. They kept walking on the dark trail and, shortly, surprised two full grown lionesses hiding in a ficus tree, a mother and daughter? Real potential danger! The warriors formed a single line and kept walking and pounding their spears, again appearing too formidable to be attacked, even by two mature predators.

This is how the night progressed. No adult male lions were seen in the trees. No Simba. It was almost like they knew not to be there! The warriors chewed Miraa, a relative of cocaine, to stay awake. Leboo didn't chew, he was sending thought-messages, trying to contact Sobo. He knew his friend was roaming somewhere west of the Serengeti in the Ikorongo area—where safaris didn't go. A week before, Sobo had sent Leboo a vivid image of himself rubbing trunks with a female elephant and would now have to work his way through a phase known as musth, a wild state of sexual energy that lasts about month—with no shortage of bravado. Leboo smiled to himself.

It was 3:00 a.m. when the warriors reached the flat basin of the giant crater. It was black-dark with the moon down and no stars for subtle illumination. So, they sat in a circle and meditated around a fire made from blackthorn wood. The wood smoke would keep the fisi away. Koinet was in charge, at dawn they would attempt to ambush a large male lion—the Lion King of one of the prides. Leboo would just watch, while sending out telepathic warnings to all male lions.

Sobo was swimming in the deep, cool water of Lake Victoria—sixty-nine-thousand square kilometers of fresh water—a long way from his aunts, cousins, and the boy. It was his first time in deep water and swimming came naturally. He simply marched into the water and kept going until he was over his head, then kept moving his legs while using his trunk as a snorkel.

Some natural force, maybe advice from the cave spirits, had prompted him to explore north up to the great lake. Along the way he'd been shot at by poachers from the Kenya side of the Mara River, the famous river that gets crossed by thousands of zebra and wildebeest during their migration every February through March.

Two AK47 bullets had lodged in Sobo's rump just deep enough to be an aggravation—Lake Victoria's water kept flies away and soothed the pain. His intelligence had directed him to escape and not charge the poachers, who'd already killed a bull elephant crossing the river. Sobo was a happy elephant except for the pain in his arse.

Luck had not been with the Maasai hunters, they did not kill a male lion. Leboo was quite content about that but hid his positive feelings. Times had changed and just being on the hunt was enough to qualify him for warrior status. It really didn't matter: he'd already made up his mind. He would move in with his uncle Sironka in Arusha and train to become a park ranger. He had to help stop the insane killing of elephants and other wild game.

Leboo, upon finishing his training and earning his ranger stripes, sent Sobo a telepathic image of himself sharply dressed in his new uniform. He had to gaze intently into a mirror, frame a clear picture of himself, then blink his eyes rapidly while thinking of Sobo. That was the telepathic procedure to send an image.

The next morning while having breakfast with his uncle—hot cornbread with honey and very black Tanzanian tea—a very clear picture appeared in Leboo's mind as he stared out the window.

"What do you see?" his uncle asked him.

"Sobo!" Leboo replied, smiling.

"What's he doing?"

"Standing next to the baobab tree." Leboo kept smiling.

"What are you going to do?"

"Send him a picture of me holding a large watermelon."

Postscript:

Think about this: The Maasai elder who told me most of this story swore in Enkai's name that it happened. Names have been changed except for Sobo's.

Poaching continues to be a major problem—rich Chinese will pay any price for ivory. It was good that President Obama destroyed the six tons of ivory that had been in the U.S. Government Repository in Denver—only a symbolic gesture, but it sent an important message.

In the 1800s it was estimated there were twenty million elephants in Africa. In 1979 there were 1.3 million, and today (2018) you might find fifty-thousand. Poachers kill over one-hundred per day. Any zookeeper will affirm that elephants are intelligent, empathetic, emotional, social animals. They have the largest brain of any animal, possibly excepting the sperm and blue whale.

Visit www.worldwildlife.org and adopt an elephant for $8.00/ month!

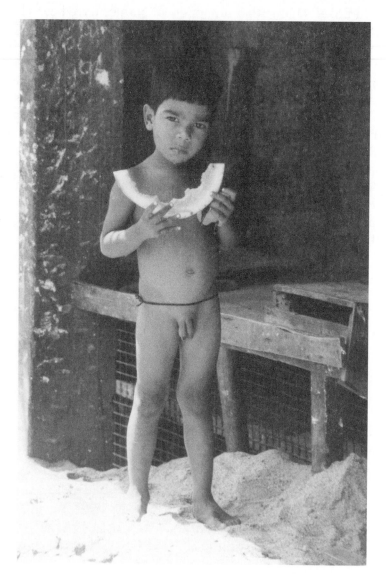

Ali's son in Taman Negara jungle

3

Inside Taman Negara
Where Eagles Dare and Tigers Hide

*P*rologue:

Taman Negara is a National Park in peninsular Malaysia's tropical rainforest. It's estimated to be 130 million years old, 75 million years older than the Amazon. Its 4,343 square kilometers are located six hours northeast of Kuala Lumpur: three hours by road to the town of Kuala Trembling, then three hours by boat to the national park.

It was June of 2003 when I visited Taman Negara with Doctor Charles Watkins, a consulting mycologist who was helping me solve a stubborn fungus problem that plagued banana plantations in Malaysia and Indonesia. After a month of dedicated field work using probiotics to enhance soil biodiversity and inhibit the fungus, we took a needed break and visited Taman Negara. I had been here in 1995, but this was the first time for Charles—new territory for the young PhD who was born and raised in Oklahoma.

Day One, Early Morning

Deep in the Malaysian Jungle, Ali held the seven-foot blowpipe steady, resting it on the railing of the camouflaged hide—a hut on stilts. He quietly loaded a poisonous five-inch dart into the pipe. Then, with his lips on the pipe's mouthpiece, he aimed the weapon at a leaf monkey in a nearby tree. Charles and I watched quietly without moving.

"Puhh," he blew into it with a short burst of air, like blowing a single note on a bugle—a calibrated puff. The dart sailed silently and accurately, hitting the monkey in the chest. It felt nothing, or maybe something like a mosquito bite, just enough to make it change branches. After a couple of minutes, the monkey started itching and scratching itself as if suddenly developing a massive flea infestation. After five minutes it fell out of the tree, dead. The poison, made from the sap of the Ipoh tree, was very toxic; the small amount on Ali's dart was enough to kill a horse.

Ali whistled loudly, twice. An elder kera (long-tailed macaque) came out from under the hide and retrieved the dead monkey, dragging it to Ali by one leg—then started jumping up and down displaying its long canines in expectation of something. Ali unwrapped a piece of hard candy and gave it to "Mac" who immediately chomped it in half, then chattered like a crow that had just escaped captivity.

"He do anything for candy," Ali said. "I name him Mac." I had specifically requested an Aboriginal guide for the week, there were only a few who spoke English. Ali was at the top of the list.

He was a cross between the Batek and Semokberi people, the result of tribal intermarriage that had become common. He had no last name and was simply listed by the Malaysian government as Orang Asli—one of the original people. He was tall and dark-skinned with wavy black hair—a young man who wore a permanent smile.

"This is considerably different than deer hunting in Oklahoma!" Charles remarked, in his low-key Sooner style.

"You haven't seen anything yet!" I responded. The young scientist was on his way to being enlightened.

Ali carried the leaf-monkey carcass by its tail as we walked to his village; he told us his family loved eating monkeys. His wife would skin it, wash it, then hang it in the sun for a day, which would deactivate any residual poison. Then pieces of it would be grilled on sticks, satay style, over an open fire.

"Family like Tabasco on monkey meat." Ali said, grinning.

"Where do you get Tabasco in the jungle?" Charles asked him, speaking slowly, emphasizing nouns and verbs as I had advised.

"Brother trade spiders for Tabasco," was Ali's short answer. I mentioned to Dr. Watkins that the general store in Kuala Trembling sold it along with other ecotourist supplies, including an impressive selection of mounted spiders, centipedes, and beetles—big ones.

After we crossed a wobbly suspension bridge over a deep ravine and got wet double-stepping an overflowing stream, the green canopy of trees opened, exposing a panoramic view of the world's oldest jungle. Hundreds of bird species combined with countless cicadas and other insects to produce a strange jungle melody. Blowing a whistle loudly quieted the cacophony for a minute or so before it restarted. I gave Charles a demonstration.

"The cicadas sound like they're cutting plywood with power saws. Loudly!" Charles remarked, while using binoculars to examine some of the three hundred species of birds that called Taman Negara home. I knew he liked birds.

"You won't see the cicadas; they're a bit small!" I teased him.

"I'm looking at a Dicrurus paradisens!" he announced, matter-of-factly.

"Ah, a greater racquet-tailed drongo!'" I replied.

He nodded, looking amazed. "How did you know that bird?"

"It was described in the middle of a guide book I arbitrarily opened at the guesthouse this morning—there it was, looking like a crow spackled with white paint and sporting a split tail longer than its body. Just like that one," I pointed to the living version Charles had in focus.

We kept following Ali in the direction of his home—the Orang Asli village. It was a small village of about fifty people. Since hunting provided their main sustenance, living in an area where wild hogs were abundant was a priority. Fish and birds were plentiful along with fruits and yams, but pork was a preferred protein source, the Orang Asli relocated as necessary to find it. Their palm-thatched shelters were easily reconstructed anywhere in the huge national park.

One standout feature for me was the tribe's attachment to colorful western clothes which were sold in Kuala Trembling using

Malaysian ringgits earned from guiding and selling bugs. Many natives, wearing bright tee shirts, shorts, and flip-flops, stood out in contrast to everything else primitive. Shortly after I had made notes on this, Charles was quick to point out several topless women and a bunch of naked kids—and two older men who only wore leather jock straps. Bob Dylan was right, "The times they are a changing." More were naked when I was here in the 1990s.

"It's not Oklahoma," I reminded Charles with a grin. He just kept staring at the nakedness.

After touring the village, Charles and I assured Ali we could find our way back to the guest house in Kuala Tahan. Rice noodles, yams, and chicken were on the menu for dinner—hopefully including the cantankerous rooster that had crowed half the previous night.

Day Two—Jungle Fishing

Let me tell you more about Doctor Charles Watkins before we go fishing: He was twenty-six years old, single, clean-shaven with a medium build and had inherited green eyes and brown hair from his mother. He earned his PhD in mycology at the University of Oklahoma in 2001 and was interested in working for my company—I was testing him as a consultant first. Seeing his scientific skills in practice over the four weeks we had been together in Southeast Asia had impressed me. This trip was, except for one spring vacation to Cancun, his only time out of the USA. He was a mycologist, a mold scientist, and knew things I didn't know about pathogenic fungi—like the Fusarium fungus that was killing banana plants.

Charles was also a bass fisherman, average by his own admission. I had told him to bring along a medium-size spinning rod and reel plus several favorite shallow-running lures in red, yellow, and silver. When we'd landed in Kuala Lumpur at the start of the trip, he'd been anxious to show me his lure selection. He was well prepared for jungle fishing.

The Trembling River was the major waterway running through the park, but there were adjoining rivers that branched off into remote areas which all had good fishing. I recalled from my trip in 1995 that the connection with the Tahan River came first after leaving Kuala Tahan village and went as far north as the Lake Berkoh rapids—a good place to catch kelah from shore. But that was eight years ago.

Kelah are unique freshwater fish in the carp family that can exceed twenty kilos. Found in Malaysian rivers and lakes, they liked to eat palm-oil nuts that fell off trees near shore, but the real challenge and fun was to catch them on artificial lures like Rapalas.

Unlike other varieties of carp, the kelah was famously delicious—a true delicacy in Southeast Asia and a prime gamefish in Malaysia. I've eaten them in China where an imported two-kilo fish sold for three hundred U.S. dollars, five hundred if alive. We planned to release all but one or two (for lunch)!

Ali arrived in a wooden boat at 7:30 a.m. A short conversation resolved any mystery; he would take us on the Tahan River to a secret fishing spot near Lake Berkoh.

We headed upriver going north. The wooden boat was long and narrow with a canvas roof. A forty-horsepower outboard motor with a long propeller shaft was set on a tilt. It smoothly moved us along, and except for the yattering motor noise, the boat ride on the Tahan River was something special—curving and winding through dense jungle with exotic trees and broadleaf plants hugging the shoreline on both sides. Parts of the river were under a full botanical canopy where large neram trees hung over the water, connecting with other nerams on the opposite shore. Primal biodiversity surrounded us. When we saw motion in a tree, like a tall merbau with its edible seed pods, a leaf-monkey would often pop out of the foliage to check us out.

Like most first-timers, Charles, wide-eyed and excited, kept turning his head to look around. Then, just after he had settled down, we came upon two Asian elephants giving each other a bath just offshore. Ali immediately slowed the boat and turned toward them.

"Rare to see here!" Ali said, surprised. The elephants were usually farther east.

His voice caused the elephants to back up onto shore, stepping over a freshly- downed tree that they'd probably knocked over for lunch. The two young males, both about seven feet tall, were squirting each other with their trunks when we first saw them. I'd seen others do this in India. When fully grown, these teenage pachyderms would be about two-thirds the size of an African elephant.

"Could they be twin brothers? Charles asked. The two were identical.

"Maybe," Ali answered. Although uncommon, Asian elephants were known to have twins. We watched them disappear into the jungle; even when out of sight we could still hear them trampling the thickness.

"Great sighting!" Charles was thrilled. It made me recall the first time I saw wild elephants in Africa—they were crossing the Ewasco Nyiro River in Kenya's Samburu Reserve, obediently following each other one after the other in a straight line. I was pleased to see the excitement in Charles' face.

Ali upgraded his smile and finger-combed his wavy hair, probably still wondering how the "brothers" got this far west without being spooked by tourists. Taman Negara was a huge park, the largest in Malaysia. The elephant herds tended to stay away from tourists.

"Ali, is Lake Berkoh still good for catching big kelah?" I asked as we continued upriver. I had fished it in 1995.

"Still good. I bury bait in ground." Meaning he had buried palm-oil nuts near the shoreline somewhere. They had to be buried downstream from the Tahan rapids, an unnavigable expanse of rocks. It was the end of the line for boats but a great place to take a swim, where water rolled through pools and around big rocks.

Charles and I helped Ali tie our boat to a big tualang tree about a hundred yards south of the rapids where the river widened. The tree had a wide trunk and was at least 250 feet tall—that boat wasn't going anywhere! No tigers spotted!

"Ali, how many tigers have you seen in Taman Negara?" Charles asked.

Ali, thought for a few moments, then held up three fingers.

"Three tigers," Charles confirmed. Ali nodded. "This year?"

Ali shook his head; apparently, he hadn't understood Charles.

"In how many years?" I asked him loudly, remembering from my prior trip that a tiger was exceptionally rare to see. The odds of seeing a tapir or sun bear were better. We already knew the odds of seeing elephants were good.

"In my life!" Ali answered. "Three tigers in my life." Charles, surprised, seemed to relax after that. Tigers would be great to see from an enclosed hide, but not so much out here in the open!

We kept walking the shoreline away from the rapids toward Ali's secret fishing spot, minding our fishing rods so they wouldn't tangle in trees draped with hanging epiphytes.

After walking the shoreline for about fifty yards, Ali pointed to red and yellow stains on the ground—his buried palm-oil nuts. The water was cool and clear, purportedly safe to drink. Nevertheless, I used a tube attached to a 0.2-micron filter and took a drink. Bacteria averaged one (1.0) micron in size while most protozoal parasites were ten microns or larger. The water tasted fresh.

We started casting from shore. The first fish engulfed a red Rapala on Doctor Watkins' rod—on his third cast.

"It's a nice six-pound kelah," I estimated, excited about the fast action.

"It fights like a big largemouth bass!" Charles shouted as he reeled in line. The fish nosedived when it saw shore and took line off the spinning reel. Charles kept medium pressure on the fish until it tired.

"It's a beauty," I announced as Charles grabbed its lower lip like a good bass fisherman would, then proudly held it up. Salmon-red scales covered the upper half of its body, changing to ivory-silver on its lower half. Adjoining scales were hexagons in a perfect matrix that would have pleased a mathematics professor. The fish's dime-sized, ebony eyes stared at us as Charles released it.

I took my yellow Shad Rap off and snapped on a red one, same color Charles had used but a fatter, shad-shaped lure. I cast it five yards farther out from where Charles' Rapala had landed before his fish hit. I didn't wind in line at first but popped the lure with a single jerk of the rod and let it go still—then popped it again.

"Here's another nice one," I exclaimed after a kelah slurped in the Shad Rap and swam down and away, pulling hard. After setting the hooks I let the fish run and take line, watching it fight in the clear water.

"This one's not going to be as cooperative as yours," I alerted Charles. Ali was looking up at the sky as I made the fish feel the resistance of the graphite rod, getting the kelah to come up and splash on the surface. "It's fighting as hard as an equal-size king salmon in Alaska!"

"Sea eagles!" Charles shouted as two white-bellied sea eagles circled twenty feet above us, then swooped down, eyeing the splashing fish. Four eagle eyes focused on the kelah.

"Uh oh!" I exclaimed. "Been there, done this with seagulls in Canada."

"They're male and female sea eagles, big ones!" Charles affirmed. They were black with white-edged wings that complemented their white bellies.

"You sound more and more like an ornithologist to me," I razzed Charles.

"Birds are just a hobby of mine," he blurted, just as the huge female eagle swooped down sharply, wings spread, tail feathers dragging water, talons extended, aiming at my fish. My rod buckled, and the drag on the spinning reel buzzed loudly as the eagle soared up and away with the fish. Both eagle and fisherman (me) became electrified by what was happening. All I could do was hold the fishing rod up and let the eagle fly in circles with the kelah in its grips. The smaller male followed the female—both were screeching loudly: kikiki . . . cawcawcaw . . . kikiki . . . cawcawcaw!

I had hooked a seagull in Canada once when it tried to eat a musky lure. I had to slowly pull it to the boat and net it, almost hooking myself while unhooking the squawking gull. I released it just in time, as its calls had summoned dozens of other gulls that appeared ready to lend help—by dive-bombing me! I had never seen or heard of that happening with an eagle.

I saw the sea eagle trying to improve its grip as the thrashing kelah almost got loose. That was when the eagle hooked itself. One of the hooks on the Shad Rap had penetrated the bird's leg—deafening screeches erupted. Looking down at me, it must have sensed I had something to do with its predicament. In the next moment the fish came loose from the lure's other hook and fell into the lake. Now I was fighting the eagle in the sky with just the Shad Rap hooked to its leg. Echoes from the eagle's obstreperous screeching collided with new, angry screams in an alarming disharmony—all other birds and bugs had gone silent.

"Eagle mad!" Ali concluded. "I cut line."

"No! Not yet. Cutting the line will leave the eagle trailing over fifty yards of tough monofilament—it could tangle in trees, vines, or whatever." I kept the line tight as the big bird took more of it off the reel. This was uncanny; I was fishing a flying eagle!

Ali and Charles just watched; there was nothing they could do. I was almost ready to have Ali cut the line and let the eagle deal with dragging it when it swooped down at me in a blur, aiming for my head with its talons. I dropped the rod and ducked, hands over my head, intentionally diving to the ground—just in time!

The rod was pulled high into the air over the lake. When the eagle flew up, it was attached to the line that was attached to the lure that was stuck in the eagle's leg. I could see the big bird trying to bite the lure loose while flying sideways. Lying on the ground when Charles and Ali rushed over and pulled me up, I was stunned but not harmed.

"Never see this—eagle almost take your head off!" Ali exclaimed in English followed with aboriginal expressions, obviously disturbed! His tribe only fished with spears, not fishing rods. A speared fish didn't jump on the surface and provide a target for sea eagles.

"Are you okay, Stan?" Charles, upset, stammered out the words.

"I'm okay, should have let Ali cut the line!" Sometimes doing the right thing turns out to be the wrong thing. A shiver went down my spine. What were the odds of this happening? I looked up and watched the giant bird going crazy with the rod still hanging from it in midair.

Finally, the wildly swinging rod, about a hundred feet in the air, pulled the lure loose and fell into the water with it. The sea eagles, still screeching, flew away in the direction of the Indian Ocean.

"We need to catch lunch—one fat kelah," Ali informed us. Charles accommodated the request. I no longer had a fishing rod.

Charles did well fishing in the jungle. Why did I have any doubts? Ali carried the doctor's freshly-caught, four-pound kelah as we walked back toward the boat and dry rocks where he built a fire. The three of us shared a simple lunch: one scrumptious—five-hundred-dollar—kelah fish that had been roasted on a stick. Primal deliciousness!

Day Two, After Fishing

"It's a Malaysian pied hornbill!" Charles was excited. "Its scientific name is Anthrococeros convexus. He has eyelashes like other hornbills. They're the only birds that do."

"I knew it was a hornbill by that banana-shaped helmet above its bill." Once again, I was amazed at Charles' bird knowledge. The more I thought about it, the more I realized that many of my scientist friends had science hobbies separate from their vocational specialties. In fact, we would hold debates outside our fields of expertise—just for fun as a check on who knew something different to talk about. Mine were minerology and cosmology; I knew them like Charles new birds.

The marvelous hornbill was in a fig tree close to the Tahan Hide where we were hiding. The bird had nabbed a small lizard and was holding it by the belly with its long yellow bill. Knowing we were watching, he played with the lizard which was trying hard to get away. Then suddenly, no more playing around, the hornbill flipped the reptile up, gulped, and swallowed it. We could see the bird's neck undulating as the live lizard wiggled its way down the throat. I swear the hornbill appeared to nod at us before flying away—probably just a swallowing reflex.

"They're mostly frugivorous—the lizard was an exception. He's probably off looking for a papaya to peck open for dessert." Charles' eyes sparkled as he provided more detail. I was affirming that this talented young man had both the demeanor and intellect to fit in well with my other employees.

The Tahan Hide, one of six in Taman Negara, was an elevated wooden hut with chairs and bunk beds—borderline adequate. It was the closest one to our guesthouse, and where we would finish our second day.

The best time to see big animals was at dawn and dusk and, sometimes, in the middle of the night. If you planned to sleep in a hide, you had to notify the authorities in advance.

"Ali, did you see any of those three tigers from this hide?" Charles asked him.

"No, village too close."

"Where did you see them?"

"All by Kumbang Hide, deep in jungle." He pointed northeast.

"Recently?"

"One last year."

"Eight years ago, I slept in that hide!" I commented. "Saw a tapir, a barking deer, and lots of psychedelic birds—no tiger."

"Can we go to it?" Charles was quite serious, surprising me.

"It's a seven-hour trek . . . one way," I said.

"We can go tomorrow—stay night?" Ali said. "Leave early."

"It was a great hike through the rainforest back in '95. I saw a foot-long centipede and two atlas beetles fighting—they looked like 7.5-ounce Pepsi cans with horns." Micro-memories had just come back into focus.

"I'm up for it," Charles said, anxious to convince me.

"Okay then, we'll do it!"

With that settled, Charles scanned for more birds outside the Tahan Hide. Dusk was approaching and insect-eating Scops owls should be around. I opened my backpack and found the amber bottle of insect repellent I had formulated in our company lab in Minnesota. It was a mixture of four essential oils: tea tree, cedarwood, rosemary, and peppermint; one percent of each in Almond oil fortified with vitamin-E (to keep the oils from oxidizing). I opened the bottle and put some on my cap, elbows, and knees—creating a pleasant olfactory aura, a grassy-woody-evergreen version of peppermint. Then I handed the bottle to Charles. Sundown was at 7:00 p.m. Bugs got thick an hour before—they could tell time.

"Tell me again what insects your formulation repels?" Charles inquired.

"It's a good one for insects in full canopy rainforests where there's not much wind. Works well for flies, gnats, ticks, and mosquitos— and a few unknowns."

"I wonder if it has any anti-fungal activity?" Charles was dabbing it in various places on his body.

"It does, but would be too expensive to use for the banana problem."

Charles laughed, picturing himself dabbing banana plants with the essential oils. "Right, that's where your onsite cultivation of anti-fungal probiotic bacteria comes in . . ."

"You know it!"

It was a good time to talk shop, two hours before sundown with not much happening outside. Charles had brought a tin of Dutch hard candy in various flavors—refreshment energy while we talked. I started the discussion.

"Well, Doctor Watkins, after a month in Malaysia, can you now appreciate the magnitude of the Fusarium disaster in banana plantations?"

"Absolutely!" Charles asserted. "I didn't realize how devastating it was to the rainforest, not just here in Malaysia but Indonesia too. Freshly cleared rainforest can only be used one time, for one crop of bananas, before becoming too infected to replant—requiring more rainforest to be cleared!"

"Do you think the plantation managers understood what we were teaching them—how our onsite brewing technology produces high-strength probiotics (active, beneficial bacteria) at low cost and is a natural alternative to using chemical fungicides that lose effectiveness with continual use?" I asked Charles.

"They understood it was vital to keep a banana plant's rhizosphere (root system) dominated by probiotic bacteria, not harmful fungi. And they much preferred using the non-toxic probiotics—they hated breathing fungicide spray!"

"Great, that's right out of our company song book!" I remarked. "The Cavendish strain of banana is grown extensively in Southeast Asia for export. It's found in all the major grocery stores in Japan, Australia and the USA. By promoting monoculture, not rotating with other crops, the soil becomes deficient in microbes that deter pathogenic fungi, like Fusarium. Probiotics restore the beneficial, competitive microbes but trillions of them are required per hectare! So, we have to brew them onsite . . ."

I was happy with the progress Doctor Watkins was making in understanding and applying our technology; it would take a lot of weight off my shoulders.

A sizable Anopheles mosquito, apparently not deterred by the essential oils, landed on my arm. I swatted it and applied more of the oil formulation.

"You've got to apply enough," I reminded Charles, while rubbing it on in a dozen different locations. Charles did the same. The hide became infused again with the pleasantly augmented peppermint aroma.

Our shop talk had put Ali to sleep. We would wake him before sundown. The plan was to watch for wildlife until 8:00 p.m., then head back to the guesthouse in Kuala Tahan while Ali went back to the Orang Asli village. The following day we would trek the super-forest to Kumbang Hide and spend the night.

Ali, sitting up in a wooden chair, was snoring.

Day Three: Trek to Kumbang Hide

Charles and I had a 7:00 a.m. sunrise breakfast in Kuala Tahan village: eggs, toasted flatbread, and papaya juice. As we were sitting outside, I warned Charles not to break bread with the congregation of birds under our table. I had made that mistake in Africa once. Dozens of the winged denizens, alerted when I had shared a piece of toast with two of their comrades, converged on my table and consumed everything organic, including the rest of my breakfast! The resort staff was not amused.

"Don't worry, boss, I'm not going to feed them. It's tempting, however, there's an amazing gathering of different species."

"What do you call those multicolored parrots—Roy G. Bivs?" I quipped. They were brilliantly splotched with a complete rainbow of colors. Six of them avidly consumed bread crumbs on the floor.

Charles laughed at the rainbow's acronym, "I don't know their name, but they are red, orange, yellow, green, blue, indigo and violet. I'll have to look them up in that guide book you found in the guesthouse—the one that opens to the right page."

"Are you packed and ready for two days in the jungle?" I glanced at his backpack on the chair between us. Mine was on the floor being investigated by one of the unidentified parrots.

"Got everything you advised, plus a field guide to wild Malaysian mushrooms!"

"Ah, that's exciting! Just don't ask me to eat any—I almost made that mistake in Belize."

"I know, you believe all wild mushrooms are poisonous. The more I study fungi, the more I discover you might be right. The edible ones just kill you slowly, like smoking or nitrites in bacon. Cultivated varieties are generally safe—provided they are fed pathogen-free fertilizer!" Charles explained.

"That puts a new twist in keeping them in the dark and feeding them dung—gotta feed 'clean' dung! But the mushroom drama does have another side: In Belize, I've seen shamans cure cancer by activating the immune system with traces of highly toxic mushrooms— amounts less than a millionth of a gram!" I finished my papaya juice.

"I'm sure we'll see a few of those ultra-toxic varieties on our trek," Charles was excited and ready to go.

We were prepared to spend the night in the Kumbang Hide. It would be a seven- hour trek on paths mostly through dense jungle. Dressed in shorts, tee shirts, and good-traction hiking shoes, we had both managed to keep our backpacks under ten pounds. We each carried a liter bottle of water; additional water would come from fast moving streams and be filtered onsite (at 0.2-microns). We didn't take raingear; if it rained we'd get wet—it was already 34 degrees Celsius in the shade. Freeze-dried lasagna was on the menu for dinner; we didn't want Ali cooking up any leaf monkeys!

Ali arrived bright-eyed and smiling at 7:30 a.m. He was looking quite fashionable for a jungle guide, wearing red Nike shorts, a white collared shirt, and new flip- flops.

"Are we ready, Mr. Stan?" the indigenous guide of wavy hair and few words inquired, honoring my seniority.

"We're both ready!" I assured him.

It started as a comfortable walk in the 130-million-year-old jungle. Ali was easy to follow at a pace of about three kilometers per hour—slow by hiking standards or when out for exercise, but not when watching for tigers.

Ali took a shortcut to a trail that would take us close to where we were yesterday, then onto Tabing Hide before the long trail to Kumbang Hide. His shortcut went through a bamboo forest, and once in the middle of it any tourist would be lost. He picked several young bamboo shoots for us to chew on as we wormed our way through the vertical poles of the Buluh Rakit. We walked in a line with Ali in front and me in back.

"Watch for spiders," he told us just seconds before I saw the first one and almost walked into it—a hand-size whip spider suspended between two bamboo poles, graphite-black and big. Quite alarming with eight-inch legs and massive pincers.

"Whoa!" Charles exclaimed, seeing a different spider.

"Friendly spiders: no poison, no web, no bite," was Ali's short lecture. We stopped and watched them.

"Do you know anything about these fearsome creatures?" Charles asked me in a curious voice.

"I know a few facts from my first trip: They're cousins of scorpions, not spiders. They walk on six-legs, not eight; those big pincers, pedipalps, are used for catching the bugs they eat. And have eight eyes but can't see well."

"Now it's you who is a horse of a different color, sounding like an entomologist, not a biochemist."

"No, I hate spiders, won't go near them—nonvenomous scorpions are okay," I assured him, hoping for accuracy in what I remembered.

Ali smiled and picked up the larger of the two and put it on my arm—it danced its way to my hand while giving me the eye(s).

"That would scare the excrement out of me!" Charles backed up. "Me too, if it was a spider!"

We came out of the bamboo forest on the east side of the Trembling River and connected with two small boats that took us across—water taxis, three passengers maximum per boat. Several species of birds flew over us on the river. Charles had his binoculars out and focused on them. The doves—colored like the Green Bay Packers playing at home—were Janbow Fruit Doves. I remembered them from my last trip.

Once across, in just ten minutes, I pulled out my 1995 map of Taman Negara's trails and asked Ali to show us the intended route. There was no one trail from Tahan Village to the Kumbang Hide, and trail sign directions could be confusing if they didn't agree with the map. If you looked at more than one map, the trails often looked different. Ali stared at the map for a few seconds.

"Follow me. Map wrong," he declared. We followed him, walking north parallel to the Tahan River for sixty minutes. Then, where the trail turned east we followed it for another thirty minutes, crossing a questionable suspension bridge before arriving at Tabing Hide, our first stop.

Not one board on Tabing Hide had changed since I was here in 1995—it was still a small garage on stilts requiring a twelve-step stairway to get inside, where two mattress less bunk beds kept several folding chairs company. The hide's red-painted plywood exterior clashed with the malachite jungle.

"Ali, why didn't they paint it green—or brown?" I asked him.

"Government gets red paint free."

"A perfectly good reason," I quipped.

"Maybe that's why you never see tigers here, big cats stay clear of red?" Charles speculated. Ali understood and laughed.

A Polaroid photo of a tapir taken at night lay on the table inside the hide. "Probably five hundred pounds!" was written on the back. The strange animal was shaped like a midget elephant with a stub of a trunk and a pig's ears. Its front end was black and its rear ivory-white—about sixty-forty favoring black. According to the guide book, the three-toed Malaysian tapir hadn't changed in tens of millions of years. As with crocodiles, turtles, and sharks, it seemed that once nature attained a certain degree of perfection, further evolution stopped. This would suggest mankind was in its evolutionary infancy, and like Jimmy Buffet had suggested in the song Fruitcakes: "Maybe they took us out of the oven too soon."

Leaving Tabing Hide, where we only saw the tapir's photo, we headed back to the main trail which restarted between trees overtaken by jungle vines that twisted into knots and circles—actually, a plethora of weird shapes. It was quite dramatic, if not spectacular. Certain vines had hardened into the various circular shapes, some large enough to drive a truck through! Others looked like pythons the way they had crawled and twisted around trees. Of the ones that hadn't hardened many could be swung on Tarzan-style. I demonstrated . . .

Ali signaled Charles and me to sit on a log while he carved a pointed stick from a downed tree branch. He looked back, grinning, challenging us to figure out why he was carving a stick. I didn't even try to guess.

With stick in hand, he squeezed between the two of us, sat down, and started drawing shapes on the ground.

"Animal tracks, footprints!" Charles deduced.

"You guess, I draw," Ali told Charles, knowing this was his first visit to the park.

Ali drew a circle bigger than a dinner-plate with four silver dollar size toes. "Asian Elephant," Charles said, laughing.

"He started you out easy," I smiled at Charles.

Ali drew a cloven hoof next. "Some kind of deer," Charles said, quick on the draw.

"Right, a barking deer—looks more like African impala tracks," I claimed.

Ali nodded, then drew a ten-centimeter-wide upside-down mushroom with three big, oblong toes. Charles scratched his head, thinking. Then, remembering the photo, blurted: "Tapir!"

Ali smiled and nodded again. Next, his stick produced an eight-centimeter oval with four pointed toes and a heel mark. This one got a lot of head scratching from Charles. I could see his scientific mind deliberating. "Might it be a sun bear?" He asked, uncertain.

"Good onya, Dr. Watkins!" I said in Australian. "May the sun-bear spirits bathe you in good vibes." Ali smiled big at Charles.

Last, he drew a lobed, saucer-size triangle with four serious claws. Charles and I looked at Ali, then at each other.

"We need to know this one!" I said to Charles. Ali stood up and growled an approximate imitation of a tiger, which signaled Charles to take a second look at the footprint, making sure he had no recognition doubts. I took a second look, too!

We were about one-third of the way to Kumbang Hide and had passed the junction that led north to Lake Berkoh. The trek from here would take at least four hours depending on stops. Between the parallel running Tahan and Terenggan Rivers was the super-forest—acclaimed internationally by botanists and zoologists. Only a small percentage of trekkers went this way—most guides promoted the shorter, half-day trails. Going from Kuala Tahan to the Kumbang Hide this way required a two-day commitment.

The correct trail was now the only trail with no fellow ecotourists in sight. After a gradual uphill stretch, it was largely straight and flat with many small stream crossings. Ali picked up our pace.

I perceived a serene wildness as we looked ahead to a long stretch of trail under full canopy. Many different deciduous trees were dominant, but frequently mixed in were towering palms that allowed us to peek through to the sky.

The water was moving fast in the first stream that crossed the trail. Ali kneeled and took a drink from the stream—Charles and I drank from our water bottles. We watched a fifteen-inch yellow snake attempt to devour a large tiger nymph, a butterfly-moth with grey translucent wings streaked with black veins and geometric splotches—a collector's prize. The snake had the insect's abdomen in its mouth while the wings flapped with enough force to lift half the snake out of the water! Finally, it had to settle for just the abdomen, leaving the wings floating lifelessly down the stream. Small event, rare sighting.

"We almost saw a flying snake!" Charles remarked.

The stream was only ankle deep but that was enough to thoroughly wet our shoes—good traction and laces were a must. We stomped the water out while, marching on while Ali looked around for animal tracks.

The jungle cicadas were back to sawing plywood—they were the loudest insects and could produce up to 120-decibels (dB)—equivalent to standing next to a jet engine. Noise is measured on a logarithmic scale, so if you put a cicada producing 90-dB next to another producing 90-dB, the result would be 93-dB not 180-dB.

They can disable their tympanic membranes to protect themselves from hearing loss—from their own sound!

They love the full canopy jungle where there is no shortage of tree sap to feast on—xylem sap as we biochemists call it, a rich soup of amino acids and minerals.

"They're much louder than the ones in Oklahoma!" Charles asserted.

"Those Sooner State bugs hibernate underground for seventeen years! These guys here come out yearly, they never cool off."

Ali plucked a two-incher that was climbing a tree and ate it. A common bug for natives to eat.

"How does it taste?" Charles seemed somewhat stupefied.

Ali chewed it loudly, making a crunching sound, then raised his eyebrows in delight. "Want one?"

"No, thanks." Charles gagged. He said it made him recall an unhinged entomology professor who claimed: Those cicadas instantly break into pieces on the first bite and taste like shrimp due to their high lysine content. But their wings can stick in your throat."

"Thanks for the detail on that, Doctor Watkins." I needed a shot of Crown Royal, or at least a beer, to expunge the thought of eating one! "The microbiologist in me could imagine the plethora of unknown viruses that Ali just consumed." Raw insects are inundated with viruses!

"Try that whistle trick again." Charles grinned. He was looking a bit older today.

We examined the super-forest with emphasis on small details for the next two hours. Charles had spotted some robust caramel-colored mushrooms that looked "edible," but his field guide identified them as kulat asu, their Malay name, and warned they were extremely toxic—causing kidney failure. These harmless-looking mushrooms, which closely resembled a common edible variety, could kill you with one bite!

Charles tested Ali: "Are these okay to eat?" Charles pointed to the mushroom suspects.

Ali looked closely at them, then picked one and smelled it. "No!" he shook his head, pointing to his kidneys.

Charles was impressed. "This mushroom would have stymied many mycologists!"

"There are old and there are bold but there are no old, bold mushroom hunters," I remembered a shaman in Belize instructing me.

I don't know what awakened my appetite: a snake eating a butterfly, cicadas loaded with viruses, kidney-destroying mushrooms, or hiking for miles, but I needed a healthy snack that came from the tame side of Nature. I unzipped a side pocket on my backpack and took out a bag of organic trail mix. Charles' eyes lit up when I showed it to him.

"If we wait much longer to eat something we'll spoil our appetite for freeze-dried lasagna later." I didn't have to explain any more.

"That wouldn't make any sense," Charles admitted while reaching into the bag and grabbing a handful. I offered some to Ali, but he shook his head. It was quieter now, and I believe he'd continued eating cicadas—reducing their numbers?

We sat down on a log twisted up with vines, ate trail mix, and drank the rest of our water. Charles had his binoculars and was examining birds as usual.

"Don't see any sea eagles," he joked, while taking another handful of nuts and raisins.

"We'll be using the 0.2-micron filter at the next stream we cross." I held up my empty water bottle. For the last three hours we had been the only homo sapiens on the trail. There would probably be others at the Kumbang Hide, those who had taken a boat on the Trembling

River through its wild rapids. It was only a forty-minute walk to the hide from the boat drop-off.

We continued our trek through the famous super-forest. When we came to another stream about six-feet wide and knee deep, clear water moving fast, I got the filter out and began filling our water bottles. Ali had Charles behind him as they walked off-trail downstream a short distance from me.

"Stan, come here when you're done, you have to see this!" Charles called, in an elevated voice. He and Ali were about twenty yards from me, bent over looking at something on the ground. After filling the two bottles, I went over to see what they were looking at.

I immediately recognized the four footprints. They were from a big cat—a tiger!

"Ali says they're fresh—made today, not long ago! Look how deep they are in the mud," Charles' casual demeanor had morphed into serious-mindedness. Almost as if all our tiger talk had just been small talk to pass time. After all, Ali had only seen three tigers in Taman Negara in his entire life!

"Big tiger!" Ali affirmed. "Heavy tiger."

It sent a chill down my spine—fresh tiger footprints, broad daylight, no gun, no hide, fully exposed, alone in the middle of a super-forest. Just a few worries. I had envisioned a comfortable evening in the Kumbang Hide—twenty-feet above ground, door shut, sitting quietly with binoculars looking out through a thick plate glass window. These footprints were a game-changer. When I'd hiked in Sumatran jungles, also tiger country, a government guard came along carrying an AK-47 assault rifle.

"Scary, but exciting too!" Charles stammered. I told him I agreed, and that many times in my adventures I had experienced scary things that also had an exciting component. If forced into action without a plan, fear becomes a negative force. Winning must be a forethought, inspired by excitement and confidence that factor out acting foolishly.

Ali had his knife out, a foot-long Australian bush knife that an Aussie man had given him as a tip. He began cutting a thin bamboo tree down with the serrated edge of the knife. I knew his plan. I dug into the bottom of my backpack and pulled out a small spool of stainless-steel wire. His eyes lit up when he saw it. In ten minutes he had a seven-foot pole with the bush knife wired to the end of it. I dismissed the thought of taking out my Swiss Army Knife with its two and a half-inch blade.

"Okay, we go now," Ali insisted. "Maybe I fight a tiger."

Charles and I walked behind him.

Motivated by the fearsome foot prints, we moved at an even faster pace now, maybe five kilometers per hour. Walking fast had a calming effect on us. Ali was pumping his pole-knife vertically, up and down, keeping rhythm with our pace. I didn't know what he was thinking, but his lustrous ebony skin glistened whenever a ribbon of sunlight penetrated the canopy. Aboriginal poetry in motion! He was happy with us, I could tell; we paid attention to the little things and didn't keep nagging him to find big animals. He knew that we knew they were all here in Taman Negara! The best answer he would give persistent tourists that kept asking where the big animals were, was: "They are hiding."

We needed them to keep hiding just awhile longer until we got to the hide.

Day Three: Kumbang Hide, 4:00 p.m.

When we got to the Kumbang Hide we were alone. We felt invigorated, not tired. Our last two hours had been uneventful except for sighting six wild oxen called guar or Seladang in Malay. They were in the Terenggan River a hundred yards from us, all were rainy-day grey and wore "white socks"—some could go fierce if agitated. The thought didn't bother us; we were within sight of the hide by then.

We made ourselves at home in the hide, the biggest and best-kept of any I'd been in—worldwide. Its wide picture window looked over a large clearing surrounded by jungle. Several black vultures soared high over the far edge of the ecotone where the clearing dissolved into the jungle—likely investigating something to eat.

Charles and I sat down at the hide's wooden table and cleaned the lenses on our binoculars; they would get a workout later. Ali went outside to check the location of the saltlick that was usually around—a prime spot to view tapir and barking deer at dusk and dawn.

I was just starting to unpack and sort things out for our special dinner when I noticed a note stuck to the viewing window.

It was written by someone named Julie. The note was explicit: "We heard a tiger roar last night, about 2:00 a.m. I think it was in the clearing with the saltlick, we couldn't see it. My boyfriend said it was a tiger, he's from India and he knows. I hope you see it, stay safe. Julie."

"Hmm…" I showed it to Charles who raised his eyebrows. We could hear Ali coming back up the stairs.

"I make small fire, boil water for Mr. Stan," he said. "Tiger tracks by saltlick; two days old."

"There was no date on Julie's note," Charles mentioned.

"Hmm… This is exciting." I said.

That's all Charles needed to hear: "If you need help fixing dinner, shout. I'll be glassing the ecotone!" He was sitting on a bench in front of the window. It would be dusk before long.

"No worries, I can handle it. Keep those ten-power binocs in focus!"

I made dinner for the three of us; Ali didn't argue, he happily joined in. Dinner was an uncomplicated event, its preparation involved adding boiling water to three packages of freeze-dried lasagna, then stirring them for five minutes. I even brought a small bottle of Tabasco along for extra zing. Ali liked that.

Charles and I dozed off somewhere around 4:00 a.m. Ali told me he stayed up all night but was sleeping when I woke up at dawn. I swore I heard a tiger roar! Charles said I was probably dreaming. Ali wasn't sure . . .

Postscript:

Our probiotics significantly reduced Fusarium infections in bananas. Brewing probiotics on-site became a dynamic process—new strains of probiotics had to be developed to counter new strains of pathogens. Asian universities and research institutes got involved and the word spread.

I hired Charles as Director of Research for my company. He stayed for five years before taking a position as an associate professor at a leading university in California. He was able to continue consulting for us.

Hopi ancestor's pueblo dwellings

4

The Hopi Prediction
Cosmic Connections

*P*rologue:

One way to get to the Tuwanasavi, the "Center of the World," is to take Interstate 40 west out of New Mexico and go two hundred miles to Winslow, Arizona—then north eighty miles on Arizona Highway 87 to the second of three mesas. That will put you in the geometric middle of Hopi country!

It's a 2,439-square-mile area with the Grand Canyon in the distance to the west, Monument Valley to the north, Canyon De Chelly east, and Castle Butte south—a substantial chunk of the Old West.

About ten thousand Hopi live in twelve pueblo villages today in the region that encompasses these mesas. The Hopi first arrived at the end of their migration out of the Rio Grande valley in 900 A.D. They're farmers, not hunters. They plant corn and beans— the core of their sustenance—and raise sheep. When they're in a ceremonial mood they dance with supernatural beings, the Kachinas.

These dances follow the beat from a cottonwood drum and the dancers wear multicolored clothing and bizarre Kachina masks with horns or feathers and slits for eyes. Some masks look like space helmets shielding black buggy-eyes. Hopi elders claim Kachinas represent an intermediary between humans and Star People (sky gods).

The name, Hopi, translates to "peaceful people" but their history has been plagued with violence. Tribes of Paiutes, Utes, Comanches, and others have historically attacked Hopi villages, kidnapping the women and children while killing the men. Sometimes even the neighboring Navajo attacked to steal food when rain was scarce. But according to Hopi legend, when such attacks became overwhelming the attackers could somehow be turned back with help from the sky gods who flew down in shining shields. Of course, few non-Hopis believed this.

Planet Earth currently exists in the Fourth World, according to the Hopi. The First World was destroyed by fire (a meteorite or volcanism), the second by ice (the Ice Age), and the third by water (the Great Flood). The Hopi say we're about to enter the Fifth World with the coming of the Blue Star Kachina. And it will be a rough ride that begins with the star, a meteorite, falling to earth causing strong earthquakes, violent volcanism and associated perils. The final sign after the Blue Star is sighted will be the cessation of Hopi ceremonialism—their Kachina dances will stop.

Albuquerque, New Mexico, March 2008

I was lying in the morning sun at the motel pool. A Ford van packed with my company's booth and exhibition materials was parked behind the motel. I had driven straight from Kansas City, thirteen-hours, and arrived at 2:00 a.m. My ultimate destination was Anaheim, California, and a health-food trade show called Expo West.

The March sun was pleasant, and after a hearty breakfast of Huevos Rancheros, it was easy to doze and reenter last night's dream.

Hopi Land – 1820

"The Navajo come for your corn and sheep," Spider Woman told the Hopi tribal chief after walking down the ladder into his kiva. It was late afternoon in the old Oraibi village on the third mesa.

"How many come?" He asked her.

"Many hundreds."

"More than last time," the chief murmured. Last autumn he had given a small food-gathering party of Navajos six sheep and all the corn they could carry. "Now they come with many warriors to take all our food and maybe kidnap our women and children."

"You must put up your strongest defense!" Spider Woman looked him in the eye, knowing he was more dove than hawk.

"Where are they camped?" He replied.

"They have campfires in the north—on the flat ground. One day from here."

"They will smoke magic mushrooms in their tobacco tonight and will sleep excited," the chief surmised.

"You need to fight them!" she insisted.

"Go tell kalatakmongwi (warrior chief) and his clan leaders from the Bear, Coyote, and Eagle clans to come to my kiva for a smoke. We must decide our defense strategy. "

The warrior chief and the three clan leaders were collected by Spider Woman and brought to the tribal chief's kiva—a wide, circular, enclosed pit—twelve feet deep and lined with clay bricks. A fire burned in a hearth in the center of it illuminating six fearsome Kachina figures painted on the walls. The men climbed down the kiva's ladder and sat on a circular stone bench near the fire. The tribal chief stayed seated when he welcomed them.

Sensing the urgency, they began smoking and discussing strategy. It was clear their warriors would be severely outnumbered and would have to hide in rocks around the mesas to fight. Forming traditional lines directly exposed to the oncoming Navajos would be suicide. The Navajo Nation was a hundred times larger than the Hopi Nation.

Lone Crow of the Coyote Clan, sitting next to the warrior chief, advised he would order the Hopi warriors to wrap themselves in heavy buckskin as protective armor. And tell them that battle with the Navajos would require much bravery and skill; accuracy with their bows would determine survival of the Hopi Nation. In the past they'd defeated war parties of Comanches, Paiutes, and Utes by fighting from the tops of their pueblo houses and accurately shooting their arrows. But these war parties from distant tribes were always fewer than a hundred warriors—not many hundreds as their Navajo neighbors now presented.

Red Bear, of the Bear Clan, sitting on the other side of the tribal chief, said he would take control of the tribe's weapons, checking supplies of battleaxes, lances, and bows, then disperse them among the warriors as they painted fierce Kachina faces on each other. "It must be done this night!" he asserted.

Night Hawk, of the Eagle Clan, sitting alone, said he would lay out the defense perimeter around the three mesas, placing emphasis on the third mesa and Oraibi village. Every rock hiding place would hold a warrior. Women and children would be told to hide deep within the largest kivas—pulling in all ladders. The roofs of the pueblos would be occupied by their best archers.

The tribal chief and the warrior chief inhaled the smoldering tobacco, passing the long pipe, saturating themselves with nicotine. Then, in unison, they said to the clan leaders: Go now and do what you said you would do!

As the two chiefs smoked, they chanted, alternating the frequency of their vocal cords—high pitches with low pitches—sounds meant to alert Pokanghoya and Polongahoya, the warrior gods.

With the morning sun came an unexpected realization: All the Navajos were riding horses! More horses than the Hopi warriors had ever seen. The Hopi had no horses! They could see the leading horsemen in a long line just ahead of a giant dust cloud created by an uncountable number of horsemen following behind. They were covering the flat terrain rapidly and would arrive sooner than expected at the rocks below the mesas.

"They look more like Comanches than Navajos," Lone Crow, looking out from the rocks, declared. "They want more than corn and sheep!"

"So, it is what it is," Red Bear stated. We'll fight them standing on our feet!"

The Navajos came on in a galloping charge, yelling and yelping. It was the formula for a massacre. The "people of peace" were about to face extermination.

"Shoot at the horse if a Navajo slides down its backside to avoid your arrows," Red Bear instructed his warriors. "Kill the horses!" Dust from the hooves of the strong Iberian horses flew up, producing opaque clouds with near zero visibility. Navajos were falling and colliding with each other after the flat terrain turned rocky.

Most of the Hopi's arrows missed hitting anything, but some horses were killed. Navajos on horseback swinging battle-axes on ropes were effectively killing the Hopis who were not hidden well. But being hidden well was not working either; visibility was so bad it was impossible to aim an arrow. Those Hopi with long lances were able to stab at horse's legs as they came by. Buckskin armor had already saved many Hopi.

The heinous odor of desert dust mixed with blood and horse manure penetrated the horror, putting a noxious accent on the lethal mayhem.

"Lie down and shoot your arrows up at the horse's bellies! They make a silhouette against the blue sky," Night Hawk shouted to his warriors.

The battle dispersed into a wide area at the base of the third mesa. It was obvious the Navajos would eventually reach the top and endanger the Hopi women and children in Oraibi. There were too many of them!

An unarmed Navajo scout with four feathers in his headband approached Night Hawk from behind. "Go and defend your village, get out of these rocks. There are too many of us. We will kill all of your warriors out here."

Night Hawk grabbed the Navajo scout by the neck, but before he could cut him, the scout cried out: "The sky spirits will help you! I was born a Hopi and got kidnapped by the Navajos as a child—I've got your blood in me."

Night Hawk released the Navajo scout, then turned to face two oncoming Navajo horsemen swinging battle axes on ropes. He ducked both axes as they whizzed by him. When he got up on his knees with sand in his eyes, they had turned and were coming back, swinging their axes lower. His thoughts switched to the women and children in the kivas atop the mesa. His wife and two young sons were there. What will happen to them? He thought, knowing he was about to be killed. Then, all in an instant, there came intense streaks of brilliant blue light that hissed like a rattlesnake—both Navajo warriors flew off their horses, dead. Night Hawk couldn't believe he was still alive.

There was a pause in the Navajo attack as they regrouped back on flat land below the third mesa. It was obvious when the dust settled that many of their warriors and horses had been killed. How could this be? Many of the dead had no wounds, no arrows stuck in them, no bleeding slashes from a battle ax or a lance. Just dead from falling off a horse? So many? The Navajos were good horsemen! The Navajo war chief called for a council; they met on horseback in a large circle. "How could so few Hopi kill so many Navajo?" The chief screamed at his warriors.

The Hopi warriors watched the Navajo from a distance while tending to their own wounded and dead, a small fraction of what the Navajo had incurred. They couldn't explain the carnage their enemy had experienced.

The red-feathered Navajo war chief decided to terminate the attack and retreat. He was in disbelief of what had happened.

Night Hawk and Lone Crow couldn't believe what they were watching—hundreds of Navajo warriors creating a giant dust cloud as they rode away.

Red Bear, the oldest of the Hopi clan leaders, arrived and greeted the two of them with a wise smile. The three stood together and didn't talk until the Navajo's dust met with the horizon and it was obvious they were gone.

"Can you explain what happened?" Night Hawk asked him. Red Bear looked at Night Hawk and Lone Crow before answering—allowing a few somber moments to pass.

"We should all be dead, and our women and children kidnapped," Red Bear said solemnly, then remained silent as he pointed to the sky with two fingers.

"Did you see something in the sky?" Night Hawk stammered.

"Two flying shields landed in the middle of the horse dust in the center of the battle. I was above them on high rocks looking down; when the dust moved around I could see into it. Two long-armed, big-eyed Kachina warriors came out of each shield. All four were holding large weapons—tubes looking like a heron's neck stretched straight! When they pointed these at the Navajos, streaks of blue lightning came out of them, hissing and crackling, killing the warriors instantly, without blood or visible wounds!"

"Where are the Kachina Warriors now?" Lone Crow asked in amazement.

"Gone, back to the sky! We can thank our chiefs for alerting the sky spirits!"

I woke to the sound of the motel caretaker dragging sun-loungers around the pool, each one had a rolled pink towel on it. "Buenos dias," I said to him while checking my watch—it was 10:00 a.m. He gave me a wave and returned the greeting. I was the only guest at the pool. I had to remind myself I was still in Albuquerque!

I'd been reading about the Hopi Indians before the trip, which apparently became the catalyst for the dream I had. In it, the Hopis were fighting the Navajos in northern Arizona the early 1800s. I remember they were grossly outnumbered and about to be wiped out when the dream got fuzzy. I had driven past Hopi land before but never had time to stop and take a tour. It was only Tuesday, and I didn't need to be in Anaheim until Friday; there would be time on this trip.

I took a quick dip in the pool to insure I was awake, then checked out and quickly got onto Interstate 40 west. It was 130 miles to the Arizona state line and then around 320 miles to the Hopi's second mesa—big country!

It was 9:00 p.m. when I arrived at The Hopi Cultural Center Restaurant and Inn on the second mesa. Their phone hadn't been operating but luck was with me—they had one vacancy. A pleasant Indian lady told me she would check on which guide would be available in the morning. I was tired from the unexpected bumpy drive and I went straight to my room.

Surprisingly for March on a school day, there was quite a mix of children running around after breakfast. At least seven adults, obviously the parents, were skillfully supervising them. As I watched the kids, thinking of my grandkids at home, a tall stately gentleman wearing jeans, a western shirt, and a bowtie, approached me and introduced himself. He reminded me of a square dance caller I'd seen in Amarillo.

"I'm Ted Baxter," he said, holding out his hand with a genuine, welcoming smile.

"And I'm Stanley Randolf. Pleased to meet you, Ted. Are these all your offspring?" I asked in jest while shaking his hand.

"Actually, they are!" he said smiling. "We've pretty much taken over the Inn! Us Mormons come with big families, you know. We're celebrating the birthday and confirmation of my oldest daughter's eight-year-old twins. They're the boy and girl in blue and pink."

Both children had blonde hair and blue eyes and were dancing in a circle holding hands. "They're beautiful!" I said. We continued our conversation and he told me how excited his family was to see the Hopi Reservation—they'd driven down from Salt Lake City yesterday.

"The older ones are studying indigenous Americans in school, so my wife and I are treating the family as we celebrate the twins!"

"Congratulations, Ted!" I said smiling.

He asked what faith I belonged to and I had to admit I wasn't actively involved with any church right then but had been born and baptized Catholic. I mentioned I'd seen the Mormon slide show a couple times in the past and appreciated his beliefs.

"Well then, we both believe Jesus is God!" He said.

"I'm still trying to confirm that! Let me put it this way: he's certainly a benevolent spirit who guides and guards humanity." I could sense wheels turning in Ted's head.

"What are your plans for the day?" He asked me.

"Hire a Hopi guide and look around—I'm particularly interested in seeing old Oraibi and the petroglyphs in Dawa Canyon."

"You can go with us! I have two mini busses coming from Yuba City with two Hopi guides; they'll be here shortly. The youngest children will stay here at the pool with their grandmother, my dear wife."

"Are you sure, Ted? That's very generous!"

"I'm sure! I'll explain how Jesus and Latter-day Saints interacted with the Hopi." Ted was anxious to convince me.

"Okay then! I don't recall that part being in the slide presentations." He smiled at my comment, understanding that I understood.

"I'll reciprocate and tell you about my Hopi dream." I ran to my room to get my camera and belt pack.

The pueblo buildings and kivas of Old Oraibi were straight out of my dream. Three stories of cubical dwellings made of brown clay that had been bonded together for centuries. I could sense that nothing had changed over time except maybe activity of the residents, slower now with no urgency. The only living things moving fast were the roosters; they had taken up residence on top of the pueblo structures where defending archers had hidden in more perilous times. The roosters crowed, challenging any nearby roosters to a fight. Fighting was in their genes . . .

In my dream there had been urgency. Women vigorously prepared for attacks by other tribes: stocking the kivas with beans and cornmeal, chopping firewood, making heavy deerskin vests that repelled arrows, barricading separate rooms deep within certain kivas. Archer warriors simultaneously prepared hiding spots on the rooftops and made arrows and other weapons—but that was 180 years ago. Our Hopi guide, Gary, described various Hopi clans from the past and how they complimented each other with different skills, like the Rattlesnake, Coyote, Eagle, and Bear clans. Ted and I along with four of the adult parents walked together following Gary. The second group with the older children and two adults followed Mitch, the other guide. It was a parade through Old Oraibi, no cars or photos were allowed; March was a good time; there were no other tours.

After Oraibi, it was back in the minibuses and off to spectacular Dawa Canyon. Gary spoke English well and explained many things about the Hopi enroute to the canyon. He reinforced the spiritual nature of the Hopi people and their connection to the stars. Information passed down from generation to generation taught that Hopi ancestors, the Anasazi, originated from a planet in Lyra, the Ring Nebula, also called the Eye of God. They migrated to the Pleiades before coming to earth.

After maneuvering the van around a herd of sheep, Gary continued his explanation of the Hopi's cosmic connections: "We Hopi have serious respect for the constellation Orion, which we believe to be the origin of ruthless, murdering tribes like the historical Comanches and Apaches. In fact, Hopi villages have mathematical equivalency to the positions of the nine major stars in Orion. The three stars in Orion's belt match perfectly with three villages on our three mesas. When you connect our original nine villages with straight lines, they produce a huge image of Orion. The diagram stretches from Canyon de Chelly in the east to the San Francisco Mountains in the southwest to the town of Betatakin in the north—a huge area with our three mesas in the center. This earthly map of Orion is a constant warning for us to be vigilant—a stay in map for us and a stay out map for our enemies. We thank the benevolent sky spirits for it.

Gary then explained the major intrusions of the white man's world that had been prophesied by Hopi elders centuries ago in a total of nine signs:

"The signs predicted thunder sticks (guns), spinning wheels (wagons and cars), strange buffalo (longhorn cattle), snakes of iron (the railroad), a giant spider web (the electric grid), rivers of stone (Interstate highways), a black sea (ocean oil spills) and more. Then, after these develop, the ninth sign will appear: The Blue Star Kachina will show in the sky and will signal the coming of three days of darkness and the catastrophic end of the Fourth World. Many people will die during this brutal transition, but those who prepared will have the best odds of surviving into the Fifth World . . ."

Shortly after his encouraging commentary we arrived at Dawa Canyon (Taawaki), also called Dawa Park. The rock escarpments en-route were stunning, dark magenta-colored, iron-rich layers banded dramatically with ivory sandstone. Rounded rock outcroppings alternated with sharp spires and a geology-textbook's variety of intermediate shapes. Dawa was the mother of all petroglyph sites with somewhere between twelve and fifteen thousand petroglyphs, the only "written record" of Hopi history.

Ted and I began to explore. Gary had his hands full with the twins and the other children who asked "why" every time he explained something. That rang a few bells and made me think about my grandchildren.

"Keep explaining to them, Gary," Ted bellowed, obviously glad Gary was taking charge.

"Look over here, Ted." I was standing over a refrigerator-size rectangular rock covered with a plethora of petroglyphs, pointing to creatures with long tails curled up in concentric circles.

"I see them!" Ted acknowledged. "What do circles inside circles mean?"

"They mean 'a meeting place,'" I said. "Saw them in petroglyphs in Australia and Peru." We had talked in the van—when Gary wasn't explaining the cosmos— and had discussed our travel experiences and my dream. I learned that Ted was a Mormon bishop who had traveled extensively in his younger days.

"Look here." Ted pointed to a large Kachina-like figure holding what appeared to be a tube or a cane. "Didn't you say you saw that in your dream?"

"Yes, I did! It was the weapon used by the Kachina warriors that came out of the sky in flying shields and saved the Hopi! Night Eagle said it looked like a heron's neck." Now I was excited—talk about confirming something! "This is as exciting as the much older petroglyphs I saw in Australia's Northern Territory ten years ago; they suggested an alien presence that helped the Aboriginal people."

"I wish I had a magnifying glass." Ted replied, staying clear of the alien implications. He was looking at what appeared to be tiny ant people.

We walked on. There were thousands of glyphs to explore. Gary smiled and waved at us, apparently keeping the grandchildren happy with help from the parents. It had been my experience working with Mormons that they stressed obedience and respect when raising their children.

We came to some stick figures with large round heads and big eyes. Many had their arms—too long for normal humans—up and bent at the elbows or in a circle above their head. Some had four fingers without a thumb.

"Vetted experts on extraterrestrials, albeit not considered mainstream, have studied every shred of information about ETs. According to them, there are at least five different types: Tall greys, short greys, Nordic blondes, Reptoids, and Mantas." I explained as we walked on exploring other petroglyphs.

Ted and I had found alien glyphs right from the start; many others that followed were mundane farming and wildlife glyphs. We would have only enough time to see about ten percent of them all. Dawa Canyon was a two-hundred-foot-high red-rock escarpment directly in front of us. Seeing all the petroglyphs would call for some rock climbing and a whole day—I would come back on another trip.

"Many of us Mormons believe Jesus works with the good aliens. There are good and bad ones, you know," Ted couldn't hold it in any longer.

"That's more open-minded than most Catholic priests," I remembered Sunday school, where we were told Jesus couldn't even work with Lutherans.

"That's because Catholics won't acknowledge that The Heavenly Father is the supreme creator God and that Jesus, and the Holy Spirit, assist him as separate gods. We don't believe in the trinity as a single god. Jesus and the Holy Spirit help lead devoted people on a pathway to godhood. Heaven is full of gods," Ted replied.

"Does this require that 'devoted people' must be Mormons?" I asked him.

"Tricky question! LDS teachings are evolving. Many Mormons believe Jesus helps non-Mormons see the light and guides them, too."

"I don't imagine 'non-Mormons' would include aliens that look like lizards or bugs."

"Probably not," Ted grinned. "But the 'Nordic Whites' might qualify." Ted was surprisingly open-minded and well informed.

"The big question for me is: can any of these heavenly gods—now that there are so many of them—take on different images besides human? Giving them 'In God's Image' status to rule over the entire cosmos?"

"That's a question for another time . . ." Ted said. I agreed.

After a taco salad dinner at the Inn, Ted and I sat down with Gary to discuss Hopi prophesy. A topic of interest for both of us.

Gary was a very polite, educated Hopi man with black hair parted in the middle and deep-set eyes in a long face that was tanned beyond its natural, subtle auburn. It was my impression that the knowledge he carried made for a heavy load. He didn't laugh or smile a lot, but when he did, it was big. Young children made him smile. He was a good guide.

I started the discussion by bringing up Planet X.

"We call it the Red-Star Kachina now," Gary said without hesitation. "It's coming in place of the blue star." Amazing—he was up-to-date!

"Or along with it," Ted said.

I was pumped; this was an intriguing subject for me. Planet X or Nibiru, the biblical "planet of the crossing," is part of a small solar system that cruises through ours every thirty-six hundred years, give or take a decade or two, raising hell every time it comes!

At the system's center is a brown dwarf star called Nemesis. When Nibiru, orbiting Nemesis, comes between earth and the sun, like it was supposed to in 2003, bad news arrives: Volcanos erupt violently, great earthquakes shake everything, associated tsunamis flood coastal areas, numerous meteorites fall with iron dust that colors waters red, and the poles shift—all caused by gravitational and magnetic forces from Nibiru, which is seven times larger than Earth.

"It's happened before when it destroyed our Third World with the Great Flood," Gary declared. "We Hopis have been stocking corn and beans for eight years, since the turn of the millennium. The elders have prophesied that Hopi land around these three mesas will be a safe place to survive!"

"Deep inside well-stocked kivas!" I presumed. "NASA knows all this—but it's highly classified—only so many people can fit in a kiva!"

Gary nodded solemnly.

We all took a drink of pink lemonade. There was no alcohol allowed around good Hopis and Mormons! I could have used a shot of vodka in mine but being a well-mannered "when in Rome" kind of guy, I settled for the unadulterated version.

"The big unknown with us Mormons is when. It could be next year or in ten years, 2025 seems to be the outermost deadline," Ted stated. Gary agreed that "when" was the only uncertainty.

"Of course, you guys (Mormons) have been prepared for a 'feces-hitting-the-fan event' for years with your basements full of food," I added with a smile. "My wife and I helped a young Mormon family move out of Milwaukee once. It took most of the day to just move their food. I'll never forget the weight of ten gallons of honey after carrying a drum of it up from their basement."

"Honey never spoils! We've got a stock at home in Salt Lake." Ted was quick to respond. "Garlic is a universal medicine that's good to stock, too—it gets better with age!"

"There are blue Kachina dolls that hold corn stalks in one hand and beans in the other. You can buy them as a reminder to prepare." Gary suggested. "Hopi shake them when doing the Bean Dance. Fresh sprouted beans have saved many Hopi in tough times."

The three of us took another drink of pink lemonade.

I drove to Anaheim for the trade show the next day, following old Route 66 (I-40) most of the way. It was another pleasant day in the American southwest.

Postscript:

I promised Ted I would give him a call on my next trip to Salt Lake City—and he promised to take it easy on critiquing my misunderstandings of LDS beliefs, and that what was taught in The Book of Mormon was, to a large extent, up to an individual's interpretation. The objective of this story, beyond a bit of Hopi enlightenment, was to encourage people to do some basic preparation for tough times.

And pray for help from above before they start happening. Hopefully we won't need help from long-handed, big-eyed Kachinas with laser guns.

Beach People in India

5

Beach People in India
Adventures in Bridging Cultures

$\mathcal{P}$rologue:

Adventure can involve many different activities, some planned and some that arise unexpectedly. One way to define adventure is to do something good that is challenging and hasn't been done before. This story is derived from experience gained during my several trips to India in the late 1990s. All the events occurred as described, but over a longer period than the story's condensed several days. There are benevolent forces—private groups of people—who seek to solve intractable problems that exist between different cultures and belief systems by funding "projects" that focus on bridging the gaps and misunderstandings. These anonymous groups are not connected to any government. One of their priorities is to find and develop talented local people into management teams who promote and guide the process.

Totally incidental to my business purposes for travelling to India, I was fortunate to have met a married couple that was involved with such a project.

Madras India, 1997

There were cows on the beach—white, lop-eared cows; some were red with small humps. All were lying in the sand. It was midday in southern India and the breeze coming off the ocean was cooling them. Most were looking away from the glare of the ocean. When people walked by, the cows showed no concern—they were sacred.

People were on the beach, too—and in the water—but nobody was swimming or sunbathing. They were dressed in everyday clothes, and those in the water were only ankle or knee deep. Women in long, Indian dresses were trying not to get them wet. They would hold their dresses up a few inches with one hand and use the other hand to help explain something to someone. The bottoms of their dresses still got wet. There were also people meditating, arms spread apart, facing the ocean. An older woman in a black burka was being held up by two heavy men in knee deep water; she was wet from her waist down and couldn't stand up. Two women standing in the water had been talking to each other for quite some time, paying no attention to anybody else. And some people were just standing on shore looking out—there were no young children on the beach.

Behind the beach was a line of green trees, growing mostly in sand, and beyond them were brown hills.

A couple of miles further south there was a fishing village. It was in an area with considerable tidal debris; chickens competed with sea birds for whatever was edible. Houses made of local thatching were on the sand beyond the high-tide line. Thatching covered most houses. It was hard to imagine them staying dry inside in heavy rain. Wood skiffs without motors along with various nets and buckets were scattered on the beach. Occasionally, a cow would wander into the village and go wherever it wanted to go; after high-tide there would be seaweed for it to eat.

Next to a pathway behind the village, herring was being dried on plastic tarps lying flat on the ground in the sun. Whenever fishermen came in with successful catches of herring, everyone helped prepare the fish for drying. Women carried salt down to shore in baskets on their heads. Children helped unload fish from the boats. Men sharpened knives and got ready to gut fish. The process, when done correctly, was simple and effective: Entrails were removed with a single cut that left the heads on; the fish were then rinsed in seawater and salted. This was done on shore around the boats. Women carried the prepared herring up to the drying tarps where men, sitting in fish, laid them out and applied more salt. The fish required frequent sorting and turning—drying took several days. Poor salting or incomplete drying were the main causes of failure. These fish were staple food for the village and used to barter for fresh fruits and vegetables at local markets.

It was a simple way of life, very rural—some would say primitive. Yet, these village people were not starving. They stayed healthy, washed their clothes, and had time to relax. The beach was their life.

Beyond the village going farther south there was a long stretch of pristine beach. A road came down to a development of new houses and shops where a tour bus had stopped next to a billboard announcing Orange Crush in India. Tourists were milling around. An American couple who had seen enough shops decided to stroll down to the beach.

"Mr. and Mrs. Carpenter!" the bus driver yelled.

"Yes, Suresh, we won't be long, we're just going to the beach," George Carpenter replied loudly.

"We leave in one hour," Suresh answered. "Don't be late." He was an older man, backup for both the scheduled driver and the guide and wasn't happy about doing double duty. He didn't like tourists who required special handling.

"Okay!" Mary Carpenter yelled back. They were already across the road and on the beach.

George and Mary took their shoes off; she had a shoulder bag for carrying them. They walked straight into the water. The ocean breeze felt good on the hot afternoon.

"This is much better than being on the bus," Mary joyfully declared. The bus air conditioner had been straining to keep warm from turning into hot.

"Absolutely! We should have hired a taxi with working A.C. guaranteed." George said. "Best Tours of India gets a failing grade today."

"Well, next time…" she said while kicking some of the cool ocean toward him. "It's my first time in the Indian Ocean."

He squeezed her hand as they walked ankle-deep in the ocean. The clear water tickled their feet with thousands of tiny seashells rising and falling as gentle waves rolled in. "This is the Bay of Bengal; it's fifteen-thousand feet deep out there and thirteen-hundred miles east is Thailand." George explained in his professorial tone as he pointed straight out at the water." Rather deep and wide for a bay, don't you think?"

George Carpenter, a professor at a leading university in the U.S., was in his prime, forty-three years old, six feet tall, with brown hair and blue eyes. He had the habit of rubbing his chin when in deep thought. He'd met Mary in graduate school eighteen years ago. She was devoted to him, a very smart brunette with sparkling blue eyes.

"I prefer your non-professor tone," she told him with a wink, knowing he was just showing off. "You've been to Thailand a few times."

"Yes, I have. Doing research for my PhD years ago."

"I hope we find more candidates for The Project—yesterday wasn't so good for that," Mary said, excited about helping George with The Project.

George Carpenter had been working in North India for three weeks before Mary joined him in Madras. He had degrees in biological science and the humanities, a rare combination. He was interested how rural people in countries like India bridged the transition between old and new culture, and how science and technology played a part. Preventing poverty from becoming a destination for the young generation was a top priority for The Project! He believed that successful bridging of different cultures required a dedicated human element: Young, smart, strong-willed individuals with turbocharged souls. They could be anywhere in society; they needed to be found and developed. And there was private money to do that!

"Hey, look over there," She said, pointing left. There were three young boys with a sack of seashells on the beach. They were sorting through them and laying them out on the sand. All three stood up waving, so George and Mary walked over.

"My name is Atma, these are my brothers Sahar and Chiman, they are twins!" Atma announced in perfect English. The three boys were dark skinned with straight black hair, big brown eyes, and dressed in clean white shirts, black shorts and flip-flops. Atma was the oldest at fifteen, the twins were seven years old.

"We sell seashells by the seashore!" Atma announced. His gleaming personality was something any salesman would pray for. The twins sprouted big smiles as they watched their brother talk.

George introduced Mary and himself. Amazed by Atma's pleasant formality and clear English.

"Are you interested in looking at some fine seashells?" Atma asked with authentic charm and enthusiasm.

"Yes, but, first things first," Mary declared. "Tell us what your names mean." She remembered this was the first question the Navaho guide asked their tour group last year in Monument Valley, Arizona. It stuck with her as being important.

Atma came to attention like a soldier, saluted them, put an arm around each of his brothers, and said: "My name means soul and spirit. Sahar's means sun and dawn. Chiman's means curious!"

"Those are wonderful names," Mary said smiling.

"Do you live around here?" George asked.

"No, we live in Madras. My uncle brings us here to sell shells on weekends."

"What kind of school taught you to speak English so well?" Mary asked Atma.

"Public school, but my teacher was the reason, not the school."

"Did the school have lots of good teachers?" George asked.

"Not many. I've only had one good teacher in eight years, for grades six and seven. I'm in grade eight now with a bad teacher. My brothers have a bad teacher too. Bad teachers don't like teaching!" George thought about Atma's answers; the bad-teacher problem was worldwide. He was impressed with how clearly Atma used English contractions in his speech and awed by his overall demeanor.

"Let's have a look at what shells you have," George and Mary sat down in the sand next to the shells and motioned the boys to do the same. Atma did a head roll that meant yes in India and told his brothers to sit down in Hindi.

Atma started talking about the shells: "These are volutes; these are miters; here are purple cone shells from deep water, and over here, bonnets and cowries."

"Did you find these here?" George asked, pointing at the beach.

"Yes, right here is excellent for shells, and north of here, too, but not as far as the fishing village," Atma explained.

"Do they wash up on shore?" Mary asked. "We saw only tiny ones on our short walk."

"Sometimes, but they are mostly broken when they do," Atma replied. "My brothers are good shell-finders. Right after a storm is best. There is a reef out there—storms loosen shells from the bottom and wash them in. The first high tide after a storm is the very best. My brothers stand knee deep and shells hit their ankles—they grab down quick and catch them. Other shell finders come out too; there's competition!" While Atma was talking, Mary, listening to him, was also picking out some shells. Chiman and Sahar were showing her popular types.

"How much for these four?" Mary asked Sahar. He put up ten fingers.

"Ten Rupees?" she asked. Sahar moved his head in a circle.

"He means ten each," Atma said. "It's about twenty U.S. cents."

"That sounds very fair," Mary smiled. She opened her shoulder bag and pulled out a fifty Rupee note. Sahar was going to give her ten Rupees back, but she shook her head no: "Your tip." He didn't understand. Atma explained in Hindi then Sahar smiled. While this transaction was going on George had been looking through the bag of shells that hadn't been laid out yet.

"Do your brothers speak English?" George asked Atma.

"Just a little—they understand better than talk. They mostly learn from me."

Mary had been listening and thinking. She knew George had to be thinking as well—thoughts that went beyond seashells. George was sitting in the sand rubbing his chin.

"George has a special collection of seashells from his travels!" Mary told Atma. "Mine is pretty but not so great." Atma's eyes lit up.

"Would you like to see something very special?" Atma asked George.

"Yes, certainly, I was about to ask if you ever see any rare cone shells?" George knew the Bay of Bengal occasionally gave one up.

Atma, with a gleam in his eye, removed a silk pouch from his pocket and opened it—taking out an object that he held with both hands. George stared at what Atma was holding.

"Here, hold it," Atma said. George carefully took the object from Atma; he was speechless for a couple of minutes while he examined it.

"Wow! It's a Glory of Bengal cone shell. The pattern is amazing! And its giant size!" It was almost as large as the can of Orange Crush Mary had earlier. "Unbelievable!" George had never seen one except in a book. "Where did you get this?"

"Right here, where you were walking. Last year. It was on the wet sand just before sunrise, just after a storm!"

"This is an amazing shell, very rare! It could be the largest specimen of this species in the world—I'm not kidding!" George said while Atma listened and moved his head in agreement. "This cone shell lives in deep water, most are small and caught alive off the bottom in fishermen's nets. But to find one in perfect condition, this size, on the beach, is incredible."

Collecting natural specimens was something George encouraged his students to do. Sea shells, rocks and minerals, butterflies, fossils and insects, for example, were all collectable and collecting specimens of Nature's Creations kept young minds healthy. Too many young people were bored much of the time. This was a dangerous symptom that could lead to using drugs to escape life's realities.

"You can buy it from me," Atma said.

"George, you should buy it," Mary encouraged him.

George was thinking on a different wavelength: This boy could be developed to fit The Project—I need to keep the discussion going. "Atma, did you know the snail that lived in this shell was very poisonous? It could shoot its dagger-tooth into a victim and inject a paralyzing neurotoxin. The Glory of Bengal has killed fishermen who picked them from nets by hand!"

"I did not know that, George you are a smart man! I want to learn more about these things, like ocean science."

George put his hand on Atma's shoulder: "I can help you do that! And thanks for the compliment." George was checking for the patronizing habit common in India and was pleased Atma had avoided it; he did not overdo the compliment.

"So, Mr. Atma," George said to the fifteen-year old boy, "what is your price for this marvelous sea shell?"

"One-hundred U.S. dollars" Atma said without a pause. "It's worth much more in a shell shop if you can find it."

George conferred with his wife. "Of course!" she said. George looked at it again. Its pattern of snowy mountains connected to each other with small orange-caterpillar designs running over them was exceptional.

Atma's price was fair. George nodded to Mary. She opened her bag, took out two fifty-dollar bills and gave them to Atma. They would buy groceries for his family for over a month. The thought pleased her. George carefully watched Atma's reaction. Atma put the shell back in the silk pouch and handed it to George.

"Thank you! I will use this money to help feed our family," Atma's brown eyes reflected the ocean in a golden hue as he spoke. He put his hand out to George and they shook hands firmly. Everyone was pleased, including the twins.

George and Mary talked with Atma about India and his aspirations for the future. They were impressed to hear how well he was informed about old and new India. They asked about his parents, more about school, and what was happening at the locals' beach. George wrote down Atma's mailing address and told him he would Federal Express a package of information about The Project he was working on. Something for the future that might interest him.

Atma's eyes lit up again, "A real Federal Express package for me?"

"Yes sir, and you're not too young for it! The information is in English and Hindi," George explained. He could see Atma was excited.

"I'll be sixteen in one month!" Atma declared, affirming his interest and maturity.

"Happy Birthday in advance!" Mary said, smiling with the words.

"I'll keep in touch with you!" George confirmed as they shook hands again.

Mary, keeping track of the time, looked at George, and pointed to her watch. She knew Suresh would leave without them if they were late.

"We gotta go—watch for the package!" George reminded him. They hugged the boys and said goodbye.

Back at the bus, George asked Suresh about the fishing village and the locals' beach that Atma had mentioned. Suresh was disturbed by the question. He told George it was not a place the tours included. It was old, dirty India. Very rural. Modern Indian youth were moving into the big cities. Government was cleaning up these old areas and selling the real estate for development.

"Your tour tomorrow will stop at a modern fishing village with shops selling souvenirs, ice cream and beer!" Suresh told them. George and Mary did not like what Suresh had said. They wanted to see old India with people who could sustain themselves. It was one of the reasons they included the state of Tamil Nadu on their itinerary. George and Mary talked over dinner at their hotel in Madras about how important a visit to the fishing village and locals' beach could be for The Project.

"How could a country with a billion people, eighty percent rural, be so naive?" She asked him.

"Destruction of old cultures without acceptable alternatives throws people into poverty. A destiny that's hard to reverse," George lamented. He had walked through the slums in Calcutta where desperate people were everywhere. They were living in cardboard boxes, picking through garbage for food—no toilets, no clean water, no medicine. Moves to correct such extreme poverty were in the planning stages with private investors. The Project was currently aimed at correcting borderline poverty—rural communities that were partly self-sustained but needed help to become more independent. Minimal dependence on a central government was congruent with opportunity, freedom and happiness.

"Good morning, Mr. and Mrs. Carpenter," The head waiter welcomed them. "It's another bright, warm day in South India!" The breakfast restaurant was quite pleasant with wide windows looking out into the hotel's magnificent flower garden.

"Good morning Raj, how are you today?" Mary asked. George, reading The Times of India newspaper, looked up smiling. "Good morning Mr. Raj."

"Very well, I am very well! How was your dinner last night?" Raj asked. He knew they had eaten at the hotel's restaurant.

"Let's say it was an adventure! A better one than the night before!" George reported. Food at hotel restaurants in India was often presented in large buffets, usually on long tables with meat dishes on one side and vegetarian dishes on the opposite side.

"So, you took Raj's advice?" Raj asked him. He was a handsome, middle aged, Indian man who was born in Agra. After studying western culture at Saint John's College, he became a tour guide at the Taj Mahal. He was a professional waiter now and wrote a weekly column for the Madras Star, a newspaper for tourists.

"Yes, he did!" Mary answered, before George could. "He ate only from the vegetarian side with me. None of those curried meats that kept him up the night before."

"She's right! I was totally impressed with the vegetarian dishes. Even Eggplant—couldn't believe all the ways it was prepared. The mushroom noodles and coconut rice were fabulous. And how you guys use cardamom and coriander to add flavor to veggies is wonderful. Marvelous deliciousness! I slept like a baby."

"Don't forget to mention the mango soufflé we had for dessert," Mary added. George put both thumbs up.

"Welcome to modern India!" Raj said. "I will tell other guests your food story!"

"Let me ask you a question, Raj." George was rubbing his chin.

"Of course," Raj replied.

"You told me yesterday that you got your degree at Saint John's College in Agra, a Christian college. You also told me you were born and raised a dedicated Hindu. How did you bridge the difference?"

"Very well, actually. I began by making lots of Christian friends; was always willing to help them with their homework. And I learned to play Cricket! But I'm still a dedicated Hindu!"

"Who speaks the Queen's English!" Mary inserted.

"Marvelous!" George said. "Never change!"

"Never will! Enjoy your breakfast," Raj had other guests to tend to.

"Charming man," Mary remarked.

"Yes, and smart." George was impressed with Raj; with his credentials and charm he would be a perfect fit for The Project. Before they left Madras he would talk with him in more detail and arrange a Federal Express package. The package was a starter kit for how to get involved with The Project if, of course, the person had the dedication and desire to do it. How to get different cultures to cooperate and understand each other required a unique skillset—Raj had it.

After breakfast Mary checked their tour schedule for the day. She was showing it to George. "The tour of the Shore Temple at Mamallapuram is something we should see, it's south of here, beyond where we were yesterday," she pointed to it on the map.

"That will take up the morning," George figured, hoping she would suggest what he had in mind for the afternoon.

"Lunch is part of the tour and it's near the Shore Temple. We could skip the afternoon tour in Mamallapuram and hire a taxi to take us to the fishing village and locals' beach," Mary suggested.

"This is one of a thousand reasons why I love you so much," he gave her a big kiss.

The bus ride to the Shore Temple was very comfortable—it was in a new Mercedes bus. Also, the tour guide was not the driver, her name was Aasha. She spoke English, French, German and, of course, Hindi. She was young and smart with a perfect makeup-free Tamil face—not a single flaw. She was dressed in an Indian blouse embroidered with flowers and western-style shorts and cowboy boots. George made note of her clever choices.

"It looks like Best Tours of India paid attention to the complaints from yesterday!" Mary said.

"Proof of God," George said.

"Which God?" She asked him. "Brahma, Vishnu or Shiva?" Then she stuck out her tongue at him.

Sitting behind them, Aasha had heard this. She touched Mary on the shoulder and said, "Excellent reply!" The three of them got into a conversation. The Shore Temple was about an hour south of Madras—they had time to talk.

The two spires of the Shore Temple rose from an elevated granite foundation and could be seen for miles by fishermen in the Bay of Bengal. They were welcome guideposts, having an almost theatrical effect when viewed from the ocean. Since their construction in the eighth century, these spires have provided spiritual enlightenment and guidance. Below the spires was a complex of caves and chambers with stone sculptures of Brahma, Vishnu and Shiva—Hindu's holy trinity. These three divinities are avatars, descendants of the Supreme Being. Their purpose, respectively, was for the creation, maintenance, and annihilation of the material world…

The day was warm and humid, like yesterday, but inside the stone temple there was a cool dampness.

"Here is the reclining sculpture of the God Vishnu. He is responsible for maintaining the world and providing love," Aasha told the tour group. Then they walked on into another room.

"And here is the God Shiva," Aasha pointed to a stone panel showing Shiva with his four arms; his right leg was resting on a baby rhinoceros.

"Isn't he the bad God?" An older woman on the tour asked. "The God of destruction?"

"No, he is an important God because he will organize the destruction of the material world. The world cannot last forever; its destruction must be organized properly at the right time," Aasha explained.

"Then Brahma can create another world!" A white-haired man on the tour professed. Mary and George just listened.

George kept rubbing his chin as he was thinking, there are close to a billion Hindu believers in India! He was aware that the "Hindu trinity," Brahma, Vishnu, and Shiva, was a much-simplified explanation of Hinduism. A version that could be accepted and understood by the west—maybe an important bridge. The numerous "assistant gods" that interfaced with the Hindu trinity were too complicated for most westerners to take time to understand; like all the saints in Christendom. Thus, Christianity and Hinduism may be on common ground after all, separated largely by semantics. Some believe Jesus spent time in India.

The universe was a complex phenomenon and the Supreme Being might, indeed, require help in organizing it including, someday, the end of it. Maybe I should put a statue of Shiva in my office to add that perspective, George thought.

The tour of the temple and surrounding gardens lasted over an hour. Whenever their tour emerged from the cool dampness of the stone rooms, they got hit with the heat of the day. The gardens were

well kept with dark green grass and red flowers that complemented the Temple's granite spires and yellow beach. The group spread
out and headed in the direction of the beach where there was a cool
breeze.

"Stay together, everyone!" Aasha yelled as she ran to keep ahead
of them. George and Mary were somewhere in the middle of forty
tourists.

There was action in the water. People were swimming and floating
on plastic rafts; some were playing games; kids were splashing each
other. There were English, German, and a few Chinese kids playing
their version of Marco Polo while throwing beach balls. The throw-
er would yell "Marco!" and the catcher would holler back "Polo!"
Adults were sunbathing. Mostly these people were foreigners on vacation, but a few locals did mix in. One of the older ladies in Aasha's
tour group remarked, "Look at all those beach people having fun!"

"These tourists are from the hotels in Mamallapuram," Aasha
mentioned to George and Mary. Some from the tour group walked
in the water with their shoes off. "Do you see there are Indian adults
swimming?"

"Yes, we do," Mary acknowledged.

"More every year," Aasha said. George and Mary nodded.
Different cultures are starting to mix, a good sign. George thought as
he rubbed his chin.

"Aasha, what does your name mean?" Mary wondered.

"My name means hope; thank you for asking."

"Beautiful," Mary said. "Very appropriate."

"Aasha, where's that modern fishing village we've heard about?"
George inquired.

"It's up ahead, not too far from here. It's mostly a village for tourists to shop. The boats are new and painted with bright colors. They
stay on shore; tourists like to have pictures taken in front of them."

"Not a place we need to see," George told Aasha. He explained
their idea to take a taxi to the old fishing village and locals' beach.

"I know where they are," she said. "But we don't tour them." We
are scheduled to have lunch at the Sea Shore Garden Restaurant, very
close. I can order a taxi to pick you up after lunch," She smiled. "I
understand."

The three of them talked on the way to the restaurant. George
was inspired by Aasha's demeanor and multilingual skills. She was a

marvel. He would have a Federal Express package sent to her. Today had started out to be a good day for The Project.

The open-air restaurant on the beach had a thatched roof. There were pink and blue striped wooden boats in front of it. Two European ladies by were standing by them having their picture taken. A young Indian boy had a monkey on a rope. It was mostly gray with a red face—the kind you sometimes saw running around the beaches. It was doing back flips and collecting money in a cup. The boy gave it one peanut per flip.

Inside, the restaurant was crowded with tourists and a few locals. Sand covered the floor and sea breeze served as the air conditioning. A red and green parrot was caged and eating a banana, holding it with one foot and peeling it with its beak. Most of the tourists were drinking beer and eating some strange looking soup. George asked for an English menu. The couple at a table next to them recommended the fish stew—the strange soup.

"We'll have two bowls of fish stew and two cold beers," Mary told the waiter. "What kind of beer do you have?"

"Very excellent beer, brewed in India! Very excellent. We have Kingfisher, Tiger, and Cobra beer. Kingfisher is the favorite," the waiter answered. He was dressed like he worked at a five-star hotel. "Very excellent hat, young lady, very excellent." Mary was wearing a simple sun hat, one that folded up. "And those beautiful pearl earrings, so beautiful." he added.

"Here we go with the patronizing," George whispered to Mary.

"George, be still." She was enjoying the compliments. She ordered two Kingfisher beers. The waiter then switched his attention to the two blonde Swedish women who were looking at the parrot. He whistled sharply, and the parrot whistled back. That got the two women to look at the waiter and smile.

George assumed the waiter had learned bad habits along the way. Learning to please tourists can be a problem; the temptation was to overdo it. Tourists were, with some exceptions, not the best at bridging cultures. They tended to produce insincere relationships.

Aasha found them a good taxi; she knew the driver and he spoke English well.

"Gagan will take good care of you—he knows people at the fishing village and he meditates at the locals' beach." Aasha said proudly, she was dating him. "He will show you authentic beach people."

Aasha hugged George and Mary and said goodbye, winking at George.

"That was a wink for the future," Mary teased. George knew it.

"Hello, Mr. and Mrs. Carpenter," Gagan was standing by his taxi. He was tall and young with black hair and thick black eyebrows.

"Hello Gagan," George shook Gagan's hand. "Call us George and Mary, please."

"My pleasure. I understand you want to see the old fishing village?"

"That's right," George replied. "Aasha said you know people there?"

"Some people, I had an uncle there. He died last year."

"We're sorry for your loss," Mary said.

"Thank you, thank you for saying that," Gagan replied, as he combed his hair with his fingers. His pleasant smile defined him. He was born and raised in Delhi and had spent a year in America learning about the west. He worked full-time now in computer programming in Madras and drove a taxi on weekends for extra income.

"We can go two ways, the main road or the back way. The back way is more scenic."

"How much longer is the back way?" George asked.

"Maybe an hour, driving straight. More when cows are on the road."

"We have time, let's go that way," Mary replied. George nodded.

The back road turned sharply west, off the main road, and ran along a river with green hills behind it. There were small farms with vegetable gardens and livestock; pigs and chickens ran loose. A giant brown sow was followed across the road by her eight piglets. Gagan stopped to let them cross.

He drove on through a small farming village where women washed clothes in clay tubs, laying them flat on grassy hills to dry. From a distance, the hills looked like multicolored quilts. "This is old India," Gagan explained. "These people sustain themselves and are doing fine."

"They sure know how to use the ground in old India." George could see. "Sure do," Mary agreed. George and Mary enjoyed the perspective Gagan was providing.

"Are other villages around here like this one?" George asked.

"It's about fifty-fifty," Gagan answered. "Some are self-sustaining, some are not. The ones that raise pigs successfully do the best."

"Remarkable," Mary added.

There was no road that ran directly into the fishing village — four-wheel drive vehicles could drive over the sand, but not the taxi. When they got close, on a hill above the village, Gagan parked and they walked down to it.

There was a flurry of activity. Boats were coming in and going out. Large schools of herring were close to shore and easy to net. A net was pulled by two boats--flat skiffs running parallel to each other with the net between them. Two men paddled each skiff. When the net bulged with fish they pulled it in and dumped the fish in the boat. Then, buried in fish, they paddled the skiffs to shore where most of the village was waiting. Older kids had rubber gloves on, men were ready with sharp knives, women with plenty of salt. Everyone was ready for the fish.

Gagan recognized two men he knew and talked with them briefly. They were in a hurry to get to the fish. Boats were coming full of fish that needed to be cut and salted quickly, then taken to the tarps to dry.

"It's a very busy day for them," Gagan remarked.

"Will they mind if we watch?" George questioned.

"No; because I'm here, they won't mind," Gagan answered. "They are worried it might rain. Rain means wet fish that will spoil, there is no ice in the village. They can keep some fish in plastic bags with extra salt, but after a short time they will spoil if not dried. The monsoon season is a slow time, they often eat fish stored from the dry season. Today is a good day for them!"

Gagan walked George and Mary through the village. He talked with a few more people he knew and translated what they said. One fisherman had caught a large seela fish that was too big to dry — it was hanging from a pole and dripping blood. This fish would be dinner tonight for several families. There was significant sharing between families in the village; many of the people were related. It was a large family of families. Gagan was pleased by the sincere interest George and Mary expressed.

"I'm so glad we came here," George said. "As a university professor, I can truly appreciate the challenges these people face to sustain themselves." George was impressed with how Gagan could bridge the gap between being a computer programmer and an expert guide for old India. He would fit perfectly in The Project.

"It's a bit different from how the boy with the monkey at the lunch restaurant sustains himself," Mary commented.

"Or, the well-dressed waiter selling beer and fish stew!" George added. And how about that parrot; he was the only one getting a free lunch!"

"These people you mention rely completely on tourist money!" Gagan emphasized. "And without tourist money, the parrot would have to live in a banana tree."

Mary agreed. "Life has worries, even for parrots!"

"Where's that locals' beach where you meditate?" George asked, changing the subject, wanting to keep the conversation upbeat.

"Not far, north a couple of miles," Gagan answered. "Aasha told me you wanted to go there."

"Let's do," Mary said. They walked back up the hill to the taxi, then took a few more minutes to look back at the fishing village. The activity hadn't slowed, everything was about fish down there.

As they drove away, Mary told George to show Gagan the rare seashell he bought from Atma. George showed the cone shell to Gagan and explained that he collected seashells. He added that he was impressed with the young boy who sold it to him.

"Atma and his little brothers!" Gagan said. "I know his uncle! The twins are learning business from their older brother."

"Small world," Mary said.

More bridges. George thought.

The locals' beach was back in the direction of Madras. There was an asphalt road that wound down to it off the main road.

"Look at all the people standing by the water." Mary was eager to get closer.

"We'll park here and walk down," Gagan said. There were three other vehicles and a few bicycles parked in the small area above the beach. Most people walked to it.

There were about a hundred people at the beach; most were standing on shore looking out at the ocean. Some were standing in the water.

"The women are dressed in colorful blouses and sarees!" Mary was thrilled with the femininity. A cool breeze ruffled the women's sarees; some of them were wet. Gagan led George and Mary between the lines of people, right into the middle of the local crowd. Some locals stared at them — the ones unaccustomed to seeing tourists on their beach.

"Nobody has a swimming suit on!" George exclaimed, "Just everyday clothes."

"They don't swim. See those standing in the water, arms spread open and looking at the ocean with their eyes closed?" Gagan said, pointing to several.

"Yes," George acknowledged. They're meditating, right?"

"Yes," Gagan answered. "Meditating clears the mind; it allows your body to relax so your mind can focus. After meditating I can solve tough problems. You can ask the spirit world for help when meditating."

"Tell us your secret method; Aasha said you had one," Mary asked Gagan.

"I'm happy to tell you! I stand in the water knee deep looking out, arms by my side, eyes open. I let a few minutes go by. Then, I close my eyes and open my arms wide, palms facing the water. I take a deep breath while counting to four, hold it while counting to seven, then exhale for a count of eight, touching my upper teeth with my tongue when exhaling. I do it four times, then think about nothing. I completely clear my mind and continue facing the ocean, arms open and eyes closed until I see a school of six silver dolphins. Nothing else. The dolphins are swimming in my mind. They live in my mind. When there is nothing but the dolphins, there is no sense of time. At some point, unconsciously, I switch back on; my eyes open and I rejoin the world. Relaxed. Refreshed. And with greater focus!"

George and Mary Carpenter were stunned, looking at Gagan as if they could see inside his soul. They stayed silent and looked out to those who were meditating. George was rubbing his chin. The Project must enlist this man! He thought.

"Would you like to try it?" Gagan asked them.

"Do they all do what you do?" George asked.

"I don't know. Everyone meditates in their own way."

"I'm afraid," Mary said. George put his arm around her, "You'll do fine," he kissed her.

"I'll go with both of you," Gagan was excited for them.

"I'll use your dolphin technique. Do you think I can look for blue dolphins instead of silver ones?" Mary asked.

"Why not? The door to the universe has a wide opening!" Gagan assured her.

"Let's go then," George was overflowing with emotion. "We must send the young people we've met a message—a soul message. The world needs them, and The Project will provide the path."

He took Mary by the hand and gave her another kiss as they walked out, knee deep, shoes on, into the ocean. Gagan followed just as a cool breeze blew over them.

Postscript:

This story is based on the author's experience in India in the late 1990s. Then, as now, there exists a great disparity between people of old, rural India and the people of modern, urban India. This disparity increases as one travels south but exists to a significant extent everywhere in India. There is a misunderstanding of what defines poverty, which is often confused with being rural. Abject poverty exists in the slums of India's largest cities where people get less than one-thousand calories of food per day. But, there is certainly rural poverty where people are not self-sustaining, even when surrounded by agriculture. Rural villages that self-sustain must be encouraged and used as models, not destroyed in the name of urbanization or globalization. Local cultures must be preserved, and poverty must not be the outcome of governmental activity.

In 2016, seventy percent of India's 1.2 billion people were considered rural. Both conservative and liberal policies have failed them.

One key to bridging their disparity with modern society is to utilize talented young people in an organized manner, and do it through private funding. These are the tour guides, taxi drivers, waiters and local youth. Aasha, Gagan, Raj, and Atma are examples of them. But they need to be developed and nurtured. This is the goal of The Project.

Great Barrier Island—New Zealand

6

New Zealand Deep Drama
A Whale of a Tale

*P*rologue:

In February of 2017 it was confirmed that New Zealand sits on top of a previously unknown continent—Zealandia. Although ninety-four percent submerged, its 1.9 million square miles makes it the world's seventh largest continent—almost the size of India. Viewed from space, Zealandia has the shape of a giant boot with its toe pointing south. In its midsection is another boot, a smaller one, with its toe pointing north—New Zealand. Somewhere around 60 to 85 million years ago, this "new" continent broke off from Australia, floated east, and sunk.

An active tectonic-plate boundary runs diagonally through Zealandia's midsection and continues fifteen hundred miles northeastward to Tonga. This is where the Australian and Pacific plates meet as part of the notorious Ring of Fire—a huge area of volcanic and seismic activity that encircles the Pacific Ocean.

Where the plate boundary runs parallel to Zealandia's shallow Lau Colville Ridge, the Pacific Ocean plunges to over twenty-thousand feet deep. This is where our story begins.

South Pacific, North of New Zealand, January 2002

The sperm whale was twenty-two meters long and weighed close to sixty metric tons. Its lower jaw held twenty-six pairs of cone-shaped teeth that each weighed a kilogram; with its mouth closed, they fit perfectly into sockets in the upper jaw. These huge teeth were for holding prey, not chewing it. This was a giant male sperm whale, maybe the world's largest, and surely a rival to Melville's fictional Moby Dick.

"Mo xiang jing!" Captain Xi barked at the three officers in Mandarin confirming that a whale was directly ahead. The monster sperm whale appeared when the submarine's sonar alarm sounded and automatically turned on the outboard floodlights. Their depth was 915 meters in 1,700 meters of water. "Report the animal's dimensions."

"Twenty-two meters long, three-point-five meters wide at midsection," Ensign Zhang reported in Mandarin, Shanghai dialect. The whale was monstrous, now visible through the submarine's thick glass ports and on the widescreen video monitor. The sub's lights had surprised it in the cold- dark of the Twilight Zone, eighty-five meters above the Midnight Zone of total darkness. It was a bright summer day on the surface.

"Again," the captain ordered. He either didn't understand the ensign or couldn't believe what he'd heard. The ensign repeated in Mandarin, Beijing dialect.

There were four men in the small DSV—deep-submergence vehicle. They were investigating the loss of two top-secret, nuclear-tipped torpedoes and hadn't expected a giant whale to show up.

"Click, click, click" sounds reverberated from the speaker connected to the sub's external hydrophone. Very loud clicks!

"They're coming from the whale's anterior," Wang, the science officer asserted, looking at the sonar screen.

"You mean its mouth?" the captain's question was touched with sarcasm.

"No, its nose and head are involved. The whale forces air from its nose into its head where it resonates with different organs and then comes back out the nose, louder."

"Too much information—just say nose," the captain instructed Wang, a stern-faced, humorless young man from Hangchou who reported to the CPC (Chinese communist party), not the military.

Sperm whales produced the loudest sounds in the animal kingdom—up to 230 decibels. They could stun their prey with sound. In Mexico's Sea of Cortez, pods of young sperm whales chased schools of Humboldt squid, machine-gunning them with loud clicks. Some whales are ventriloquists and can throw their clicks, totally confusing prey.

The giant, block-headed, high-humped, blue-gray cetacean slowly maneuvered to see the DSV better. The research submarine was about one-third the length of the whale, which was now clicking in a cadence spaced out like Morse code.

"He's echo-locating us!" lieutenant Wong, second in command, spoke up. "Hopefully the whale realizes its clicks are rebounding from something inorganic, not food or another whale."

Captain Xi moved the craft in reverse, trying to maintain a constant distance from the whale which was streaming past them vertically now. The whale extended and retracted its ellipsoidal eyes, attempting to see through the blinding flood lights. The sub would have no defense should the whale attack—its two electric motors were not designed for speed. This was a deep-water, slow-moving, exploratory laboratory—water and pressure-proof but not whale-proof!

"A sperm whale's huge block head is made for ramming! It's full of spongy junk tissue that absorbs shock," The science officer instructed. The naval officers, including the captain, didn't care to hear something they could figure out. It was not possible for Wang to play down his connection to the CPC.

"It would not be smart to move away; it could catch us with one tail kick," the lieutenant asserted. The captain agreed.

"A male sperm whale is the ocean's largest predator; only a pod of very hungry orcas (killer whales) would dare challenge it. So with such credentials, it can afford to be curious and temper its aggression if it judges something un-edible or not hostile," Zhang, the well-educated ensign, contributed. The captain smiled at him approvingly.

After several more passes, clicks less intense, the whale slowed as the captain hovered the submarine at a constant depth. They were only twenty-meters apart.

"Dim floodlights," the captain instructed Zhang.

"To how many lumens?"

"Down to five thousand with more diffusion," the captain answered. They had been at eighty thousand lumens undiffused! "Now we'll let him get a good look at us and confirm that we're not edible or hostile."

The huge mammal drifted toward them, neutrally buoyant like the sub. They eyed each other. The monster intentionally nudged the sub, causing it to tilt and yaw. The captain steadied it by relocating its ballast of liquid mercury contained in a tubular network. Through the portholes the men could see the whale's many scars: circular scars from squid, its favorite food; some saucer size from a giant squid's suction cups; and some deeper and irregular—from orcas?

"Many decades of mysteries here!" the captain remarked, immersed now in respect for the giant, ageless mammal as he slowly backed the research sub away from it.

"How many amp-hours left on the silver-zinc batteries?" The captain asked Zhang.

"We're all right, just forty percent discharged," Zhang reported, checking the Power Management Display.

"What about oxygen reserves and carbon dioxide absorption?"

"Both are less than thirty-five percent exhausted," Zhang confirmed the Life Systems Display.

The DSV was the underwater equivalent of a manned space satellite in terms of life-system functions. The ensign had control of all systems, the lieutenant provided backup and security. The science officer had no authority underwater, only back at headquarters during debriefing. And the captain was charged with insuring smooth interaction between the men.

IQ wise, Zhang was just below the genius level. It was common for the Chinese military to slow the advancement of such individuals, as they could present threats if allowed too much power. Captain Xi, who was no dummy himself, was aware of this but mostly worried about Wang while happily challenging Zhang.

"We're in working order," the captain declared, "The CPC trawler should be here in two hours. I'll explain to them why we didn't find the lost nuclear torpedoes!" Wang, stern-faced as usual, didn't look at the captain.

The captain would have preferred a pickup by the Chinese navy. He wasn't amused by the thought of explaining their lack of success to communist bureaucrats more tenacious than blood-starved wood ticks. Their mission had been to locate two secret torpedoes armed with tactical nuclear warheads that had rolled off a Chinese destroyer in a storm. Just one could sink an American Nimitz-class aircraft carrier and its six thousand sailors!

The sub came up slowly to a four-hundred-meter depth where the ocean was calm but still in the disphotic, or Twilight Zone. They would hold at this depth until pickup rather than getting bounced around higher in the water.

Photosynthesis stopped at the bottom of the euphotic zone, two-hundred meters deep, as did most of the sea's biology. But life did persist much deeper, and at least one 'sailfish' hung out eight-thousand-meters deep where the pressure was eight-tons per square inch! NASA likened this pressure to what a strong woman would experience holding forty-eight 747 jet aircraft at one time.

The captain, now with time to kill until pickup, authorized Wang to recite all he knew about whales . . .

Suddenly, the outboard hydrophone registered loud clicking mixed with unusual gulping and belching as the sonar screen blinked a large, green image.

"What in Mao's Mother's name is going on?" the captain barked in Mandarin.

Zhang turned the floodlights on full.

"The whale has returned!" the lieutenant exclaimed. Captain Xi turned the research sub around 180 degrees without changing depth to face the sonar image.

Then, in front of them, an astonishing sight appeared. A colossal squid was in a life or death fight with the sperm whale! Its eight anaconda arms were hooked and suckered to the whale's face, twisting and squeezing.

The squid's arms sprung forward from its head, which connected to its torso, which was the size of a rhinoceros. Two eyes—midnight black—each as large as a human head, stared at the whale. The squid's siphon pulsed jets of water causing the giant cephalopod to lurch back and forth, while its arms kept it attached to the whale's face. It was trying to contact the whale's eyes with the club ends of its two tentacles, each four times longer than an arm. The colossal squid was attacking the whale!

"This is not to believe!" the captain uttered in Mandarin. Wang and the second officer, Lieutenant Wong, were glued to the portholes while ensign Zhang gave the captain whatever information he asked for.

The sub started to rock and pitch in the turbulence created by the fight. The captain switched to auto-stabilization to calm things down—liquid mercury raced in pipes from one ballast chamber to another, keeping the DSV level.

The whale swerved abruptly as the squid kept suctioning and twisting, wildly changing the position of its eight arms while trying to hook the whale's eyes. It was not possible for the squid to bite the whale with its beak and radula as its arms impeded flat contact. Its main strategy was to force an arm or tentacle into the whale's blowhole and smother it. Sperm whales could only stay underwater for roughly an hour. The squid never had to come up.

"This is a colossal squid, much larger than a giant squid. Its name is Mesonychoteuthis hamiltoni—there's no Chinese name," Wang mumbled in amazement. "Nobody will believe this; there has never been one seen alive, much less in a fight with a whale"—he was having trouble finding the right words in Mandarin to describe it.

"Good! Your comrades won't need to believe it, because you're not telling them!" the captain asserted. "We were looking for the lost nuclear torpedoes, and the water got rough down deep—understand? We had no radiation readings except for background on the Ratemeter Scalers. That's all they need to know!"

Wang now stared at the captain but said nothing.

The captain stared back, then told Zhang to dim the floodlights while he backed the sub, putting more distance between them and the fight. They were rocking and rolling despite auto-stabilization.

"Look at it, the squid is glowing purple!" Zhang said excitedly, recognizing the improbability of ever seeing this again. "Intense purple luminescence is coming from under the squid's mantle. It's glowing! The whale is trying to bite into the squid's head in front of its huge black eyes—but the arms are in the way." Every time the whale tried to open its mouth, the squid's siphon would jet water and pull its arms tighter, preventing the whale's mouth from opening.

"Squid and their cousin, the octopus, are smart. Put a mud crab in a jar in front of an octopus and it will unscrew the lid to get to it—a favorite food. This squid is doing everything possible to keep the whale's mouth shut!" It was lieutenant Wong's turn to impress with his knowledge.

"Turn the floodlights off," the captain ordered.

The squid's bioluminescence, produced by trillions of photoactive bacteria under its exoskeleton (mantle), created a macabre picture of a giant whale head stuck to an impossibly large squid.

"The luminescence is blue now," Lieutenant Wong remarked.

The whale had managed to bite into the squid's gills when its jaw pressure briefly overwhelmed the suction grip from two arms. The squid jolted erratically.

"It's bleeding from its gills; that changed the luminescence. A squid's blood is blue from a copper protein that carries oxygen, not an iron protein (hemoglobin) as in red blood." Wang was attempting to get back in charge of technical details.

"The squid's jetting black ink now!" the captain said. The ink sack that all cephalopods have had been pierced, and black, melanin-rich "ink" pumped out the siphon. None of this was good news for the squid. The whale shook its massive head as the squid started to come apart.

When Zhang turned the lights back up they could see the whale's huge jaws disconnecting the arms from the squid's head.

The whale swallowed the arms whole. The first of its four stomachs substituted for chewing; it crushed and macerated the squid's appendages before the three enzyme-rich stomachs took over digestion. Then the whale, scarred in many new places, eyes intact and functioning, attempted to feast on the main course—the enormous rhino-size torso of the colossal squid. It was just an average day . . . deep in the Twilight Zone.

Auckland, New Zealand, February 2002

It was noon when I arrived in Auckland after a four-hour flight from Sydney, an hour longer than usual due to 100-mph headwinds. It's a bit farther from Oz to En Zed than it appears to be on most maps!

Julian Clark waited for me at the luggage conveyor for Air New Zealand. We were happy to see each other and, as usual, had many things to talk about. We got started while waiting for my suitcase. Julian was our business partner in Kiwi Land and, like other partners around the world, was dedicated to using probiotic microbes to solve tough problems. And we were working on a tough one here! Our mission for the trip was to evaluate whether probiotic microbes could stop an incurable fungal disease that was lethal to the magnificent, native kauri trees.

"We'll head straight to GBI on the SeaLink Ferry—going flat out it will take over four hours to get there by water." Julian never wasted words explaining the weather—I could see it was overcast and windy. GBI translated to the "Great Barrier Inland" (Aotea in Maori) that guarded Auckland and environs from the mean swells of the Pacific—strategically positioned ninety kilometers out in the Hauraki Gulf. It was home to many endangered kauri trees.

"You've let your golden locks grow since last winter (August)," I mentioned as we sped away from the airport. Julian didn't want to miss the ferry, it would mean a lost day if we did. He was a modestly stout, middle-age Kiwi with yellow hair and artic-blue eyes—and had a good head for any business fueled by science. I'd met him three years earlier at a marine science seminar in Honolulu.

"I get it cut twice yearly by a Maori lady in Christchurch—whenever I go there."

"Let me guess; that would be two times."

Julian, testing me, grinned as we pulled into the parking lot for Auckland's Wynyard Wharf—the SeaLink's horn was growling pre-departure tones.

"We'll have to hustle." It was two-hundred meters to the ferry from where Julian parked. I noticed a Chinese trawler in the harbor that looked like it was carrying one of those mini research subs.

"The Chinese are here," I noted, as I pulled my suitcase across the gravel parking lot thankful for its large, fender-protected wheels — cheap suitcases with small wheels had caused me expensive delays in the past.

"We see that trawler often, carrying a DSV sub. They're always looking for something; they come in for supplies." Julian explained, trying to keep up with me while swinging his briefcase; he had no suitcase. The SeaLink's crew could see us running toward them.

Inside the ferry we settled down and ordered a beer — the bar would soon be pitching and yawing once the ferry got into the wind. The scenery was marvelous in good weather; I'd been here before.

"How's that Double Brown?" Julian asked me. It was DB Breweries' backpacker favorite. A six-pack of 330 ml cans could feed you for a day.

"Two of these and I won't need dinner," I assured him. It was a full-bodied amber lager brewed on New Zealand's North Island. It appeared that out of the forty or so passengers, Julian and I were the only non-tourists.

A redhead wearing a Maui Rays sweatshirt was standing nearby at the bar. It was a standup bar that didn't allow much wiggle room. "Normally this would be a warm summer day in February — that cold south wind is spoiling the ambiance," She exclaimed.

"That depends," Julian contended.

"Depends on what?" she responded.

"On how it affects the kauri trees." Julian pulled a photo of a big one out of his briefcase and showed it to her. "These trees are native to New Zealand and can live for two thousand years — they tower over fifty-meters high. The largest on GBI is over four meters in diameter."

"Too much wet weather spreads a soil fungus that kills the trees; cold weather slows the fungus down, so cold windy days without rain like this can help the kauri." I added, then held three fingers up for the bartender to see. When three cans of DB Double Brown arrived, I gave Sarah one and told her it would be a good substitute for lunch. Her name had been called out by two other ladies: Qantas flight attendants standing at the end of the bar.

After making brief introductions, Julian and I continued discussing kauri trees with Sarah while the ferry continued to rock and roll. Given the weather, it reminded me of a boat trip in Scotland last year, where the windows were fogged same as here—a cold, windy day spent in Loch Ness looking for Nessie? But that was eleven thousand miles from here, too far for Nessie to swim.

By the time we reached Tryphena Harbor on GBI, the wind had calmed, and the day brightened enough to expose the jagged, high-walled, emerald-green geology of the island: A rock-solid 285-square-kilometer oceanic barrier, GBI guarded the North Island of New Zealand's archipelago. Its eastern shore faced the open Pacific Ocean where relentless swells punched into its rocky cliffs and long white beaches, while deep sheltered harbors and sandy bays graced its western shore. It was a true wilderness with a population of just over three residents per square kilometer.

Julian had an SUV rental ready for us in Tryphena at the southern end of the island. He had rented a small cottage near Whangaparapara Harbor on the calm western shore—pleasant and desolate. Sarah and her two flight-attendant friends would meet us later at the Currach Irish Pub on Blackwell Road and continue the kauri tree discussion.

"Tena Koutou (Greetings) Mates," Mick Gooden hailed us in Maori when we arrived at the rental cottage.

"Kia Ora (Hello) Mick," Julian returned his greeting.

"Mr. Randolf, great to see you again in our wilderness."

"I'm happy to be back, Mick. Kei te pehea koe? (How's it going?)."

"Hah, you remember your Maori."

"Yup, just like you taught me."

"It's going good—look in the truck." The back of Mick's pickup was full of wooden signs that read:

Healthy Kauri Trees Ahead
- Scrub your shoes

- Spray your shoes
- Keep to the track
- Stop the threat of Kauri Dieback Disease.

"Need to put several of those signs on each trail. We'll be busy chaps in the wop-wop (outback) tomorrow." Mick grinned.

"Aye, that's the right message!" Julian proclaimed. "You better run, Mick, or you'll be late for church." He was the backup minister who began his sermons in Maori and finished them by quoting passages from the Bible. It was sermon time.

"Meet me at the Aotea Track head at eight bells in the morning," He shouted.

"Hei konel ra (see you tomorrow)," I shouted back as he drove off.

Mick had a Maori mother and a German father. He grew up an Aucklander and worked for the Department of Conservation (DoC). He and Julian were old friends; it was Mick who convinced Julian to help solve the kauri-tree dieback problem. I planned to take soil samples for lab tests and then submit a plan to the DoC for using our anti-fungal probiotics (beneficial soil bacteria) as a natural treatment. Pathogenic fungi don't do well when our Bacillus probiotics are around—they don't appreciate competition!

When we arrived at the Currach Irish Pub, the only pub on GBI, we could see Sarah with her two flight-attendant friends, Joy and Judy, at the bar.

"Hope you don't mind, but we've switched from DB to Guinness!" Sarah declared. The three ladies toasted our arrival, holding their frothy glasses high.

The pub was quite contemporary, not an old rock-wall cellar with locals huddled in dark corners drinking pints like I envisioned from times in Dublin, but something brighter and cheerier, like a place you might see in Pismo Beach, California.

The five of us began by reintroducing ourselves. It had been a bit too jarring to do it properly on the ferry. Sarah worked in the office for Qantas in Honolulu. Joy and Judy also worked for Qantas but at thirty-five thousand feet over the Pacific Ocean.

"What are you guys eating?" I asked Judy, who was just about to take a bite of a fish filet.

"Some kind of Dory fish and chips. Here, try one."

I took a bite. It reminded me of Chilean sea bass in Santiago. It was good.

"The fish's name is John Dory, there's one on the wall." Julian pointed to the fish. The big, mounted, flat-headed fish that looked down on us.

Our conversation changed directions and subjects as the five of us got to know each other. I ordered additional Dory filets, chips and Guinness for all of us. The chips came with vinegar, like in Canada.

"What trees were we talking about on the ferry?" Sarah asked.

"Kauri trees," Julian confirmed.

"The tall, silver ones we saw horseback riding in the mountains behind Wellington last week," Sarah reminded Judy and Joy.

"What could endanger those wooden brutes?" Judy asked.

"A microscopic fungus called Phytophthora agathidicida. One gram of soil contaminated with it can infect a tree that's twelve centuries old—and kill it," I explained.

"We have to educate the trekkers and tourists on how to prevent the fungal infection from spreading by properly cleaning and disinfecting their shoes and staying on the trails. Tomorrow we have sixty trail signs to install that explain how to do it." Julian elaborated.

"We're working with both the Maori Tribal Council and the New Zealand Department of Conservation—first to educate the trekkers, then to test a possible natural cure." I added.

Sarah whispered something to Joy and Judy. They nodded. Then she looked at Julian and me. "Want some help?"

The following day, Aotea Track, 8:00 a.m.

You can imagine the surprise on Mick Gooden's face when Julian and I showed up with the three attractive females ready to help—all dressed for work in bright, Hawaiian attire that included broad sunhats and Maui Ray sunnies. The weather god had answered our toasts—it was a blue-perfect day in the Southern South Pacific.

"Blow me down and send all my money to my mother!" Mick bellowed.

The women didn't give Julian or me a chance to say boo. They introduced themselves to Mick and cleared up any concerns that they'd been shanghaied.

Sarah checked out the pile of signs in the back of Mick's truck. "They're for real," she shouted.

Mick took control. "Good onya mates for finding these working lassies; we're gonna have fun doing some important work. Here's the plan . . ."

Mick unfolded a map showing the main roads on GBI and where they intersected with tracks (trails) including the popular the Aotea Track. "We need to put a sign at each major intersection."

We followed Mick in our rental SUV—his truck was dirty and had worn out leaf-springs. Areas on the road that were not sealed were rutted. The petrol-operated post-hole digger did most of the work. We would stop where a trail intersected the road, dig a hole, plant a sign, take a quick look around, then move on. I felt like Chevy Chase in the 1983 movie Vacation.

In most places, the kauri trees we could see from the road were young ones mixed in with rimu and kahikatea trees. But when we came on a grove of giants—towering silver-speckled skyscrapers shinning in the sun—it required pause. In two blinks, I was standing in Sequoia National Park in California surrounded by the kauri's redwood soulmates.

I had been taking soil samples in the rhizosphere (root zone) of various-sized kauri trees, using disposable foot coverings whenever going off-trail. These samples would be lab tested for the phytophthora fungus and, if present, for susceptibility to our different probiotic strains. On my next trip to GBI we should have enough information to start field trials.

We saw the island in one day and all sixty signs had been set to educate trekkers.

The hot tub at the lodge where the ladies were staying was a hot 104 F. We had talked about going to island's Kaitoke natural hot springs—heated by underwater volcanic activity—but it was dark after dinner and we decided to leave it, and the rocky trail to get to it, for another time.

Sarah, Joy, and I sat in the hot tub while Julian and Judy sat on the rim with their feet in the water. Mick was reciting Maori poetry interspaced with translations. He had his arms stretched out, holding onto the tub's rim, eyes closed. It was a poetic story of what happens when the various giants of nature clash. And how the outcome can influence the balance in the spirit world.

He told of an enormous squid fighting a huge sperm whale. The squid had attacked the whale. Whales only attack squid to eat them. Squid only attack whales to kill them. Confrontations between such giants is most significant. The intention of the attack is what separates good from evil. Vital to man's successful existence in the physical world is the implicit requirement that evil stay in balance with benevolence. Mick finished by singing an old Maori song telling of God holding a scale that had doves in one pan and demons in the other—the pans were in balance.

"Can we talk about whales?" Sarah asked as she kicked her feet.

"Sure, why not?" I said, Mick had started it and was now asleep.

"Scientists and politicians are saying that global warming is killing whales," Sarah said. "Is that true?"

"Global warming or killing whales? I quipped.

"You know what I mean!"

"I don't know the answer to that question, ocean warming may reduce zooplankton numbers that many whales depend on as a food source. There is some warming, but it has little to do with people driving cars and trucks around! Or making tea on a wood stove. Or cow flatulence."

"What's causing it then?"

"Many thousands of undersea volcanoes, seventy-five thousand of which are over a thousand meters high. Just fuming and hiding underwater!

"But they've been there forever; why now are they such a worry?"

"Changes in our solar system have switched them on. The earth's rotation is changing. Gravitational and magnetic effects are occurring on a massive scale. The volcanoes are waking up. It's a cycle that has happened many times before!"

"Do you know this for sure?" Sarah kept on.

"With ninety percent confidence!" I answered.

"What's the solution?" she asked.

"There is very little man can do to make a significant difference. If the warming continues without interruption, we will need to start relocating people away from the coasts and prioritize research on crops that grow in deserts," I said.

"This explains why China is building all those mega-cities inland! Huge empty cities just waiting for coastal refugees," Julian added.

"Yup. There is one thing that can offset the warming short term: the sun. If the next eleven-year solar cycle, or the following one, is less active (fewer sunspots), things will likely cool down."

"Pray for nature to help us," Sarah lamented.

I slept well in Julian's rental cottage. This place, this island, was a true wilderness. It was early, and we wouldn't see Mick until noon—he had two DoC scientists meeting us in Port Fitzroy for a discussion on antifungal probiotics.

We had bacon and eggs for breakfast, and then at Julian's suggestion, we drove over to Whangapoua beach where we had planted a sign yesterday.

Julian knew I collected seashells and the east-facing Whangapoua beach was a great place to find them early in the morning. We parked by our sign and walked to the white sand beach.

"What are all those birds doing?" Julian exclaimed as we walked in their direction. They were in the air, in the water, on shore, all circling a pink mass. Strangely, owls were mixed in with seabirds and vultures.

"Probably a whale carcass," I suggested.

When we got closer, we both could see the pink mass was no whale!

"Can you believe what we're looking at?" I said in amazement. We both ran toward it, waving our arms and yelling the birds away. They reluctantly moved off the corpse.

"It's half of a giant squid!" Julian said loudly. "Only the second one I've ever seen, this one is much larger."

"Actually, it's one half of the torso of a colossal squid! Different species!" I said in disbelief. The size of the eyes gave it away. Few have ever seen one—and here in front of us was a fearsome fraction of, arguably, the rarest of ocean monsters!

"Something ate all the arms off, left the head, beak and giant eyes, then bit the torso in half!" Julian explained, with his tee shirt pulled up over his nose.

The odor was extreme, like the five-pounds of bait squid I forgot about in the trunk of a rental car one August in Key West! I took a more detailed look at "the thing." The eyes, each the size of a human head, had not been pecked at by the birds; they looked right through me.

As we walked back to the SUV, I thought about sperm whales. One of them probably won a great victory here. Cheers for balance in the spirit world!

Postscript:

After returning to Minneapolis, I received a letter from Julien. He explained that he and Mick had met a Chinese sailor named Zhang in Auckland who might be available to help us with our kauri tree efforts. It was at the city administration building and Zhang was waiting for his number to be called—he was applying for a resident visa. He was happy to meet Julien and Mick and explained his situation in clear English. The research sub he had been assigned to, the one on the trawler in Auckland's harbor, had been decommissioned and he had been discharged. No more details were provided to him, typical of the Chinese government.

As Julien and Mick waited with Zhang, recognizing his intelligence and many skills, they offered their support, and the possibility of him helping with the kauri trees. Just as Zhang's number was called, he asked Julian and Mick to please wait, he had a "whale of a tale" to share with them.

The Indian Ocean kisses Bali

7

Return to Bali
Manta Rays, Soul Enlightenment, and Primate Thieves

*P*rologue:

Bali, Indonesia is a small tropical island east of Java. Complementing its popularity as a tourist destination is a special heritage: unlike the rest of Indonesia where Islam predominates, in Bali an evolved version of Hinduism prevails and is practiced by eighty-three percent of the population. Many positive aspects of other religions are incorporated into Balinese beliefs, while dark aspects are rejected. A strong localism exists; rules in one village can differ from those in another. Religion is viewed more as a guide of acceptable customs rather than a dominating force.

Balinese Hinduism includes reverence for Buddhism and its commitment to spiritual guidance and a civilized respect for life. The concept of spirit embraces many forms of natural phenomena including plants, animals, oceans, and mountains.

A fundamental belief in Bali is that order in the universe is sustained by a force known as dharma and opposed by a disordering force called adharma. Achieving balance between these two forces is required before a person can escape the never-ending cycle of reincarnation—this sought-after state of being is called Moska.

Bali, Indonesia—February 2003

The ocean is calm in the dark, overcast night. Wading shallow, parallel to the beach, the bottom feels sandy and smooth. I splash my hands in the water and create blue flashes with my fingers—awakening bioluminescent phytoplankton. When present in large numbers, these plankton illuminate the breaking waves. But tonight it's calm, and my hands produce the only waves. I sit down waist-deep and celebrate the stillness. Looking out at the Java Sea, several ships hug the horizon.

It has been a long day. My flight on Garuda Airlines from Hong Kong to Jakarta was delayed, so I missed the early connection to Bali. Sitting now in the cool ocean provides welcome therapy after a day of hot, humid travel. My hotel room is close, just beyond the beach. Artfully arranged next to its door are fruit and flower offerings for the good spirits. I'm happy I've returned to Bali.

After flying thousands of miles, I find it's important to quiet the drums of business and take time to recalibrate. It may take a few days or a week to do this. The process involves an evaluation of my priorities—what I do, what I believe, how I interact with others—what the future holds. It helps me decide whether I need any fine tuning or, maybe, a complete change of frequencies. The island of Bali is one of my favorite places to recalibrate.

Sitting on a rockpile on a hill behind the resort I study the ocean in Amed Bay through polarized binoculars. It's just after sunrise, and I can see beyond the turquoise shallows deep into the cobalt-blue water. Dozens of coral reefs are visible before the water deepens; vibrant with life, they create one of Bali's famous spots for scuba diving and snorkeling. A boat is optional; you can walk in from shore.

Mount Agung looms behind me to the north, an active volcano responsible for the black sands of Amed beach and a lethal eruption in 1963; from here it's an almost perfect cone 3,142 meters high.

A traditional jukung fishing boat floats slowly over a sunken World War II Japanese patrol boat—one that didn't make it home. I had snorkeled over it last year. Out in front of the jukung a frenzy of whitetip reef sharks circles a huge, seven-foot leatherback turtle that's rapidly pumping its massive flippers. Five-foot reef sharks don't alarm the giant turtle, but tiger sharks would. In open water the turtle can dive over four thousand feet deep to avoid tiger sharks and stay down for eighty to ninety minutes! His mission this morning is to find jellyfish—a favorite food—in fertile Amed Bay. A hundred years ago the same turtle, but smaller, was likely swimming with the great-grandfathers of these reef sharks.

Leatherbacks are the largest of the seven species of sea turtles— this one easily weighs over a ton. They told me at the dive shop in Denpasar that he was around; one this size is a rarity.

"Amazing animal, that leatherback!" a stranger coming up the trail remarks. The turtle is easily recognizable without binoculars.

"G' Day," I say, turning around. "Do they get this big in OZ?" He was unmistakably an Aussie, so I'd switched to Australian vernacular.

"Never saw one that size in Brizzie (Brisbane). Five years in the slammer if you kill one up here!" Bali was "up," north of Australia.

"Good reason not to do it," I reply. "Are you bunking in Kuta?"

"Aye mate, with a bunch of banana benders from Queensland. They're a bit crook, had too much amber fluid last night."

"Tell them to take B-vitamins next time—before they pop the tinnys."

"Yeah," he says. "What's that do?"

"Activates the liver to metabolize alcohol faster, keeps you from getting rotten." I was having fun with him.

"That's ace, mate! I'll give it a go. It's great to meet a Yank who knows how to talk."

The Aussies love Bali. The town of Kuta near the airport is called Ozzie Town by the locals—rooms go for as low as five dollars a night. We introduce ourselves and talk awhile more. He's flying back to Brisbane in the morning. Mick Limerick is an authentic Ozzie—I jot his name and phone number down in my notebook before he leaves me with a "good onya" for showing him the turtle.

"I'll buy ya brekkie in Brizzie on my next visit!" I shout to him... I have an uncle who lives in Brisbane. Mick gives me a thumb up as he heads back to the trail.

I sit back down on my favorite rockpile on the hill and reach into my backpack for the bag of rambutans I bought yesterday. The hairy red fruit opens with a quick twist, exposing a white nugget that smells like a strawberry and tastes like a grape dipped in pear juice. I eat three; these Balinese red-haired (ciliated) rambutans are exceptionally tasty. I never visit Bali without eating a dozen or so.

After wiping my sticky hands on brown grass between the rocks, I begin scanning the bay with binoculars again. I'm certifiably into my first Balinese morning, looking for giant blanketfish, as locals call them. The dive shop has reports of several in Amed bay—they claim one has a "wing-span" of almost thirty feet. Think about that: when one of them swims above a scuba diver, undulating like an enormous silk blanket in a mild breeze, its shadow blocks the sun leaving the diver in the dark. Manta birostris is its scientific name—the largest ray in the world.

"What are you looking for?" A lady in hiking attire asks. The trail behind my rock pile is becoming popular.

"Giant manta rays," I reply.

"We saw three while scuba diving yesterday." She points to the deeper water north of the sunken patrol boat. "Shimmering purple blankets! Our instructor told us they were feeding on patches of zooplankton beyond the reef."

I stand up, hand her the binoculars, and tell her to look just beyond the jukung fishing boat.

"Nice, I can see deep into the water with these! What am I looking for—the rays?"

"No, a huge turtle." I move the binoculars slightly while she looks through them, over to where I had been watching the smiling reptile. Spotted facial markings formed a perfect smile around the mouth of the big guy.

"I see it, a giant leatherback. Wow!" She watches the turtle for a couple minutes. "We didn't see him yesterday." Then she looks at me... "I know you! You gave a lecture in Hawaii last year at the university—on using probiotic bacteria in aquaculture to reduce pollution."

"Yes, I did." She has blue eyes and short blonde hair under a white sun hat and is about five-foot-five and forty-something—but she doesn't look familiar.

"You probably don't recognize me; it was a big audience in the auditorium that day and dozens of students wanted to speak with you after your presentation. I'm Susan Parker, I teach Marine Ecology."

"I'm certainly pleased to meet you, Susan! If I stare at you long enough it might trigger my memory." She laughs and winks at me.

"Let me see if I can find those big rays for you," she says. "We were diving farther north and further out from shore." She still has the binoculars.

"There's a dense band of plankton where the deep water starts; it's translucent brown not green, so it's zooplankton." I point north.

"There they are, the three of them, on the deep side of the plankton bloom." She hands the binoculars back to me.

"Spectacular! Look at the wingspan on that giant male—almost thirty feet!" He's leading the other two 'smaller' twenty-five-foot mantas, probably females. He's royal-purple on top, white underneath, with white tips on his dark triangular pectoral fins (wings). All three mantas are undulating smoothly, gliding through the water. "How close did you get to them?" I ask her.

"We were ten feet below them, in the dark under their shadows. They didn't bother us— it's the big sting rays you have to watch out for."

"You know it—close relatives of the mantas, but they're carnivorous and respond to threats. Last year in Tahiti, my son and I were snorkeling with a guided group off the island of Moorea, hand-feeding dozens of sting rays. They surrounded us; all were the size of garbage can lids. They would swim past us, turn upside down to expose their mouth, then eat pieces of squid from our hands. We presented no threat, fed them lots of squid, no problems . . ."

"We don't do that in Hawaii anymore; inexperienced tourists wouldn't follow instructions and they'd get stung!" She added.

Unlike sting rays, mantas are harmless plankton feeders, and some have been around over a hundred years—like the amazing thirty-footer. Looking again for the three of them, we can see they are moving slower now, over large coral humps.

"They're looking for a school of sergeant majors; a cleaning-station crew," Susan surmises.

"You're right, blue ones!" Dozens of blue sergeant majors begin approaching the rays and start eating parasites off the protective mucin layer covering their skin. The rays are in Fish Heaven—undulating in place like pet dogs being groomed at a talent show.

The sergeant majors are about the size of a Minnesota bluegill. Being very territorial they are quite aggressive toward each other, but fortunately for the smaller sergeants, there's plenty of skin in the game. From a five-inch fish's perspective, there's an infinity of mucin to eat.

Susan and I talk more about the ocean and its ecology and Bali's uniqueness. She invites me to join her and several fellow biology professors for dinner at their hotel in Nusa Dua—she says they would appreciate a biochemist's perspective. I have no plans for the evening and am happy to accept. Recalibration often involves the unexpected.

Nusa Dua is on the Bukit Peninsula in south Bali, about ninety kilometers from Amed Bay. Its broad, bone-white beaches contrast with Amed's black sands. I'm looking forward to the dinner event.

I had plenty of time to visit the Taman Ayun Temple in Mengwi, west of Amed Bay. Taman Ayun is a superb example of Balinese-Hindu architecture—rows upon rows of pagoda-like towers are mixed in with pavilions, ponds, kemboja trees, orange bunga flowers, and calico cats. But for me the attraction is the peace and solitude, more than at the tourist crowded shore temples. I explore it all . . .

When ready for a little meditation, the kind that evens out the emotions and clears the mind, I take off my shirt and rub on coconut oil spiked with carrot-seed and red-raspberry oils—about SPF 40—one of several versions of natural sunscreens I formulated. Commercial sunscreens contain compounds that poison coral reefs—and possibly people, too!

I sit down next to a small calico cat on a bench in the outer courtyard of the temple. The cat licks the sunscreen on my arm as I glance at a long row of maroon, multi-tiered pagodas. Strangely, the small cat's raspy tongue creates a mesmerizing sensation. I pet it on the head while looking out over a pond where birds are standing on lavender lotus flowers; they're shaped like blue jays but are completely white. I make a mental note to look them up in the Audubon Field Guide sometime.

I take off my shoes, close my eyes, rub my feet in the freshly cut emerald grass, and try visualizing The Source—The Divine Oneness—the way the Aborigines taught me in Australia's Never-Never. I quickly become at ease and two hours disappear. When I wake up, I distinctly remember my dream's tour guides, a very competent team of avatars: I recognized Moses, Jesus, Buddha, and Gandhi, but there were others—and they all pointed to an infinitely bright kernel of light in the distance and explained that it was The Source of all love and knowledge.

"Meet Mr. Stanley Randolf; he's the biochemist from Minnesota who was studying Amed Bay with binoculars this morning," Susan Parker announces to her fellow professors. "I'm pleased he could join us tonight."

I begin shaking hands with the four other professors; three are men except one who is another Susan.

"You two could pass for sisters," I say, looking at the two Susans. They are attractive young women close in size, shape, coloring, and age—both are marine scientists!

"Susan Horner doesn't wear eyeshadow like I do—she's one-hundred percent organic!" Susan Parker remarks. All the men laugh including yours truly. Ms. Parker has on a red dress; Ms. Horner an "I Love Bali" tee shirt with white shorts. The three male professors are in local disguise, wearing colorful Balinese silk shirts. I have on a Batik Indonesian shirt from Sumatra that's printed with a score of jumping tigers. With my dark tan and neatly-combed hair, I approximate an Indonesian biochemistry professor.

We all order something to drink from a small Tiki bar that's outside in a garden dining area surrounded by three swimming pools. It's a new beach hotel and I need to stretch my neck to see the Indian Ocean behind all the development. "It's not as remote as Amed Bay," Susan Parker whispers to me.

It's a pleasant warm evening under the southern stars. The head waiter seats us at a round table covered by a tablecloth printed with a kaleidoscope of tropical fruits. He seats the two ladies first, then us men. Professor Gerald Cummings, the renowned senior ichthyologist, has no clue that his shirt perfectly matches the tablecloth.

The two Susans start tearing with laughter as soon as Dr. Cummings sits down—he's literally an extension of the tablecloth! Without much expression and likely difficult to humor, he can't seem to figure out what's going on. Neither could I or the other two professors in the first

127

several moments—we'd been deep in the Amazon discussing its zoology before sitting down. But then we burst out laughing too, as does the head waiter. Gerald looks confused, probably thinking he missed a joke.

"Gerald, stand up," Susan Parker tells him, wet-eyed and still laughing.

"Did I miss some joke?" Gerald mumbles.

"Stand up!" Ms. Parker repeats. Gerald, surprised at her insistence, stands up. "Look at your shirt!"

He looks down at his shirt, then the tablecloth…the perfect match registers. A sly grin slowly appears on his face, but before it can grow into a smile, it morphs into a stern professorial gaze.

"It's a setup . . . somebody's fooling with me! You two girls!" He points at the two Susans but can only hold a stern face long. Everybody is laughing now, including guests from other tables. Finally, Gerald starts to laugh at himself. I order him a second Crown Royal Manhattan.

Delbert Johnson, the short, polite, portly professor who teaches Invertebrate Zoology, proposes a toast to Bali. Wilmar Wessel, the tall, thin professor who specializes in Amazon zoology and looks like Jimmy Stewart, seconds the motion. We all take a drink of something alcoholic except Susan Horner; she drinks lemon water. "There is no worry about purity of the ice, the government controls it. Not so for tap water," I explain. I make sure the bartender uses Perrier from a freshly opened bottle. Drinks in hand, we get into a lively discussion before the food arrives. Specifying Perrier water gets everyone talking about germs.

"Can scotch kill germs in the local tap water?" Wilmar asks me.

"Only if you order a double and let it sit for an hour before drinking it," I reply, getting a few chuckles. It's apparent they need to ease into having a biochemist around.

Dinner is an outdoor satay barbeque. Two chefs in tall white hats bring out the food—steaming sticks of meat and veggies with various dipping sauces. There are multiple selections: skewered chunks of lamb, pork, grouper, and shrimp that have been marinated in a secret sauce then grilled over hot charcoal. All look superb. A grill wheeled out next to our table keeps everything hot. The variety of separately skewered local vegetables competes with the meats for first place in the scrumptious-aroma category. Satay is easy to eat; you just slide a morsel of meat off its stick into your mouth. I started with the grouper and lamb, dipping them into spicy peanut sauce first. Everyone is talking while holding onto a meat or veggie stick.

Our discussions span almost every aspect of biology but focus mostly on marine science. I describe the remarkable leatherback turtle I had been watching in Amed Bay when Ms. Parker came by. That got Wilmar going on turtles in the Amazon.

After Wilmar paused, Susan Parker mentioned the three manta rays she'd seen scuba diving and then again with me on the hill. "The huge male had giant eyes and a stunningly-wide mouth that revealed its filter-feeding apparatus," she said, taking a drink of her martini.

"It could have covered a big part of the infield at Yankee Stadium," I interject, then devour two kabobs of lamb.

"That, indeed, is a big manta ray; big mantas have the largest brain of all fish," Doctor Cummings confirms. "These grouper kabobs are quite good," he adds, holding one up. "Were the reef sharks bothering the rays?"

"Not really, they were whitetip reef sharks, not the more aggressive silvertip or greys," she replies. Reef sharks are known to work together to herd schools of fish into valleys of sharp coral then eat the wounded.

"Some sharks are smarter than others," I remark. "I've seen quite a variety while diving and snorkeling around the world. The dumb ones scare me the most. Smart sharks blend instinct with acquired acuity and seem less likely to attack divers, great whites excepted." I take a drink of my vodka gimlet and notice Ms. Horner is on her second veggie kabob—no meat for this lady.

"Big mantas mainly fear killer whales and deep-water sharks, like tigers and hammerheads—great whites probably get after them too, but I haven't seen any reports of it." Doctor Cummings comments. "A lot goes on deep in the oceans that we have no clues about!"

Wilmar, inspired now, tells us that on a previous trip to Bali, a large male manta ray completely cleared the water on a jump meant to impress female rays. "I could tell by the way he looked at me he was a wise old blanketfish." Wilmar says sipping his scotch and water.

Just then a gust of wind rustles the water in the swimming pools and blows the napkins off our table. After a few seconds it's gone, and everything is back to calm. Susan Parker combs her hair and straightens the collar on her dress; Susan Horner disregards the sudden breeze.

"Do fish have spirits?" Ms. Horner asks openly, out of the blue. "After all, we're in Bali where locals believe all creatures have spirits."

The question gave the group pause. For some reason, everyone is looking at me for an answer. I had to think fast.

"I believe they do—I saw proof today," I respond, matter-of-factly.

"Oh, really?" Gerald Cummings remarks, with a curious smile. "Please share the details with us."

"It happened when I was sitting on the rocks overlooking Amed Bay this morning—before Susan Parker came by. While watching the reef sharks swim around the giant turtle, I happened to scan the binoculars past a flat rock on the beach. And there it was—hard-to-dispute proof!" I pause, doing my best to look serious.

"Yes, go on," Gerald insists. Both Susans are staring at me. Delbert and Wilmar are sporting puzzled grins. I hold up my last stick of skewered grouper and eat the last morsel on it, chewing slowly while looking at everyone. Susan Parker begins to smile, probably figuring out what's coming next.

I explain: "On that flat rock was a tiny temple made from sticks, brown grass and black sand. Quite intricate! An arrow design made from small pebbles pointed out to the coral humps and numerous fish. A lovely rainbow of Balinese flowers circled the temple which housed four perfect sardines on a bed of sea lettuce in a small courtyard. Obviously, an offering to the many fish spirits from dedicated Balinese believers. What would be the sense of making an offering to spirits that didn't exist?"

Everyone is quiet, not knowing if I am serious or kidding. They had all witnessed similar offerings outside houses, shops, restaurants and other places—Balinese Hinduism on display. While they try to mentally sort this out, Susan Horner speaks up, "Having a spirit doesn't mean they have a soul."

Here we go, I thought. She just pressed the launch button that could take us beyond good humor!

"Aren't they the same thing?" Delbert asks. With his expertise in invertebrate zoology, he probably has trouble believing snails and crabs could have spirits or souls.

"No! They're not," Ms. Horner asserts. "The spirit defines the individual creature—its intelligence, personality, habits, instincts, etc. When the creature dies its spirit, which is basically an operating manual unique to each creature's DNA, loses ability to function; it becomes part of a random, rudderless, energy field—where ghosts and demons reside. The soul is something entirely different, creatures don't have souls; humans do—or, better said, souls have humans. They are multidimensional spheres of eternal consciousness, part of The Source. Each has its own specific frequency and has experienced many lives! Souls agree in advance to take up residence in a specific human body. A fuzzy life plan, defined by a person's spirit, leaves plenty of room for free will." She pauses and takes a drink of her lemon water then winks at Gerald, attempting to disarm his unbelieving expression.

Ms. Parker adds: "Some people diverge from their spirit's predetermined fuzzy path more than others. You can think of your spirit as a game plan for a football game—your life. As we all know, games don't always follow a plan. The results—win or lose—are largely up to you and your free will. The soul experiences the actual paths that you take in life and, if you listen to its voice, it will assist you in making the right decisions."

"Animal spirits run mainly on instinct; some also demonstrate learned behavior," Ms. Horner explains, "like the smart sharks Mr. Randolf mentioned. But they have little or no responsibility for their actions. Souls do! And souls understand there is a future; animals live for the present not knowing another day will come."

The women are working in tandem! Delbert seems to be thinking about their answers to his question.

"Is there any scientific basis that our pineal gland is involved with the soul?" I challenge Ms. Horner. "I'm aware this small pinecone-shaped gland in the center of our brain regulates circadian rhythms by producing melatonin but may also have other duties."

"There's likely a connection," Susan Parker answers. "Small pine-cone shapes have inundated religious literature and art since ancient times. In the 1600's Descartes called the pineal gland the 'seat of the soul,' the place where our thoughts originate."

"But that has been debunked by neurologists; thoughts originate in the cerebral cortex from neural processes!" Gerald is quick to point out, his stern look still in place.

"There are studies where certain drugs reportedly facilitate a soul's movement in and out of the body by interacting with the pineal gland—at birth, at death and other times. This is common talk among scientists in Brazil," Wilmar interjects, then begins consuming a veggie kabob.

"I believe much of that has been debunked as well," Gerald says, turning towards Wilmar. "I thought you mainly studied the Amazon's wildlife in Brazil?"

"People are part of that wildlife!" Wilmar replies, smiling at Gerald while eating a cube of jackfruit off the veggie stick. "What kind of vegetable is this?" He holds another one up. "It tastes like a pineapple-flavored potato."

"It's nangka, or jackfruit," I tell him. "A staple food in Bali. Grows on trees in the lowlands and can easily dwarf a watermelon. You're eating a piece of a piece of a seed pod."

Hearing this, Wilmar eats the second piece then proceeds to question Susan Parker about the pineal gland.

"We don't know all the details of its interactions yet," Susan Parker admits.

"Who's we?" Gerald retorts, then forces a grin.

"A group of mystic Hawaiian shamans that have contact with the other side—the after-world," she answers confidently. "Susan Horner and I were invited to join their group and provide a biological perspective. It has been interesting, to say the least!"

Gerald scratches his head, while Wilmar takes another drink of scotch. Delbert sits quietly, looking down, likely in deep thought. I just smile to myself.

Ms. Parker continues: "The shamans explain that the spirit of a person defines the 'container' or body the soul occupies. Souls have a choice whether to stay with or leave a person. They say that monsters like Hitler, Stalin, and Mao lost their souls early in life. At death, they're gone forever: no after-life. They're completely deleted! She drinks the rest of her martini and looks at me. I signal the bartender and he makes her another.

"What does the world-travelling scientist, the biochemist, have to say about all this? Is there any scientific basis that humans can harbor a soul or that souls even exist?" Gerald asks, puzzled by what's going on and probably wondering how we got this far away from discussing manta rays and sharks.

"How much time do we have?" I ask with a grin. "It's a bit complicated."

"All night!" Susan Parker declares, before Gerald can answer.

"Okay then, I'll give it a shot: The nebulous soul has been defined and redefined and its existence debated for ages. Scientists have argued there is no hard evidence that souls exist, while theologians always argue that faith—believing—translates into evidence. I'm a biochemist but have old schoolmates who became smart physicists—they keep me briefed on the wild side of science." I pause and clear my throat.

"First, regarding the pineal gland's possible connection to the soul, there are some new twists. Piezoelectric calcite crystals have been found in human pineal glands. Fact, no debate. When you put pressure on them they produce electricity and light, electrons and photons. There are many forces, internal and external, that can pressure these crystals. This happens inside your head! New evidence suggests that unexplainable phenomena such as extrasensory perception (ESP) and psychokinesis (PK) may be linked to an excited pineal gland. If true, it's not a big leap to include a soul presence. How can a soul be any stranger than ESP or PK?

"That said, I'll attempt to explain some recent advances in quantum physics that are quite significant:

"One: Quantum physics provides room for souls to exist apart from Newton's laws of physics, which only explain how the everyday world works. We know now that there are eleven dimensions in space-time; we exist in four of them if you count time as one—this leaves plenty of mystery locations for souls that we can't experience with our five senses. These extra dimensions are right here—not thousands of light years away!

"Two: Equally amazing is the recent discovery that the universe is only five percent atomic; meaning the elements in the Periodic Table and all their atoms, which comprise all known substances, are absent from ninety-five percent of the universe! Instead there exists strange, ubiquitous dark matter and dark energy that we know nothing about—plenty of ephemeral substance for souls.

"Three: A discovery that truly threatens logic: there is proof now that subatomic particles, which constitute all atoms in all elements, can't exist unless they are observed by a conscious being—like a human. Think hard about this one: Consciousness can create!

"Four: There is stupendous porosity in our current reality; if the nucleus of a hydrogen atom, one proton, were as large as a pin head, the farthest extent of its one orbiting electron would be ten thousand miles away! Essentially, just open space in between. The nucleus is smaller than one trillionth of a pin head, so my example is relative. What this comparison tells us is that our 'solid world' is only an illusion—there is plenty of space for souls to set up shop—right now, right here. We exist in a great expanse of emptiness. Reality in the universe goes beyond Hollywood's wildest science fiction, but the good news is: There is now scientific basis to believe souls can exist—there is room for them, substance for them, and energy for them!"

I paused and so did the others. There was pure silence except for the Java Sea in the distance.

"You need to come and teach the shamans about this in Hawaii," Susan Parker says, Susan Horner nods in agreement. "Your words will help quell the negative influence from pervasive nonbelievers."

"I would be pleased to do that! I'm scheduled to be in Hawaii in April."

"Wonderful!" She replies. "These Hawaiian shamans are very private. They live on The Big Island; Hilo would be best to fly into for a meeting. Ms. Horner and I can arrange the details."

The three male professors keep quiet as the two Susans and I continue to talk. Both ladies explain how the Hawaiian shamans have experienced many events in the after-world; they espouse narratives that reveal both benevolent and malevolent entities in explicit detail. But the shamans don't understand how science can allow this. The science I summarized—understanding there are still many open riddles and questions—would provide powerful new tools for the shamans to use to qualify their teachings, thus allowing them to convince more people of our true reality!

There is a consistent breeze coming off the Indian Ocean now; off the Badung Strait to be specific. It's a beautiful rain-free evening in Bali. The six of us stand up from the table spontaneously without any prompting or suggestion—and stretch like it's the seventh inning in the World Series. Susan Parker suggests we walk the path behind the swimming pools leading to the beach, a spacious white sand beach. An hour away by speedboat is the island of Nusa Penida, famous for its manta rays, giant sunfish, and exceptional scuba diving.

We stand together watching the ocean, much like beach people do in India. Nobody speaks for at least fifteen minutes. There is moonlight breaking through the clouds when Wilmar restarts the conversation.

"Have you ever spent time with shamans in the Amazon?" he asks me.

"Yes, I have, in the Brazilian and Peruvian Amazon—and in Belize."

"What did they do to impress you?"

"In Peru they could levitate objects and summon interdimensional entities. In Belize there were two shamans who could cure cancer!"

"Did you see this?"

"I saw a Peruvian shaman levitate a hatchet off the ground—two feet high before it fell back down. I'm still astonished by the memory! In Belize, I spoke to people who had been cured of stage-four cancers by two shamans working together synergistically."

"No kidding," Wilmar asks with a serious look.

"No kidding," I respond with an equally serious look.

"What about entities—did you see any?"

"No, you had to take a psychoactive drug called Ayahuasca to see them. It's a tea made from a vine and shrub in Peru and Colombia—it's called the 'teacher plant.' I didn't try it but was with a group of others who did. One fellow from Belgium saw good and evil entities fighting—he found himself back in time during the Middle Ages. His explicit descriptions of specific details were hard to disbelieve—he was a plumber from Brussels."

Susan Parker comes to stand beside me. We all take a break and quietly listen to the ocean again. White frangipani flowers in trees bordering the resort property share their jasmine-like fragrance with the sea breeze. I pick up two of the flowers and give one to each Susan. Then Gerald breaks the silence.

"What about animals like manta rays?" Gerald asks. "My mind still can't get around how they can have a spirit."

"How can they not, if we consider what both Susans are saying? They require a spirit to function as distinct individuals—it's likely coded in their DNA and probably translates holographic instructions in three dimensions," Delbert declares, entering the conversation while bending over and shaking sand out of his shoes.

"Hallelujah! Delbert understands!" Ms. Horner declares. "A manta's spirit is DNA coded just like a human's but runs at a different frequency. In animals, spirit totally rules behavior. In human's, free will can override spirit, resulting in either good or bad results—the soul keeps track. Remember, spirit doesn't survive the body, the soul does. You don't need instructions on how to operate your body when it's gone!"

I can tell Delbert is bothered by something. "What's on your mind Delbert? Got some sand left in your shoes?"

"No." he looks at his feet, pausing and rubbing his chin.

"What do you believe?" Delbert asks me like he's afraid to hear my answer.

With no hesitation I answer him: "I believe our souls teleport to the after-world at, or just before, death. There is evidence the body loses a few grams of weight moments after death. I also believe our soul, once on the other side, takes part in a process with many perspicacious souls who share insight and intuitive vision that help the new arrival decide where to go next. The Buddhists profess that the eleventh realm, Nirvana, is the highest realm a soul can achieve and where it returns to the Godhead—The Source. And that along any soul's journey, experiences of unconditional love always get first-class seats."

Delbert thanks me and the two Susans. He seems relieved, satisfied and enlightened. Gerald and Wilmar look out at the ocean; appearing to absorb a therapeutic dose of wonderment. I stand with the two Susans as the Southern Cross shines down on us.

I drive the rental car back to my hotel and take a swim in the ocean. Again, it is calm, like the night before. I don't need to think or meditate, I did that earlier today. I just need to swim with one fascinating and compelling thought: Might the sea, so immense and rich with life, so catalytic to creation, so real and exceptional—have a soul?

The morning arrives with bright sun and chirping birds. After sleeping out on my room's lanai in a comfortable sun lounger, half-covered with my sarong, I walk to the breakfast buffet where an Islamic lady makes me a veggie omelet. I'm still digesting last night's satay. I think about the two Susans, still surprised at how cleverly they directed the dinner conversation. And about Gilbert, Delbert and Wilmar—what a serious threesome of zoologists.

I have a copy of an article that summarizes The Lotus Sutra—the final teachings of Buddha. I begin reviewing the part where he describes the after-world's eleven levels of existence, centuries before science discovers eleven dimensions. Good reading material to accompany the omelet.

There is a temple, of the thousands on Bali, that I like to visit. At high tide it's on an island, which becomes a peninsula at low tide— The Tanah Lot Temple. The scenery is dramatic but, due to its proximity to Kuta, tourists will be abundant. I drive to it on Bali's south shore.

I have been here before, but this temple qualifies for revisits. The iconic Hindu temple sits on large rocks at the edge of the Indian Ocean where sunsets are spectacular. Built in the fifteenth century to honor spirits of the sea, it's no surprise Tanah Lot is a popular tourist destination.

I know locals in the surrounding artists' community who create impressionist-style Balinese paintings at reasonable prices. They remind me of Monet's flower creations in the Musee d'Orsay in Paris, but here in Bali the flowers have an ocean behind them. Ernest Hemingway admired impressionist art; his goal was to write true sentences that could convey in words what the paintings accomplish visually. He may have come close.

I park the car and walk to the temple; it's low tide. The Indian Ocean crashes on the surrounding rocks. There is wind today.

One of my interests are the numerous sea snakes guarding the temple's shoreline, caves and crevices. Most average three to five feet long, an inch or two in diameter, and are silver with black bands every inch, head to tail. Regarded as holy snakes by the locals these docile creatures are, ironically, venomous. Watching tourists play with them makes me nervous—I saw a diver get bitten by one while snorkeling around Tioman Island in Malaysia last year; it took three hours before leg paralysis set in. He required an I.V. containing ten vials of sea snake antivenom! Compression and immobilization is a first aid must and antivenom should only be given if envenoming is confirmed.

After paying the snakes proper respect, a Hindu priest at the temple allows me to come into where only Hindus are permitted. I'm sure wearing my sarong and peci hat helped convince him I'm a worthy exception. I'm careful not to walk in front of anybody praying or go higher than any Hindu priest—a strict rule. I stay in back and say a prayer to Shiva—suggesting he take it easy on us all and delay any adharma. A habit of mine when traveling around the world is to appreciate other religions by attending their rituals and ceremonies when allowed.

Back on shore, sarong and peci in my backpack, I hire a foot masseur. They are men with wooden boxes filled with gadgets that reinvent your feet. I sit on a stool watching tourists walk by. The massage takes forty-five minutes and is heavenly. Every gadget is used: wooden rollers, ball bearings, brushes of different sizes, a flap of shark skin, and a rubber hammer. As tourists pass by I see them gaze at my feet—having a ball bearing between each toe while my heels are being pounded gets the most curious looks.

After paying Petu, the young masseur whose name means firstborn, I put my hiking shoes back on and walk past the souvenir stands featuring masks that expel evil spirits (entities), kites shaped like butterflies, and "I Love Bali" tee-shirts in every color. Finally finding the artists, I recognize Kadek, an older artist I met last year, we shake hands and he shows me his latest creations. I kid him about his name, which means "the second born male" in Balinese families. There are a lot of Kadeks and Petus in Bali. Last names are rare.

I buy one of his paintings which has imaginary butterflies feeding on lavender flowers on a cliff by the ocean. A perfect painting for recalibrating the mind—Monet and Hemingway would be pleased.

Beyond the artists, a small gamelan of musicians playing flutes is surrounded by monkeys—long-tail macaques—and tourists feeding them bananas. It's a monkey's life in Bali and they know it. This group is galena-gray with white bellies and pink faces. Most have a cone-shaped tuft of hair on top of their heads, except on bad-hair days when some cones get smushed.

One of the tourists, a young lady, is hysterical. A monkey has stolen her purse! A large male macaque has it around his neck; a small blue purse on a long strap. These macaques are smart. It isn't unusual for them to steal jewelry, purses, cameras, or hats, then bargain them back for food or drink. They love Coke and Pepsi—retrieving empty cans from waste containers and drinking any last drops is a favorite pastime. Giving one a full can sends it to the Promised Land, providing it doesn't have to fight off other monkeys. With sunlight behind them, the monkeys exhibit a glowing halo of fine hair, white in the sun, a couple of inches high over their main coat of gray hair. Spirit hair?

This girl's boyfriend is trying his best to bargain for the purse. He holds out a large banana, but the monkey doesn't want to trade. Not even for two or three bananas! Apparently, he's full of bananas; peelings are everywhere. Another younger monkey comes over, grabs the banana from the boyfriend, then tries to snatch the purse—the big male screeches, showing his formidable teeth. The purse isn't going anywhere.

"My passport and allergy medicine are in my purse—money too!" the girl yells, crying now. Her boyfriend approaches the monkey again, attempting to grab the purse and pull it loose. The monkey goes crazy, screeching and swinging its arms—then jumps up a nearby tree with the purse dangling from its neck.

These monkeys have learned to barter. North of here in Ubud there's a monkey sanctuary with over six hundred Macaques from five different family groups; a popular tourist spot staffed with rangers who assist tourists. No ranger is around to help this girl. Strangely, flute music plays on while other tourists just watch.

Then I remember the rambutans in my backpack. They're in a plastic bag and aromatically ripe. I go over to the tree, zip open the bag, and show it to the monkey. His eyes light up with excitement. Nobody else has rambutans and the aroma is enticing. He starts bouncing around the branch making babbling noises then ha-ha-ha-s and wiener-dog yapping sounds. I take one rambutan, then, standing below the branch he is on, I hand it up as high as I can reach. He stares at me for a minute or so, babbling, almost sounding human. Then, all in an instant, he secures his tail on the branch, reaches down, snatches the rambutan, twists it open, then eats the tasty fruit nugget.

I back away from the tree while showing him the bag. Now he's chattering and ha-ha-ing loudly. When he reaches his arm down for another rambutan, I shake my head and say no, then point to the purse. He knows I want to bargain.

The girl, still crying, and her boyfriend are standing behind me with a dozen other tourists. Put off by the crowd so close, the wise macaque keeps babbling but won't come down.

"All you guys move back." I turn around, instructing them. "Do it now before he forgets how good these hairy red golf balls taste." They all move back, and I sit down near the tree. The monkey watches my every move. I open the bag of rambutans—there are five left—take one out and show it to him. Then I twist it open and eat the nugget—spitting out the pit with drama. Every type of fanatical-primate sound comes out of him. I stand up and point to the purse and then the rambutans. This big macaque clearly understands I want the purse.

The girl who belongs to the purse has her fingers crossed on both hands and is now jumping up and down. Her boyfriend is standing next to her scratching his head, not showing much confidence in my world-proven technique.

I keep waving the open bag of rambutans for another five minutes or so while pointing at the purse. An enticing strawberry-grape aroma permeates the air under the tree.

It works! The macaque comes down the tree, cleverly leaving the purse on the branch. As he heads down I take the bag of rambutans over to an open waste container, macaque on my heels, and throw it in. He immediately dives after it.

The boyfriend, alert and ready, climbs the tree and retrieves the purse. I wave to them as I head to the car; I'm happy to have helped. There is something about going back to special places where you've been before—there are many for me in Bali.

I stop in Denpasar, Bali's capital, after the monkey-bartering event to confirm my reservation for a scuba trip to the island of Nusa Penida the next day. I want to make sure an experienced guide will be along, and that the rental equipment is in good condition; I have my own mask and fins. I'm excited to see more mantas and, possibly, a giant ocean sunfish. Recalibrating requires variety.

Postscript:

This story is based on true events. People's names have been changed to protect their privacy. I really did observe the hatchet levitate in the Amazon. I'm still astounded by it. And, I did meet the shamans on the Big Island of Hawaii that April—four elderly, Indigenous Hawaiians in excellent health. The meeting, with both Ms. Parker and Ms. Horner present, started at 7:00 p.m. and lasted until 2:00 a.m. Maybe longer because we "visited" many places. There was no concept of time!

They knew about the science I spoke of, but as pictures and symbols, not words. They were happy to add my words and qualifications. I must admit, it was much more than what I had expected. In a sentence: Reality is infinitely more complex than can be imagined, but it has a doorway that leads to a marvelously beautiful and simple world. I only got to peek through the keyhole in the door—but that was enough.

It's time to believe! Jesus and the other holy avatars are not insulted or disturbed when you accept there is a greater Source working with them. Their mission is to guide all souls to a state of Moska and into the eleventh dimension . . .

Ancient Australian Petroglyphs

8

Into the Never-Never
Mystery in the Dreamtime

$\mathcal{P}$rologue:

Mystical places exist in the vast outback of Australia. Isolated Aboriginal settlements function today as they did forty-thousand years ago. At that time, the ice age had advanced to its maximum extent, penetrating the northern hemisphere with glacial ice two miles thick that wouldn't start melting for another twenty-thousand-years.

Australia was extremely dry during the ice age, but a small number of refuge areas were able to support the early Aborigines. The center of Arnhem Land in Australia's Northern Territory was one such refuge area where rivers and marshes survived the ice age in the north, while arid grasslands and rock country dominated the south. This is where we find the bones of six-hundred-pound kangaroos, twenty-five-foot goannas, two-ton wombats and the first Aborigines—ancestors of today's Indigenous Australians.

According to their legend, Australia's Aborigines exist in the Dreamtime which has three parts: The first part is the Time before Time, when nothing existed. The second part is the Creation Time, when everything was made. And the third part, the Now Time, is the time since human creation. The Indigenous Australians believe they are direct descendants of the first beings.

None of their history or knowledge was written down by them when it occurred. Rather, it has been communicated by singing, dancing, storytelling, and rock art. Underneath what we think we know, there are new revelations emerging from the Dreamtime—finding these involves connecting with what is called the Never-Never.

Part One: Arnhem Land, Australia, 35,000 B.C.

A small clan of twenty-six Aborigines is camped within a stand of gum (eucalyptus) trees and six large termite mounds that form a circle—huts made of tree bark provide shelter and privacy within the circle. The clan relocates their camp as necessary to assure access to food and water. The current location has served them well for fifteen months.

A small fire burns in the center of the circle where three children sit eating witchetty grubs that taste like almonds. Nearby, several topless women adorned with seashell necklaces make flour by pounding wattle seeds with stones. Other women, working together just beyond the camp, are busy digging wild yams.

Two naked boys with curly black hair pound dust out of kangaroo hides draped over the termite mounds—everyone sleeps on them, so pounding out dust is a regular duty.

An older man, Tribal-Elder, whose face is encircled with a thick white beard, helps Healing-Woman crush emu-bush leaves by rolling round rocks on them. The resulting oil, a powerful antiseptic for cuts and stings, is stored in hollow gourds.

A wooden lean-to holds strips of goanna meat drying in the sun; lizard jerky is a favorite delicacy for the clan. A nearby riverbed provides water from an underground spring several meters deep.

Just north of the camp, a hill of pancake-shaped sedimentary rocks rises twenty meters off the desert. Standing on it, the clan's hunters can see clearly for forty kilometers in all directions. It's late afternoon in the middle of the dry season in Northern Australia—35,000 years before the birth of Christ!

A hunting party of five Aboriginal men, their faces painted white with pipe clay, wear headbands holding wedge-tailed eagle feathers. They all wear crushed eucalyptus leaves sticking out of belts made from kangaroo tails. The ethereal odor of eucalyptus oil dominates their scent. Each hunter carries a seven-foot wooden spear tipped with a flint arrow head. The most muscular hunter, Muscle-Man, also carries a heavy mulga-wood boomerang.

Moving one by one in a line with the tallest leading, the hunters walk toward an outcropping of red rocks and boulders. A pond, green with algae and shaded by eucalyptus and acacia trees, hides in a depression behind the boulders. Beyond this oasis to the south, the red vastness of the Never-Never becomes clear. A state of complete alertness engages the hunters, immersing them in an energy field of shared consciousness.

The hunters don't talk; they remain silent and watch the pond from behind the rocks. Animals visit at night; it's late and darkness will arrive soon.

Signaled mentally by Tall-Leader, the youngest hunter goes to get more eucalyptus leaves. Their fragrance serves two purposes: as an effective deodorant, and as an insect repellent. Ubiquitous black flies are an ever-present annoyance but don't bite—they crawl and enter every orifice of a human body from mouth to anus. Giant wasps, six inches long, are a more serious matter, as are red ants and angry bees. These insects cause hunters to miss with their spears; they are repelled by eucalyptus oil.

Right at dusk two wallabies appear at the pond. Each would be an easy kill to make with a spear, but nobody throws; their objective is to kill something much larger. The wallabies can sense the hunters, but without human odor they are not alarmed.

When Orion appears high in the northern sky, its nineteen bright supergiant stars form an image of a great hunter holding a bow above his three-star belt. Tall-Leader stares at it in reverence. The other hunters look up too, then at Tall-Leader who points to them and then to Orion, reminding the hunters of their equivalence to these special stars.

After the wallabies leave there is greater darkness which allows the clear, dry-season sky to accentuate the southern hemisphere's constellations. Tall-Leader now points to the Pleiades, The Seven

Sisters, and telepathically explains its supernatural connection to Orion. He describes how the first beings of their clan met the creator beings from the sky, and that these beings rode large stingrays from the sea up into the sky, taking men to Orion and women to the Pleiades.

The youngest hunter, Baby-Man, is suddenly alerted. He points to a wide acacia tree behind the pond. They all look down from the sky and out at the pond. There, standing up, its massive legs stretched out, is an eleven-foot giant kangaroo eating leafy vines high on the tree. This animal's two-hundred-fifty kilos of meat would provide months of protein for the clan and a great pelt for sleeping. The leader knows it's the kangaroo's destiny to be here and to sacrifice itself for them. The animal must be killed quickly without suffering. His hunters can do this.

Tall-Leader hand-signals the men to divide into pairs and approach the animal from each flank, crouched down, silently. Then he tells Muscle-Man what to do with the heavy boomerang. They all know the danger: one kick from one of those massive legs and it's all over—the victim would be on his way to Orion.

The hunters smell like eucalyptus leaves. The giant kangaroo doesn't eat eucalyptus leaves—they upset his bowels—but he's accustomed to their odor. Human scent would spook him. A slight wind provides enough rustling sound in the trees to disguise their approach. When close, the four stand up, lifting their spears, aiming for the animal's neck. They throw in unison—four spears flex and fly toward the target. Tall-Leader is the backup, he stands holding the clan's Spirit Stick, but doesn't throw it.

The kangaroo's legs spring violently, launching the huge marsupial straight up into the tree. Its head clears the first branches as the spears break off but stops suddenly when it hits the upper branches. With arterial blood pumping from four holes in the animal's neck, it falls backward, slamming the ground. Muscle-Man, holding the heavy boomerang high, throws it at the back of the kangaroo's head immediately breaking the spinal cord, ending any pain sensations. Its legs continue kicking for a short time as the muscles reflex. It's a fast kill!

Back at the village there is great excitement; there will be dancing and singing after everyone tends to the work at hand. Fire-Man, responsible for fires, sees the five men carrying the huge kangaroo tied to a pole. He jumps up and fortifies the camp fire with extra wood. Earlier, the tribe's teenagers had dug a deep cooking pit next to the fire, they see it must be enlarged—the four of them get busy with their digging sticks.

Tribal-Elder, standing next to his three wives, beams with pride and smiles—two of his sons are among the hunters!

The entire clan embraces the hunters with joy and happiness. This is a special event! Celebratory bumping and touching begins while the hunters firm up the animal's connection to the pole before rotating it over the fire. Fire-Man continues to expand the fire while pushing its embers into the pit. The odor of singed kangaroo hair fills the air. An hour passes.

Tall-Leader and two of the hunters guide the kangaroo with heavy sticks while the other two hunters rotate the pole. This takes indefatigable effort.

With its hair singed, the four hunters move the giant animal out of the fire and lay it on a bed of rocks near the pit. Then they begin scraping off the charred hair using coarse granite wedges while Fire-Man continues to push more embers into the pit. Tall-Leader comes over and uses the Spirit Stick to finish removing any hair.

"Hair gone now," Baby-Man says, looking at the swollen, massive, pink kangaroo. He speaks in an early Yolngu tongue that also requires hand motions.

"I'll gut kangaroo," Muscle-Man grunts. Using the Spirit Stick, he cuts the animal's underside from anus to neck with precision, no deeper than necessary. Then he pulls out a mountain of warm guts and internal organs. Big-Hair and Star-Man, the other two hunters, cut out the edible organs, leaving just the bowels and mesentery for eagle bait.

"Everyone eats!" Tribal-Elder declares. The raw thymus gland, liver, and heart disappear first. The four hunters fight over the liver—a friendly, brotherly fight. The liver is huge and after each hunter gets a couple of mouthfuls, Star-Man cuts the remainder into pieces, a treat for the entire clan.

After the liver fight, wearing blood-red smiles, the four hunters drag the kangaroo into the pit of red-hot embers. Fire-Man must keep working, adding embers throughout the night.

"Slow cook until morning." Tall-Leader speaks. The meat touching the fire will be well done but, given the size of the animal, most of it will be medium-rare in the morning.

The music starts. Chanting and wood-on-wood pounding blends with eerie moans made by blowing into long wooden tubes (didgeridoos). The clan dances, moving around the fire pit with arms swinging high; all types of moves—touches and bumps are allowed. Tall Leader holds the Spirit Stick high as he dances—the stars shine down on them as they thank the sky spirits. Artist-Man immortalizes the evening by painting a rock picture of spirit beings riding sting rays in the sky.

Morning brings in a hot day. "Good meat-drying day," Tribal-Elder says loudly. Most of the tribe is already having breakfast—kangaroo steaks, medium-rare. Eagles fly overhead hoping to avoid a dingo's breakfast (no breakfast).

"Cut in long strips, salt, and dry in sun," Tribal-Elder tells his wives, who are already cutting the meat with the Spirit Stick. He can see this animal will require all their salt. Salt is essential—the tribe can't live without it. "We need to visit Tree-People—trade meat for salt. It takes ten days to dry meat if sun hot, more if sun cold." Tribal-Elder communicates telepathically, only using a few verbal words for emphasis. The clan knows to look into his eyes at these times.

Twelve days later

Muscle-Man, Star-Man, Big-Hair, and Baby-Man depart to find the Tree-People, a five-day walk northeast of their current location. The Tree-People live near the Gulf of Carpentaria on bark mattresses in trees—necessary protection from saltwater crocodiles! The climate is lush and tropical around the Gulf. Since the Tree-People mostly eat fish and birds, they're happy to trade sea salt and colorful bird feathers for kangaroo jerky.

The four young men, naked except for strips of leather that protect their genitals, walk one by one in a straight line. At the end of the line, Big-Hair pulls a sled made from tree bark, carrying water in wallaby bladders and the dried kangaroo meat (jerky). The other three men carry multiple spears.

Muscle-Man has tattoos on each arm that depict markers on the horizon that they must follow: Various rock outcroppings, termite mound clusters, gum tree groupings, slopes and valleys. At night, Star-Man confirms their position by the stars.

They walk at six kilometers an hour for twelve hours the first day. Camp is simple: each man fashions gum tree leaves and dead grass into a bed—no fire the first night. They each drink a measured amount of water and eat kangaroo jerky. Gazing at the stars they notice that some are moving slowly, a frequent observation. Star-Man assures them: Some sky spirits like to move, most do not. Sleep comes easy.

Day two starts at sunrise. The four men get up, take a drink of water, and after checking Muscle-Man's left arm, begin walking again. Baby-Man drags the sled this time. He's energized and ready for it. If the terrain gets rough, two of them carry the sled on a pole. Muscle-Man carries and guards the Spirit Stick; making poles is easy using it, as are many other vital functions. They head north toward a small green valley surrounded by arid emptiness . . .

It takes two hours to walk to the valley where woollybutt and ghost gum trees huddle together. Muscle-Man retreads the sled with fresh bark and they all drink water, which is hot now in the wallaby bladders. That's when Big-Hair notices a beehive in a tree.

"Honey!" he cries out. "A treat from sky spirits!" He climbs the tree quickly and reaches into the hive while the other men surround the tree, waving their spears to confuse the bees. Back in their village, bees are controlled with a smoking torch.

Big-Hair gets stung while pulling out a large honey-filled wax comb, being careful not to take the queen. He hands it down to Star-Man while shaking his forest of curly hair. It's every man for himself as they all run from the tree.

"Big-Hair got stung on his face and hands—he was too excited!" Muscle-Man is mad. "Need torch to disperse bees. Making fire easy with Spirit Stick!" He communicates mostly with fast hand movements and a few verbal words.

Star-Man grabs a small gourd containing emu-bush oil and applies it liberally to Big-Hair's stings to prevent infection—its aroma drives a dozen additional bees from his mountain of hair. Star-Man signals for Baby-Man to come over and use his small fingers to remove barbed stingers connected to pieces of bee abdomen. Many guard bees had sacrificed themselves to sting Big-Hair.

Away from the tree, the four fearless hunters take a short break and enjoy the honey—finger food. They then proceed to the next marker on the horizon, three hours away. If they walk too slowly, their weight shifts from one foot to the other and it takes more energy to go a kilometer. If they walk fast to keep their weight even, they dehydrate more quickly. They search for a compromise.

The arid vastness now dominates everything, only widely interspersed gum trees and spinifex, a tough tussock grass, dot the extensive desert tableland, which hasn't changed significantly in 560 million years. Not since Precambrian times! As they walk in the sultriness, they need to drink more water—hot, wallaby flavored water. There's no wildlife in sight except for an occasional desert rat. The four hunters have tough, calloused feet that tolerate the hot ground—a genetic trait. Aborigines with genes for tender feet die young.

They continue northeast, but Muscle-Man is not sure of the next horizon marker, a small outcropping of rocks. They walk on. Six hours pass before they see rocks, but there are two outcroppings well apart from each other. Muscle-Man decides to head for the rock pile on the left, where one large boulder balances on another. Star-Man agrees.

As they approach the boulders they come upon pink-flowered turpentine bushes in a dry riverbed. Beyond, in the distance, a tight grouping of red gum trees matches the next picture on Muscle-Man's arm. He had picked the correct pile of rocks to follow.

Baby-Man can smell water! He begins digging behind rocks in the riverbed. Star-Man and Big-Hair harvest leaves from the turpentine bushes—a decoction from these reduces fevers. Under orders from Tribal-Elder, they must harvest medicinal weeds for future use whenever possible. Turpentine vapor is released as they pull off the leaves.

Baby-Man is digging frantically, knowing Muscle-Man is impatient and wants to leave. He overturns numerous rocks finding only dry sand under them.

"We go now." Muscle-Man commands, pointing to the red gum tree cluster on his arm.

"Water!" Baby-Man shouts. His arms are shoulder deep in the sand behind a large rock. He claws out sand from the hole with his small hands. Muscle-Man and Star-Man run to him and start digging madly with bigger hands. The hole begins to fill with water, turbid from the fine sand but clean tasting.

Star-Man starts to chant: "Hugh—u-u-u-u-u... Hugh—u-u-u-u-u..." The others join him, saluting the sky spirits. They cup their hands and drink the good-tasting water.

"Dump and refill Wallaby bladders," Muscle-Man points to the bladders in the sled, think-telling the others what to do. Water stored in bladders in the sun develops a foul taste in a short time. Replacing it will provide clean-tasting water for another two days. Back in their village, pond water is purified by adding white clay to it in stone pools. After several days the clay settles out with any contaminants and the water is safe to drink. But spring water under sand is always safe to drink.

They walk fast to the grove of red gum trees depicted on Muscle-Man's arm and then on to the next marker on the horizon. With the sun setting, Muscle-Man makes a fire. He scrapes a flint arrowhead on the Spirit Stick over a handful of dry grass—hot sparks fly and immediately ignite the grass. In bright sun, just reflections off the Spirit Stick start a fire.

"It's easy to make grass beds tonight," Star-Man declares. There's an abundance of long grass. While walking today all four men thought about dinner. They'd chewed a strip of kangaroo jerky earlier, but tonight each man would eat a large handful of witchetty grubs with honey for desert. Chewing the living grubs after dipping them in honey produced a nutritious, almond-tasting custard.

The fire is comforting as marsupial lions, soon to be extinct, become a threat the closer they get to the Gulf of Carpentaria. These fearsome lions stay clear of any fire; youngsters could be aboard in their pouches. Tonight the four men sleep safely to the music of dingo howls.

Two more days and nights pass before they see the gulf's blue water. It's Baby-Man's first time to see it. "Nothing was ever this blue before," he tells the others using his hands. He points to the hazy blue sky with one finger, then to the gulf with three fingers—meaning three times bluer.

All four are anxious to walk in the water, but it's farther than it looks. And when it becomes rocky, two must carry the sled. When they reach the beach, it's dark and not safe to go on. Farther on, giant seven-meter saltwater crocodiles patrol the river that leads to the Tree-People. Their visit would have to wait until the next day. They will sleep on the beach.

Muscle-Man builds a fire from driftwood, while Star-Man and Big-Hair teach Baby-Man how to catch mud crabs. While roasting the crabs for dinner, Star-Man points to several moving stars. "Spirit stars!"

Muscle-Man and Star-Man wake first; the incoming tide wets their feet. Muscle-Man yells to Big-Hair in Yolngu: "Move sled!" It's near the incoming tide. Big-Hair jumps up and quickly drags it away from the wet. All four men move off the beach, but not before Baby-Man's curiosity convinces him to take a few gulps of seawater. Coughing and vomiting, he shakes his head, pointing to his butt, then the ocean. Translation: "Bad water." Sunrise is moments away.

They walk parallel to the beach until they reach the river's mouth, then head inland twenty kilometers. Muscle-Man has the Spirit Stick tied firmly to the end of a pole, not a flexing spear. It cuts through thick bush and can kill marsupial lions and crocodiles if necessary.

Their walk in the lush, wet, humid jungle takes most of the day. They alternate carrying the sled. All four agree that the desert's dry, hot air is better than the jungle's wet, hot air. They have no word for humidity.

A dozen Rainbow Lorikeets fly from one tree to another. Baby-Man points to them and then to his smiling face. He's happy to see such birds. Big-Hair keeps a lookout for beehives which annoys Muscle-Man who keeps an eye out for crocs. Star-Man will not be happy sleeping in trees tonight; few stars shine through the jungle's green canopy.

The Tree-People live on the river the hunters are following. Their clan has a population of around fifty and they all live in trees. During the day the young men come down from the protection of their tree homes to hunt, but most of the women and children stay in the trees all day. Elders who venture down often disappear. The dry season is the worst time for crocodiles because they have less water to search, and trapped ocean fish are usually gone (eaten) by the end of June. Crocs normally eat several Tree-People a year, often babies that fall out of the trees at night.

Star-Man has a code to identify themselves from would be attackers—meaning hostile tribes—four raps made by hitting two stones together with pauses and frequent repeats. When Muscle-Man estimates they're close, he signals Star-Man to start rapping stones.

They walk on until they hear a shrieking whistle three times in succession. Then they respond with three stone raps. The whistle repeats. It's now safe to enter the domain of the Tree-People.

Returning home after eleven days, the four hunters are welcomed back. Their sled is filled with sea salt and colorful bird feathers from the Tree-People. It's a joyous time. The Tribal-Elder looks at the white sea salt containing all the world's elements and smiles. Bending over, he tastes it, still smiling, appreciating its life-sustaining and food-preserving properties. It would serve the tribe for several months. Then he looks at Muscle-Man thinking, Spirit Stick! It was in a leather sheath strapped to the hunter's leg. Muscle-Man, hearing the thought, unties it and gives it to Tribal-Elder who grins, holds it up to the sky like a priest would present a cross to God, then slides it into his kangaroo pouch for safe keeping. The clan celebrates the salt . . .

Part Two: Darwin, Australia 2005 A.D.

"G' Day, mate, Time to shine and rise!" Adam's cheery voice blares—I was in REM sleep when the phone rang.

"G'Day to you. What time is it?"

"Early—six bells," Adam replies. "When did you get in?"

"Late. I mean early: 2:00 a.m."

"On Qantas?" Adam asks.

"No, Garuda; Qantas was overbooked. Garuda was delayed for two hours because the cabin's seatbelt light wouldn't go on."

"Never fly those Indonesian blokes! They buy used planes from Qantas."

"I know. Sounds like your English is improving."

"Yeah, I'm giving it a fair go, so 'me' favorite Yank can under-stand," He replies. Adam Rody is my business partner in Australia, he's an authentic Ozzie with a master's degree in Aquaculture Science. He's in his early forties, tall and slim. He and I are in the business of water purification using biotechnology; reducing pollu-tion from aquaculture is one of our priorities. As a bonus, the cleaner water produces more fish or prawns per hectare. But ahead of us is an adventure week, no work!

"Go back to sleep! I'll be at the hotel in two hours, Abbey will make brekkie for us."

"Got it."

"Sweet dreams!" Adam hangs up.

I'm wide awake now. Good morning, Darwin . . .

Adam and Abbey pick me up at 8:00 a.m. at the TraveLodge. They're remodeling their house and the guest room is out-of-order, but the kitchen is functional. Their three kiddies are staying with her parents in Sydney.

Abbey begins preparing lightly-seasoned huevos rancheros to compensate for the extra picante version I ordered for the three of us in Mexico last year. It took mucho cerveza to wash them down.

"I went easy on the habañero," she says, handing me a glass of fresh mango juice. "No cerveza will be required!"

"Not yet," Adam adds. "Wait till I introduce him to eggs smothered with local Scorpion Pepper—it demotes habañero! He'll need to pop several tinnys . . ."

"Of Victoria Bitter?" I presume, smiling.

"Aye mate, best amber fluid in the world."

"I remember when you promoted it from 'Best in Australia' last year."

"That promotion was long overdue! I bought a slab last week to celebrate me new ute (SUV)!"

"Adam, say 'my' and tone down the slang. Poor Stanley," Abbey gives him a disciplining look.

"It's part of his 'Down-Under' education!" Adam asserts.

"No worries, Abbey. I'm used to it now. But I'll miss Mitsy," the nickname for his old, outback-proven Mitsubishi SUV.

"Aye, she was a ripper truck in her day," Adam laments. "But now it's Big Hondo! Honda's 'beauty of a ute…'" I laughed at that— he should copyright the phrase!

"I guess when we drive through Arnhem Land we'll need plenty of room for extra petrol, food, and gear—so size matters!" I say. Arnhem Land, in the northeast corner of the Australia's Northern Territory, is essentially a country within a country: ninety-seven thousand square kilometers of protected Aboriginal land which includes Kakadu National Park.

"Aye, this trip will break Hondo in!" Adam declares.

"What time does the professor arrive?" Abbey asks.

"Round eleven," Adam answers her then looks at me. "You packed, mate, ready for this?"

"Packed and ready to meet the professor and get lost in Arnhem Land!"

As we head to the door, Abbey hugs and kisses Adam. I only get a hug.

"Watch out for snakes," she tells us.

"Aye, Lass, I got me custom snake stick along! Cheerio!"

She just shakes her head. Seven of the world's ten most poisonous snakes live in Australia.

We go outside and get into Hondo—it's a superb vehicle—full of camping equipment, coolers loaded with food and beer, jerry cans of extra petrol, and other gear. I didn't want to ask about the snake stick; this man fights crocodiles with a baseball bat!

We meet Doctor Daniel Gurumarra at the Darwin airport. He's a native Indigenous Australian with a PhD in Paleoanthropology. His major study is ancient Aboriginal culture, and having known Adam since high school in Sydney, he invited him to come along on a dig in southeastern Arnhem Land. Adam, knowing my wide range of scientific interests, asked Daniel if I could join them. He agreed and here I am.

Daniel's a rare individual! He's in his mid-forties and has good status in the growing society of professional Aboriginals. Doctor Dan, or just Dan, is six feet tall, medium build with dark skin, a broad nose, and curly hair with streaks of silver. He speaks English clearly, and only uses the Aussie vernacular when necessary!

"Dan is one smart dinky-di (the real thing)," Adam declares as we head south out of Darwin on the Stuart Highway. I'm in the spacious middle seat behind them. Adam did a good job introducing us on a conference call before the trip, so Dan and I are already comfortable with each other.

"I know Mr. Adam has been teaching you Australian slang. So, Mr. Randolf, please teach me some American slang this week," Daniel requests in a wise baritone voice.

"It won't be as funny as the Aussie's, but I'll get you started right now: Let's 'shoot the breeze' about your doctorate thesis." Both Daniel and Adam laugh.

"My research thesis is about small groups of early Aboriginal people, ancestors of the Yolngu and Gagudju clans, and how they survived and sustained themselves."

"How early is early?" I ask.

"Between 30,000 and 40,000 B.C." he replies.

"Bloody early!" Adam exclaims.

"Those early Aboriginals lived almost identical lives to the many isolated clans that exist today. Dance, song, and story-telling tracks their history. Rock art and a few questionable archaeological finds are the only things that approach hard evidence," Daniel explains, eyeing the Fedex package he'd sent to Adam last week—to be held until he arrived. "I believe you will be surprised by what I show you this week!"

"We'll be doing a few walkabouts," Adam adds. The three of us scientists are in disguise, wearing shorts, tee shirts, and hiking shoes. Hot weather is directly ahead, and I'm stoked.

After thirty-five kilometers we turn off the Stuart Highway onto the Arnhem Highway and proceed east to Kakadu National Park, ninety minutes away. That's where Paul Hogan made his fame in Crocodile Dundee. But fighting crocs is not on our program, hopefully.

"First on the agenda is Aboriginal Rock Art," Doctor Gurumarra starts explaining: "There are three sites we will visit in Kakadu National Park—one is in a protected cave where tourists are not permitted. I have never been in that cave and I'm very excited to see it."

"Dr. Dan has tribal permits that allow us to go into closed areas," Adam clarifies.

Dan continues, "I'm quite interested in "virgin" paintings showing spirit entities that are thirty-thousand years old—or older. Sites approved for tourists like those at Nourlangie Rock and Ubirr have rock paintings that are less than one-hundred years old mixed in with some that are truly ancient; and equally disappointing is that many have been repainted in white."

So, it's the red paintings that have the best odds of being ancient!" I interject.

"That's right! Truly ancient paintings will be mostly red from indelible red ochre—made by pulverizing hematite—iron oxide—and mixing it in water to make red paint," I could see excitement in Daniel's eyes in the rearview mirror as he explained this.

"Those ancient blokes painted with rusty water!" Adam blurts out.

"And it lasts forever, like the red desert south of here." Daniel confirms.

"And like Utah's red rock country," I add. "There's a lot of iron oxide in the world." The road is smooth and well-paved as we approach the National Park.

Two of the rock art sites open to the public are south of the Kakadu visitor's center near the park's eastern border with Arnhem

Land. When we stop for a restroom break, Daniel shows one of the permits to the ranger at the information desk, then asks about access to a spot on the map.

"It's lush and mostly flooded from December through March but should be passable now in the dry season. Just watch for wet areas near the rivers!" The ranger warns.

"Tomorrow is the Fourth of July, so we should be good," I mention (July is the middle of the dry season in the NT). Adam drives south of the visitor center on the Kakadu Highway now and follows signs to the Nourlangie Rock, which is just west of the Arnhem Land escarpment. It's a large area; signs direct us to the rock art.

We see surprisingly few tourists in the Anbangbang and Nangawulurr shelter areas when we arrive. Once on the trails, the paintings jump out at us. They're clear and dramatic, larger than those made by the Anasazi in the American southwest and much older.

Daniel takes over and explains what fascinates him most: "There are two groups of spirit beings that my associates and I find quite interesting: The Mimi spirits and the Wandjina. The Mimi are tall, thin beings with triangular heads and large almond shaped eyes; their arms, legs and torso appear to be segmented."

I stare at two of them painted in white on a large slab of flat rock in a shaded depression. One is bigger than me, and I'm six feet tall!

"That long, thin one with his feet bent is a real beaut'—his head and torso look like some bug I should know!" Adam comments.

"A praying mantis?" Daniel asks?

"That's it, mate! A giant mantis," Adam agrees.

I keep to myself, thinking . . . We see more of them as we walk on. Actually, they look like some of the extraterrestrials that UFO buffs claim to see.

"Aboriginal folklore tells us that Mimi spirits taught the Aborigines how to hunt and cook kangaroos. In some of their dances they imitate a Mimi holding a type of stick or weapon. And, in stories that have been told for thousands of years, they explain how the Mimi could get sick and return to the stars if they stayed outside their caves too long." Daniel injects more perspective.

"Have these been repainted?" I ask Daniel.

"Most likely. I'm hoping we'll find only red Mimi spirits in the protected cave; I need to confirm they were painted during the ice age! Very important. These dramatic paintings in front of us are either recent creations or repainted."

"What about the Wandjina?" Adam asks.

"They're spirits, too," Daniel answers, "somewhat stocky and short with big round eyes and what appears to be a black circle of spiked hair around their heads—very symmetrical. Folklore tells they are the creative spirits that made everything during the Dreamtime. Good rock art of them is found in the Kimberley region of Western Australia." I was thinking: the Wandjina, except for the hair, describe a mysterious photograph I saw in Peru a few years ago.

After seeing these large, mostly-white stick spirits, we're ready to find indisputable, unadulterated, ancient red ones. We get back on the Kakadu Highway and head farther south. At a spot where Dr. Dan's GPS starts beeping faster, Adam puts Hondo into four-wheel drive and turns left into a dry river bed that runs through a forest of twisted tamarind trees. When the trees thin out we come to an open grassy area and scare two six-foot, blue-billed emus that have never seen anything like Hondo before. Running away from us, the big birds inflate their windpipe pouches and discharge several deafening grunts.

"Antisocial blokes!" Adam remarks.

"Aboriginal hunters can hear them two-kilometers away!" Daniel informs us.

We continue bumping along around trees and bushes while Daniel checks his GPS. "More to the left," he tells Adam, showing him the map on the handheld unit.

"Right," Adam says.

"He said left," I remind Adam with a grin.

"Right, I'm going left!" He asserts, getting a good laugh out of Daniel. "Stan is only a sophomore in Oz talk," Adam reminds Dan.

We grind our way along, now throwing mud, until we see a billabong and a river with old monsoon water blocking our way east. Adam stops Hondo and gets out. "Keep an eye out for crocs," he says as he walks straight ahead into the water. I turn around and look behind me and see a rope tied to a life preserver on top of all the food and gear. Hopefully it won't be needed, my inner-voice speaks.

Adam steps high and is only knee-deep halfway through the water. "She'll be apples," he shouts as he turns around. Back in Hondo, smelling like decaying algae, he shifts into four-low and slowly drives into the water. No problem!

"Head for the 'X' on the GPS," Daniel says, holding it up again for Adam to see. Hondo's raised chassis and big tires do the job. It takes us about an hour in the wet before we see dry land and the red rocks of the escarpment. The beeps on the GPS increase as we run south along the base of the escarpment until we see a break in the rocks and a large crevasse. The GPS now sings a loud monotone—its "bingo" signal. There's no one around and we're well away from any road.

"That's it!" Daniel says. I'm excited as I get out of Hondo; seeing the great expanse of Arnhem Land ahead is invigorating. I grab my belt-pack and flashlight; Adam grabs his walking stick; Daniel carries a four-D-cell torch, a small camera, and a notebook. We scare up a couple of eight-inch, long-hair rats as we walk to the break in the rocks.

The cave entrance is a tall, narrow gap between two rock faces. Daniel enters first, squeezing between the rock faces, then Adam, then me. Cool dampness hits us immediately.

The rock art begins about fifty feet in . . . Daniel is ecstatic! "They're all dull and muddy-red!" he exclaims. "Just like the old professor in Sydney told me they would be."

Adam and I see them clearly when I switch from spot to flood on my flashlight. "They're ridgy-didge (genuine)!" he exclaims." The thin Mimi spirits, large and well defined, have not been repainted in white. They all have triangular heads with large, black, almond shaped eyes. Some have torsos you can see into showing various splotches and tubes.

"X-ray rock art!" Doctor Dan points out. "Internal organs, good sign . . ."

I check the smooth quartzite-granite walls of the tall cave and see numerous, parallel water lines running from the floor up to a fifteen-foot ceiling. "This is an ancient place."

"There's one more age-confirming requirement," Daniel says, opening a pocket knife. He scrapes off several grams of black color from one Mimi into a small stainless-steel vial from his pocket—the black from two eyes and a foot.

"My permit allows this!" He explains. "This Mimi is already disfigured from age and not a complete specimen." He makes notes and takes photographs and tells us he must file a report with the Arnhem Tribal Council.

"What's that all for, Danny?" Adam inquires. Dan smiles at being called Danny, remembering when Adam first called him that in high school social studies class. The teacher was not amused and had sent Adam to the principal's office. It was socially unacceptable to call an Indigenous Australian by anything but his formal name.

"I'll let our biochemist explain it, I just call it carbon dating." Dan glances at me.

I explain that the black color is from charcoal (carbon). Its age is determined by the relative amounts of three carbon isotopes: C-12, C-13 and C-14. Since C-14 is radioactive and decays at a specific rate over time; ancient charcoal will have a higher ratio of C-12 + C-13 to C-14 compared to fresh charcoal.

"Smart lad, that Stan." Adam tells Daniel as he leans on his walking stick.

Daniel is confident the carbon dating will confirm what the dull red ochre signifies: that what we are looking at is ancient, early Ice Age artwork with no adulteration. We continue studying the details—the Mimi have thin, elongated bodies, segmented arms, legs, and torsos. Some show their arms spread wide apart in an arc and curved down—an unnatural position for humans. But it's their triangular heads that are haunting; the eyes look right into you! They do resemble a praying mantis—a very big one.

"Look at these coiled snakes." Daniel points to them. Perfect concentric circles that start in the middle with a tail and end in a snake head are mixed in with the Mimi spirits. "The ancient artists painted snakes as an excuse to paint concentric circles. They indicate a meeting place, according to Aboriginal legend."

"I've seen them in hieroglyphs in the American southwest and in the Nazca Lines when flying over Peru, where a huge monkey glyph had its tail forming seven concentric circles. A Brazilian general claimed they were antennas used for communication with sky spirits," I add.

"What's the dating on those Nazca Lines?" Daniel asks me.

"Between two hundred B.C. and five hundred A.D." as I recall. Not anywhere near thirty thousand B.C. or more, like this rock art!"

"Modern blokes carved the Nazca Lines," Adam quips. Daniel and I laugh.

"It's quite interesting that the concentric circle design survived human history and was used for so long in different places," Daniel says, looking like he's contemplating something.

After that intellectual bout, I open my belt-pack and bring out three Snickers bars and exclaim: "They didn't have these thirty-thousand years ago!"

As we enjoy the high-energy snack, we hear slapping sounds and pebbles falling by the entrance. We are about one-hundred feet into the cave, near where it ends, when we turn and shine our flashlights toward the entrance, but don't see anything. It sounds like a couple of garden hoses slapping dirt. As we get closer we see brown dust flying up in the narrow sunlit entrance we came through a half-hour ago.

"Snakes fighting!" I yell, seeing them through the dust.

"Big taipans!" Adam shouts, and pulls a metal object out of his pocket. We back away.

One snake is eating a long-hair rat, possibly one of the two that ran past us outside; the rear half of the rat is sticking out of its mouth. The other snake wants it. There's no way around them; they're right in the narrows.

Adam is screwing something onto the end of his walking stick, some type of large fork. "Snake fork!" he exclaims, holding the seven-foot stick straight up, fork on top. His walking stick is now a long snake stick!

"The taipan is the world's most venomous snake with huge fangs and a large venom reservoir; without anti-venom its bite is lethal," Daniel instructs in a nervous baritone.

I'm about ready to wet my pants—if an Aboriginal PhD is nervous, I should be scared shitless or worse! But snakes were never on my "Big-Five" worry list like big spiders and mozzies (mosquitos). I think now they will be!

The two six-foot reptiles are indifferent to us, at least so far. They tangle and untangle, moving around in dusty circles as their bodies slap each other. They're golden brown with white snouts and bellies,

162

and obsidian-black eyes. Mirror images of each other! The snake eating the rat makes violent swallowing undulations attempting to finish it fast; over half of the rat is a lump in the snake's neck. The rat is dead, but its tail swings free in the face of the attacking snake. The attacker clamps its jaws on the tail, and the snakes meet nose-to-nose, appearing now to be one long, twelve-foot snake.

"They're not immune to their own venom! They won't bite each other." Daniel emphasizes. However, I see venom drops on the fangs of the attacker.

Adam stands guard with his long snake stick, while Daniel and I quickly locate a large, flat rock next to a Mimi painting. It's almost a meter long, and it takes both of us to lift it. Awkwardly, we run with it over opposite Adam, four meters from the snakes, and set it down.

"Listen to me!" Daniel commands, wide eyed and calm. "Stan and I will hold the rock and stand next to the wall on the right. Adam, you stand next to the wall on the left with your stick; be ready to take first action if the attacking snake stops and confronts us. Here's what's going to happen: After the rat is fully swallowed, the snake that ate it will quit the fight and leave. He needs to find a quiet place to digest his meal—he'll disregard us and head into the cave. The attacker will be mad and follow him, going between us! If it stops or coils, Adam will fork its head into the dirt before Stan and I drop this rock on it. We must be fast and precise."

Another fifteen minutes go by before the rat is completely swallowed. The attacker snake only gets the tail. Already digesting the rat, the snake that ate it slithers into the cave paying no attention us, just like Daniel predicted. The attacking snake follows it but stops, sensing us, and hisses! Adam acts before it can coil. He forks the snake's head into the ground with the stick and holds it down. Whipping violently, the six-foot reptile slaps Daniel with its tail as we move toward it with the rock. The snake's head is pinned to the ground, but for how long?

"Drop the rock on its bloody head," Adam shouts. "Don't miss!"

Daniel and I keep our legs spread as tail slaps keep coming. This snake is very much alive—if its head gets out of the fork we're dead! "We need to hold the rock out farther, so it doesn't hit our feet when dropped! On the count of three," I yell.

"One, two, hold it out, three!"—Wommp! The front third of the snake is crushed—the rock did the job! Tail slaps continue for a nervous minute due to muscle reflexes, then go still. All two hundred pounds of me is now standing on top of the rock. The taipan is dead! We run outside, cautiously peeking back into the narrows to see the motionless taipan wearing the large rock on its head. Adam grabs the end of his seven-foot "walking stick" and pulls it free.

"In twenty-five years of world travel, this was my first snake fight!" I tell Daniel and Adam as we hike back to Hondo. "I recall reading that only two of all the people ever bitten by taipans, who didn't get anti-venom, lived."

"No worries, it was good fun—just like fighting a croc with a baseball bat!" Adam boasts, still shaking.

"What's that big wet spot on your pants?" I ask him, mostly in jest but also checking myself.

"Just a bit of Aussie pee, it's a backup snake repellent!" Adam smiles in relief.

"Very rare to see two taipans fighting. We Aboriginals call it the Fierce Snake!" Daniel explains, shaking too but in dry pants.

"Dr. Dan knew exactly what those snakes would do—London to a brick!" Adam exclaims.

"Daniel, you were 'right on the money' with your instructions. I'm just happy it's now on my 'been there done that' list."

"There's some ace Yank expressions for your notebook, Danny!" Adam quips.

We drive south on the Kakadu Highway to Pine Creek and then on to Katherine on the Stuart Highway. We miss seeing our wise Aboriginal friend, George. They tell us in town he's on a walkabout and will be back sometime. We eat a kangaroo- meat pie at a local diner, then, with no time to waste, drive to the Central Arnhem Road (Highway 24) which runs on a northeast diagonal through the center of Arnhem Land. It's 710 kilometers from Katherine to Nhulunbu, where the Arafura Sea ends and the Gulf of Carpentaria begins. But we're only going about halfway before we detour off Arnhem road to no road at all—where the Never-Never awaits.

The Never-Never is both a location and a frame of mind. The location is various places in Australia's vast Outback—far back in the bush where a special energy flows. Aborigines can feel it. The frame of mind is like a dream-state that engages your consciousness in the Dreamtime; where your success is determined by how skillfully you navigate and learn in the new reality. Once you understand the Never-Never, you will understand why traditional dreams never quite get resolved . . .

"It's two hundred and forty clicks (Kilometers) to the Mainoru Outback Store, our next stop," Adam declares. "Famous old place." The road starts out as bitumen, but after one-hundred kilometers becomes a rough dirt road with grooves, ruts, and sudden dips.

"Dusk is arriving," Dr. Dan observes, as we bounce along heading east doing ninety kilometers per hour despite the road. Hondo's heavy-duty everything is much appreciated. Mitsy would have been significantly more stressful on the old bum. There's no oncoming traffic; the desolation I expected is accented by the developing darkness.

We stop at the store briefly. There's a garden next to it and a gas pump. Adam asks two native men about road conditions but needs help from Daniel to translate. There are hundreds of native clans and languages in Australia's Northern Territory. The men, speaking in Rembarrngan mixed with their version of Aussie slang, tell us to cross the Wilton River on the downriver side and stay to the left. It's mostly a half-meter deep on that side but can be over a meter deep in the center. We listen carefully and examine the map—conditions can change daily!

The road smooths out and widens as we head northeast on the Central Arnhem Road. Bullman, an old cattle station with a population of two-hundred, is the last settlement before we venture off the Central Arnhem Road and into the Never- Never. A sign warns of no petrol for 420 kilometers. I turn around and count six red jerry cans each containing twenty liters of petrol.

Adam notices me counting them and remarks, "She'll be right." I smile and check my seatbelt. Moonlight saves us from having to cross the Wilton River in total darkness. Adam shifts into four-low and we go slowly into the moving water.

"It's a piece of cake in Hondo," I remark as we push the water aside.

"Danny, did you hear that Yankee slang?" Adam declares as we pull out of the river."

"Thank you, Stan," Doctor Dan acknowledges. "I like cake!" I smile as I sense he's still trying to connect with our near-total informality, which I assume is apart from the dialog rigidity common at the university.

"You're welcome. The phrase just came out of me; means it was easy."

"In Oz we say: 'It came good!'" Adam clarifies as he drives on in the moonlight. The road is fine now — wide, flat, red gravel, bordered by gum trees.

As we drive on, Dan mentions something to Adam, who pulls over and stops. He checks the map while Dan turns on the GPS.

"Up ahead about ten clicks," Adam deduces, Dan nods. "We'll pitch camp near the turnoff for tomorrow," Adam turns his head and tells me. "The bush is always at mate's rate (free)."

I'm impressed at how fast we get camp set up. We're in a gravel clearing just off the Central Arnhem Road. It's drier here and the gum trees are spaced apart more. Adam's new tent sets up automatically, except for staking it out. I blow up the air matrasses with a 12-volt pump while Dr. Dan builds a roaring fire.

"She'll be apples," Adam declares, looking at camp. I've heard that before.

Our dinner is simple: Subs and V.B. We bought six sub sandwiches in Katherine; they're cold in the beer esky (cooler). Adam un-bungees three aluminum folding chairs off the top of Hondo, and we sit around the fire, eating and drinking. Dan checks the date on our alcohol permit.

"Just a few differences from forty-thousand years ago," Dr. Dan comments.

"The stars have moved a bit," Adam says.

"Just a little bit!" Dan clarifies.

"I recall reading that most stars move about a 'pinky's worth' in thirty thousand years. That's the width of your little finger held out at arm's length," I mention.

"Good onya, Stan! You have accurately defined a 'bit,'" Adam exclaims.

"Excellent Stan, good analogy. I can use your 'pinky-measure' in the classroom," Dan says.

"What would the ancient Aborigines think if they could see us here now?" I wonder out loud.

"That we are sky spirits, and Hondo must have flown us in," Dan responds.

"But we don't look like the Mimi." I know Dan understands where I'm going with this.

"But what if the Mimi are just one type of sky spirit? Some of the clans up here in Arnhem Land believe the Mimi are arbitrators! That they maintain a balance and keep evil aliens from dominating benevolent aliens." I sense an increased pitch in Dr. Dan's voice.

The fire burns straight up, there's no wind. The stars compete with moonlight for our attention. Finally, with another V.B. in hand, we get into it.

"So, Doctor Dan, it's time to discuss stars that move twenty pinky-widths or more in a few seconds." This gets Adam choking on a swallow of beer that's only halfway down.

"Tell me what you know about them." Dan grins, showing his pearly-white teeth. Adam opens another can of V.B. while I describe my experience in Alaska last year.

"We were at Kodiak Island on a salmon fishing trip. I was with two friends: a retired physics teacher and an aeronautical engineer, Ted and Dean. After a challenging rough-water day on the ocean, we ultimately wound up on the lodge's deck watching stars at 1:00 a.m. Several were moving fast at satellite altitude, in geometric patterns! NASA calls them "fast-walkers."

"Moving their bloody arses!" Adam clarifies.

"Those are alien spacecraft." Doctor Dan, calm and cool, acknowledges without a trace of doubt.

That takes us into discussing five different species of aliens that Dr. Dan purports have interacted with mankind for eons and still do. And then a big surprise: He reveals that most of the funding for his dig comes from a secret UFO study group in Australia. And we are here to confirm, unambiguously, that Mimi rock art is thirty to for-ty-thousand-years old and connects with ancient manta beings that, apparently, are still around.

My mind now begins to absorb it all: If, in fact, they are arbiters between pro-and anti-human alien forces—this becomes a trip that supersedes adventure and redefines importance.

"Time to hit the air mattress." I lie down in the tent wearing ear-plugs. Adam, instantly, becomes a snoring machine! Dan can't take it; he sleeps in Hondo. I think about the pack of dingoes that con-fronted us in the past on a fishing trip—Adam and I were sleeping outside on cots with only a tarp above us. The dogs surrounded us and scared the Bejesus out of me! Adam woke up for five seconds. But that's another story.

A warm sunny morning shines into the open tent flap. Dan has the fire going and I can smell coffee. I stand up and stretch—ready for the day in shorts, tee shirt and bush hat, like Adam. But Dan is wearing a ranger's uniform.

"You look pretty formal, Doctor Dan," I say, coming out of the tent.

"I know," he answers. "We are on Aboriginal land and in the un-likely event we get stopped and checked, I need to look professional. I've got several different permits I'd have to explain.

"There's a Buckley's chance (no chance) we get stopped, but we everyday blokes understand." Adam says while filling our coffee mugs; then opens a Tupperware container of Abbey's muffins. We are on the east edge of the Wilton River Basin; two magnificent brolga cranes fly overhead, checking us out as we prepare to leave.

One thing I've learned from Adam is what I call "quick camp." It requires no more than fifteen minutes to set up and the same to take down. We follow that rule. Adam starts Hondo and we get moving, finishing the muffins and coffee in the truck (aka ute).

When we turn south, off Arnhem Road, we come upon four Aboriginal women getting ready to cook long-neck turtles. Dressed in colorful western garb, two are holding eight-inch turtles by their heads. The reptiles are alive and moving their feet, trying to swim away. The other two women are stirring embers of a fire that's about ready for the turtles.

"Hello, Ladies," Daniel says when he gets out of Hondo. Then he greets them again in two different Aboriginal languages. They huddle closer to each other and giggle. All four are dark-skinned and slender with braided black hair. The two holding turtles lift them up to show us. We nod and smile. Daniel signals them to go on and cook the turtles—we're just here to watch. They lay the turtles in the fire upside down. As you might imagine, the turtles violently move their legs trying to swim out of the fire while pulling their heads completely into their shells. It's over in less than a minute for them and they'll be ready to eat in an hour. The ladies cut the plastron (bottom shell) off and eat their meal, the turtle, in the carapace (top shell) when it's ready. Welcome to the past.

The off-road drive into the Never-Never is mystifying. For the first couple of hours it's slow going and bumpy. But we expected this. In parts, it reminds me of Africa—and seeing a massive baobab tree ahead confirms that recollection. The tree is a rare sight in the Northern Territory, more common in Western Australia.

"That must be the Supreme Being of trees for the gangly woolly butts and gums," I suggest. The tree has a huge bulging diameter and loses its leaves in the dry season—it looks like some imaginary botanical being in a Disney movie, or the fighting tree in The Wizard of Oz.

"Very spiritual tree in Aboriginal lore, we call it a boab tree," Daniel instructs. "It can save your life! The nuts can be eaten raw or roasted, and a tree like this one can hold over a thousand liters of water."

The vastness is now apparent as Arnhem Land expands and we head into something akin to absolute desolation. Dan turns on the GPS but can't get a good signal—only one bar. We pound on; Adam's dashboard compass takes priority over dead reckoning. In the distance there are substantial rock outcroppings; we turn toward them.

"I've only been this way once; I usually come up from the south," Dan says. Two more hours pass before we need to make a nature stop.

"You blokes take the men's room. I'll use the Shelia's over here," Adam jokes. "And watch out for snakes!"

The topography becomes more interesting as we approach the Parson's Range of hills; small oases appear, rock groupings with thicker trees around dry river beds. It's 39 degrees Celsius in the sun (102F); we have the air conditioning on max.

"Come to think of it, I prefer Hondo's AC over Mitsy's," I tell Adam. Mitsy had no AC at all!

"Aye, mate. Arvos (afternoons) are warm out here," Adam grins. "Dan, did you catch how Stan started his last sentence? Authentic Yank slang at its best."

"Thanks for reminding me," Dan replies, scratching something in his notebook. We travel on as I finish a bottle of water. Adam notes that a cold V.B. would be better for me, but ranger Dan reminds him our alcohol permit doesn't allow drinking while driving. We keep on moving southeast with the sun glaring down on us. Water-pond mirages quiver on the horizon. The compass is okay, but it would be helpful to have a bearing. Southeast is a big place out here!

Hondo now grinds through thick spinifex bush; the spikey grass tangles in our tires. There's no way around it. Spinifex is tough like wire and can cut into horses' legs, causing them to bleed when they walk through it. Trucks with cheap tires can get stranded if the sidewalls get penetrated. Some varieties of the Spinifex are sharper than others.

"We have steel radial tires with four-ply sidewalls, they should rip right through this stuff! Adam declares confidently.

"You could say Never go into the Never-Never without 'Ripper' tires!" I try to be funny. Neither of them laugh.

Adam shifts into four-low and Hondo becomes a spaghetti factory as the Michelin tires throw brown noodles of ground-up Spinifex everywhere. I look out and see the wake of dead grass the truck is making. Strangely, it reminds me of running a boat through thick weeds on a Canadian lake, only that wake is green and slimy. We're in a low area that gets just enough moisture in the wet season to accommodate the Spinifex.

It's a relief when we're out of it! Adam stops, and we get out to check the tires. They're hot from substantial weed entanglement. We put gloves on and start pulling weeds off the tires and undercarriage. When finished, the three of us drink a can of beer—to hell with the alcohol permit's fine print! Ahead was flat, unobstructed land that never looked so good!

After another hour of heading southeast with Dan still unable get more than one bar on the GPS, he suggests we stop and have a look around. He's out before Adam has Hondo fully stopped.

"I sense we're close to the dig," Daniel says, employing his Aboriginal sixth sense. "Look for a large road-train container!"

Adam points to the top of Hondo and glances at me; that's all the permission I need.

I dig in my backpack for binoculars, take off my shoes, and climb through the sun roof to get on top of the truck. Then I stand up and start glassing like when I'm elk hunting in Colorado. The first thing I see is a big quivering lake, obviously a mirage.

"Look more southeast," Daniel shouts. I follow his instructions.

"I see something that looks like a rectangular rock, or maybe a building? It's out a good five miles! It's red like the other rocks but definitely rectangular."

"Does it have a black top?" Daniel asks.

I refocus the binoculars. There's significant glare, and my stocking feet are getting hot. "I can't tell. Maybe. There's a hill of gray, pancake-shaped sedimentary rocks to the north of it."

"That's it!" Daniel shouts.

"Bloody terrific!" Adam echoes Daniel.

I get on my knees and look down through the sunroof and check the compass reading, then scoot down and put my shoes on. "A guy could cook a turtle on that roof!"

"Good onya mate. My crook back wasn't up to it," Adam says. I reply with a thumb up.

The three of us get back into Hondo and head southeast at 140-degrees. Adam and I are excited and so is Ranger Dan, despite his Aboriginal maturity. The terrain is sandy clay interspersed with numerous termite mounds. One lone kangaroo is resting in the shadow of a ghost gum as we pass by—nothing is jumping around anywhere that we can see. Breaks in the clay—sand shelves—slow us down. Adam has Hondo in four-wheel-drive-low again as we creep along a broken no-road.

"We're getting close!" Doctor Dan exclaims as we leave a red dust trail. Adam keeps Hondo aimed at 140-degrees southeast.

"When do we see your big discovery?" Adam asks Dan.

"Soon—it's locked in the container!"

"Aye, I'm betting it's a ripper fossil!" Adam quips.

"You'll have to decide that when you see it." Dan wouldn't say any more.

We continue throwing dust as we pass a rock outcropping and a small stand of gum trees guarding a small pond covered with algae. I try to imagine if it looked like this thirty-five-thousand years ago. Why not? What could change out here?

Finally, the rectangular container is directly ahead. "Right on the 140-degree bearing." Dan flashes an approving grin at me as Adam pulls Hondo up to it, loudly crumbling old termite-mound gravel. We can see the pancake-shaped rocks to the north.

"The door is on the backside—it will be a bit warm in there." Dan is sorting through a large ring of keys. Adam and I follow him.

"The door! It's open!" Dan rushes to the large, sliding freight door. Just as he enters the container, an eight-foot goanna climbs out above him and runs up the outer ribbing to the top of the container, then turns and harshly hisses at Dan.

Adam and I follow Dan in, keeping an eye on the giant lizard. "He's a perentie monitor, biggest in Oz—a real beaut'!" Adam remarks.

"It's hotter than a freshly-inseminated fox in an Iowa cornfield in August!" I joke using humor from an old professor I once knew, as I step into the container. Adam chuckles, but Dan doesn't hear me, he's already in the back and out of sight. The only light is from the doorway which is on the side of the container.

"It's all here! Still here!" Dan shouts in the dark before finding the switch on a 12-volt light wired to a battery.

Just then we hear a vehicle's horn! Adam and I jump out and run to peek around the end of the container. So much for being alone in the Never-Never.

"G' Day mates!" A tall Ozzie in a cowboy hat bellows as he gets out of a dusty pickup truck. "Where's the good doctor?"

Adam and I are momentarily speechless. Dan, now out of the container, smiles big. "Howard!" he shouts, quite surprised, then warmly greets him.

Daniel introduces us to Howard, then explains they're friends and that Howard Johnson is a senior member in the UFO study group in Sydney. He makes his living in the cattle business in Queensland.

"Howard's father helped my father integrate into the western world while insisting he not give up any of his Aboriginal heritage. Mr. Daniel Gurumarra, my father, then schooled me, insisting I go to graduate school. I could pick any field, he just provided the fuzzy path, allowing me to decide the turns, left or right.

"You're a bloody Junior," Adam declares, he already knew this but couldn't help himself. "Doctor Daniel Danny Dan Junior Gurumarra is the politically correct way to designate you!" Adam can always provide a good laugh, even the day after a snake fight.

"What got you to come here?" Daniel asks Howard, ignoring Adam's comment.

"I was west of Cairns on a drive-about when I called me boy. He said you'd be here! I figured you for tomorrow—picked the lock on your container to let it air out, then drove to the pancake rocks to have a look at the dig. When I came back, a monster goanna wouldn't let me go in, so I went out to that small oasis just before you drove by. I waited for your dust to settle then drove back here. Now I won't have to drink with the flies tonight (drink alone)!"

"That's right. It's great to see you! You can help us dig tomorrow," Daniel's pleased.

"I'm a good digger! Let's find a marsupial tiger's bones!" Howard declares. "That'll cork up those kangaroo-loose (intellectually inadequate) archeologists in Sydney."

"Want to see some special bones? Now?" Dan asks Adam and me. "Howard saw them when they were first discovered, but not the complete set."

"Of course." Howard answers for us.

I'm excited but still wary of Howard, I say a loud "yes" and nod while slapping my shirt and pants to get the dust off.

"Lead the way, mate," Adam says to Dan. "I forgot to add 'Mate' to your official name designation list!" This time Dan laughs.

The four of us go into the container, cautiously checking for the goanna. He's not in! We go all the way back, turn on the light, follow orders from Dr. Dan and haul out four heavy cardboard boxes full of bones. There's shade now on the south side of the container—a good place to put a giant puzzle together. Following Doctor Dan's instructions, we begin handing out bones. They're from a huge animal and each one has a number. Dan starts laying them out on the ground like a giant puzzle, starting with bones from box number one. By the time we get to box number four, the giant leg bones, we know what it is.

Each of us drinks a cold can of V.B. as we stare at the bones of an extinct, eleven-foot, giant kangaroo. It's quite a sight—not a single bone is missing, but the neck vertebra is cracked in four places.

"This is a real bonzer (cool)!" Adam exclaims. "Has to be the best specimen of the extinct giant kangaroo in all of Oz!"

"It is!" Doctor Dan says proudly. "Notice the black stains on many of the bones," Dan points to those on the giant legs. "This animal was hunted, cooked, and eaten by our first people in the early 'Now Time'—in thirty-five thousand B.C. Twenty-five thousand years before the end of the Stone Age! The charcoal stains permitted very accurate carbon dating.

Daniel continues: "Giant kangaroos, according to current thinking, went extinct fifty to one hundred thousand years ago. This perfect specimen changes that thinking by at least fifteen thousand years, which is important by itself, but it also dates a very exceptional artifact that was found with the bones!"

We all pop another tinny of V.B. and wait for Dan to tell us the rest of the story. It's obvious that Howard knows all this.

"It's time to reveal the exceptional artifact!" Daniel declares after finishing his V.B. Howard is standing beside him smiling.

Daniel opens his duffle bag and brings out a soft leather pouch. Like a magician preparing to begin a trick, he pulls out a gleaming, twelve-inch, metallic, knife-like object. Then, holding it high, he lets it catch the sun and produce a powerful reflection.

"Watch!" He points the brilliant reflection down at a Spinifex bush—in seconds it starts on fire! Then, holding the object by its handle, Daniel mutilates a second Spinifex bush, cutting it to pieces with a few gentle swings. Adam and I are captivated.

The object is glistening metallic and sharp pointed with two cutting edges and a molded handle—all one piece. One edge is a uniquely serrated blade; the other an unusual saw. Two V-shaped fins on the end of the handle make it look like a cruise missile.

"Keep watching, boys," Howard says while Daniel hands him the object. Howard moves back and away from the container, well beyond the kangaroo bones. He grips the object at the end of the handle between the V-fins. Without delay, he throws it overhand as hard as he can at the steel container.

Wizz.........Spang! The sound reverberates as the object flies straight as an arrow before penetrating the steel container. Adam and I just watch, speechless. Dan walks over and removes it; the sharp pointed nose is in perfect condition, no impact damage!

"One more test, boys," Howard states. He carefully takes the "cruise missile" back from Dan and throws on the ground. "Hand me that rock mate!" He points to a shoebox size slab of granite next to me. With both hands, I carry it over to him.

Thud, Thud—Ting, Ting! Dirt flies as Howard pounds the rock on the object as hard as he can. Then picks it up, wipes off the dirt with his shirt, and hands it to Adam.

"I'll be stuffed! It's not a bit rooted—no scratches, no dents!" Adam exclaims. "The bugger is perfect—what's it made of?"

"We've had top metallurgists attempt to analyze it. They couldn't cut it with a diamond saw or melt it with an oxy/hydrogen torch at six-thousand degrees Fahrenheit," Daniel explains. "So, we don't know what it's made of."

I'm awestruck when Adam hands it to me. Its light weight is a surprise. I examine it carefully. I'm a hunter who prides himself in owning the best of guns and knives and have never seen anything like this.

"What's your best guess?" Howard asks me.

"It could possibly be titanium alloyed with rare earth elements to be strong and light—but it would melt well below six thousand

Fahrenheit. Titanium alloyed with tungsten would be strong and survive six thousand Fahrenheit—but would be much heavier! This object is not from Hardware Hank!"

"Correct," Doctor Dan affirms.

Adam stares at it. "Aye! It's a bloody conundrum! Danny, you never mentioned this."

Dan looked at Howard. "He was under orders to keep quiet," Howard responds.

"And not anymore?" Adam asks.

"We want you to keep this object hidden in Darwin until our group can agree on a disclosure strategy. Doctor Dan's students, including my son—who found it with the kangaroo bones—have told others. Our group's office in Sydney was broken into last week, but Daniel already had the object Fedexed to your house. If the deep state's cronies find it, they'll destroy it." Howard is very serious.

"It might take a nuclear bomb to do that!" I say, not joking.

Howard nods, then continues: "This object would be a life saver in the bush! An Aboriginal could hunt with it, cut open a kangaroo with the knife, make a wood pole with the saw, make a fire with the reflections, and even kill a marsupial lion or a crocodile with it strapped on a pole. Having one would give a clan superior ability to defend itself against hostile clans and help insure sustainability,"

"Who made it? The Mimi?" I ask Dan.

"We don't know, but that's a good guess. After all, Aboriginal lore claims the Mimi taught them to hunt. And we still sing songs that speak of a powerful Spirit Stick!"

"Current UFO reports of Mimi-type mantis beings indicate they can communicate telepathically!" Howard adds. "Maybe they taught the early Aboriginals that skill too! Cogitate on that awhile."

All four of us pause for a few moments, I keep staring at the exceptional object—a genuine Spirit Stick? My science education was failing to provide answers.

"Let's go see the dig," Howard declares. "I brought a new, heavy duty rope ladder in case the old one is cactus (ruined). I intend to find a Mimi Lightsaber!"

The dig where Daniel and his students found the kangaroo bones and the Spirit Stick is behind the pancake-shaped rocks, where uranium prospectors did most of the deep digging forty years ago—an extension of their activity in the Bulman area. Records show they didn't find uranium at this site, so the hole was already there for Doctor Dan and his student team to explore. Inspecting abandoned mineral digs was common fare for paleoanthropologists. Since Daniel was concerned that low-level radioactivity might be a worry, he kept the road-train container (their base camp) away from the dig. Later, a Geiger counter confirmed there were no worries.

"All my team of students had to do last year was to go down twelve meters by rope ladder and dig a little deeper," Doctor Dan remarks. Meanwhile, Howard is already halfway down the hole on his new rope ladder.

"Picks and shovels are waiting for you down below," Daniel shouts to him in the oncoming darkness.

"I'm just checking it out for tomorrow!" Howard shouts back.

"Let's eat something, mates," Adam declares. "How does canned spaghetti and Spam sound?"

Postscript:

This story is based on true experience. Names and some places have been changed to protect secrecy and privacy. Carbon dating on the Mimi charcoal sample confirmed its age at 35,000 BC.

I can't prove that the secret object was truly alien and not dropped by some Russian uranium miner. Although the more I reflect back, the more convinced I become that's it's not from this world. Rather than hide it in Darwin, Adam suggested we bury it in Arnhem Land, deep enough to not be detected—and record both GPS coordinates and the location on a physical map so it can be found again when the world is ready . . .

For the next two days the four of us took turns on the rope ladder, digging and looking for other artifacts. We didn't find a lightsaber or meet a Mimi preserved in carbonite but did discover several fossilized seashell necklaces! Holding them, I could imagine Aboriginal ladies dancing with these strings of white cowrie shells swinging around their necks in the Never Never—in 35,000 B.C.

Author's grandson William with a nice Canadian walleye caught
before a storm

9

Big Rain in Canada
Underestimating the Power of Nature

$\mathcal{P}$rologue:

Bob and Bill Parsons were cousins and equal partners in a feed company in Iowa. Every year for ten years they had invited loyal customers to join them on a fishing trip to Canada. The summer of 2003 was their eleventh year. It was a fourteen-hour drive from Cedar Rapids, Iowa to Eagle Lake in southern Ontario. Bob was driving the company's R.V. with Bill sitting next to him; their five guests were playing poker in back.

Northern Minnesota, July 2003

"Are you guys about ready for a famous burger? Bill inquired on the RV's speaker. They had just exited interstate thirty-five east of Cloquet, Minnesota.

"At Gordy's?" Steve yelled out. He was a consulting veterinarian and a fishing trip regular.

"Yup, at Gordy's," Bob shouted back. Gordy's Hi-Hat was an old-fashioned hamburger joint founded in 1960—a traditional halfway stop for them. They could see the sign of a chef in a white hat after crossing the Cloquet River.

halfway stop for them. They could see the sign of a chef in a white hat after crossing the Cloquet River.

"They're made with one hundred percent Iowa beef!" Dennis declared, a dedicated Angus beef farmer from western Iowa and another yearly regular.

They all placed their orders at the inside counter and sat down until their number was called. California burgers were the favored item.

"I wonder if the weather will behave like it did last year. I didn't have to put rain gear on for the entire six days!" Dennis commented, then took a bite of his burger.

"It does seem like dry years alternate with wet years," Bill confirmed before mouthing a spoonful of Gordy's famous coleslaw. "Hope I'm wrong; being zipped up in rain gear all day makes for a tough outing—like two years ago."

"True, but it wasn't all bad, the rains came without much wind. We caught nice walleyes that year." Bob was always the optimist.

"But a big storm is a cat of a different color," Dennis said. "If you can't get back to the lodge, you gotta seriously hunker down somewhere."

"That's right," Bob acknowledged. "We'll have good guides with us! They know where to go when water, wind, and electricity refuse to mix peacefully!" The thought did wake up some caution in Bob: Between the gear and supplies we brought plus what the guides provide, we'll be prepared.

They left Gordy's at 3:00 p.m. and had a long seven hours to go. No more interstate highway.

"We're halfway there," Steve remarked, "I'm ready to crank on some big walleyes—can smell them frying at shore lunch!" A Canadian shore lunch was a thing to behold; the secrets were in the details. Gordy's was fine, but a good shore lunch was to die for!

For Jerry, Leo, and Carl, it was their first fishing trip to Canada; they mostly listened to what the others had been saying. They were excited too, but in a different way; only Carl had any fishing experience. For the other two this was a trip into the unknown.

The drive on U.S. Highway 53 to the Canadian border was a long 170 miles in a slow-moving RV. After crossing the bridge at International Falls they cleared Canadian customs at Fort Frances.

Two custom officials came into the RV, looked around, and asked each man where he lived and for an I.D. The taller of the two officials asked how much beer and liquor they had. Bob told them five cases of beer and two quarts of brandy, the untaxable limit for seven people. Then, the taller official asked about guns, did they have any? Bill told him they had none. The shorter official asked if they had any nightcrawlers in soil. Bob said they had crawlers, but in shredded paper not soil. And that was it: they were in Canada with another three hours of driving to get to the fishing lodge on Eagle Lake.

Most of the drive was north on Highway 502 which had no services—just trees, lakes, and big animals. Bob hated to drive it at night, and it would be dark for two of those hours! Moose, bear, wolves and big cats were at home here. A twelve-hundred-pound bull moose in the middle of the road was, indeed, something to be concerned about. They would take it slow.

Southern Ontario, July 2003

The clouds looked like mountains on the northern horizon, rising high in jagged peaks. Valleys between the clouds were dense with moisture. Fishing in July could be either wet or dry in southern Ontario. Wind direction was helpful in predicting what distant clouds might do.

Above the large island the sun was bright and the sky deep blue over a wide expanse of open water that was well south of the clouds. Four aluminum fishing boats had been pulled onto the north shore of the island.

An Indian guide named Kenny was filleting walleyes on a flat rock near the boats. It took him only four cuts to get both filets off a fish, two cuts on each side. He flipped the filets into a tin plate using the tip of his knife. The plate overflowed with boneless filets—keeping the filet knife moving fast he filled a second plate.

The fishermen followed a path going up a hill where the younger Indian guide, Waawaate, a name meaning "Northern Lights," was building a fire in a flat area surrounded by pine and birch trees. There was a circle of rocks from previous fires and plenty of dead wood to burn. When the fire was going strong he took the grill he'd brought from camp and positioned it over the fire using rocks to support it. Then he pulled two cast iron frying pans out of a burlap sack and wiped them clean with pine needles before putting them on the grill.

Bob and Bill sliced onions and potatoes while Waawaate put two, one-pound bricks of lard in each frying pan. The five other fishermen stood by watching and drinking beer.

"We can thank Steve for most of these fish," Dennis said. "That bugger always beats us."

"It's because he uses four-pound test monofilament with a one-sixteenth ounce jig, no sinker. Most fishermen use six-pound line with heavier jigs because it's easier to keep the bait on the bottom. I saw him fight a twelve-pound, thirty-two-inch walleye for an hour once," Bob remarked, looking up from slicing onions. "Steve couldn't put much pressure on the fish without breaking his line, so it was a long fight. The big fish felt only the nightcrawler when it first hit!"

"That's a big walleye!" Jerry had been reading fishing magazines. "Did you have it mounted?" he asked Steve.

"That one I did," Steve admitted. "It was my largest walleye. I let all the big ones go now."

"Steve's a republican," Bill quipped.

"How do you know that?" Steve wanted to know. He rarely discussed politics!

"Because republicans mount their fish—democrats just eat them," Bill said with a conservative grin. That got everyone laughing, even Waawaate.

"Steve's the man." Kenny said, "A fish feels no resistance on his light tackle." Steve Johnson was the only ten-year veteran of the "yearly outing," as he called it. He was tall and lanky and wore a big cowboy hat. At age sixty, still a wild spirit, he looked much more like a Texan than an Iowan. And, he was a Doctor of Veterinary Medicine and knew something about everything.

Carl, Jerry, and Leo were taking it all in. All three were younger men. Jerry was well-read on fishing. Carl had the most tackle. And Leo was part of the great unknown.

"What makes the walleye such a special fish?" Jerry asked Bob, who had just accidently squirted himself with onion juice.

While wiping his eye with his forearm, Bob replied, "Walleyes are a challenge to catch; they feed mostly on the bottom and are wary of unnatural resistance when feeding. They can spit out a nightcrawler that doesn't feel natural faster than Waawaate can finger-flip a filet in hot lard. When you feel that first tap-tap, open the bale on your reel and let the fish take line and run with it, give it time to eat the crawler. Then set the hook and reel fast!"

"And they are the best eaters of all freshwater fish, clean tasting and firm—easy to digest!" Bill added. "Much the same as black grouper are the best saltwater eaters."

"They're both quite esculent!" Steve verified.

"Right, Doctor Johnson," Jerry replied. "Whatever that means." Steve just smiled.

It had been calm all morning, but now there was a mugginess in the air.

The mountain-like clouds on the northern horizon had become larger and a thick green band ran through them horizontally. They were still a fair distance away but it was important to keep an eye on them.

"Rain coming," Kenny said, as he brought two plates of filets up the hill from his fish-cleaning rock and set them on a cooler, away from the fire. Waawaate had the lard heating in both pans; the bricks had melted. Kenny shook the filets in a plastic bag filled with flour and black pepper—lots of black pepper. His secret recipe was that simple!

"Isn't lard unhealthy; increases your cholesterol?" Dennis asked, looking at Steve. Dennis was the oldest of the men...kind-hearted, gray-haired, and very matter-of-fact.

"That's an old wives' tale," Steve replied, he knew something about lard. "The filets fry so fast in hot lard that very little penetrates the meat which stays firm and crisp. It takes longer to fry them in vegetable oil which doesn't get as hot and gets into the meat, making it oily and less firm."

"Steve is the man!" Dennis confirmed. "I believe he knows something about everything." Dennis was sincere, he had known Steve for many years and used his vet-consulting services. He had great respect for Steve Johnson.

"Big rain," Waawaate said as he put more wood on the fire. The fishermen were watching the sky and mumbling to each other, pointing to the clouds still some distance away. Jerry seemed to know something about lightning. He told the group: "Thunder travels

185

about a mile in five seconds, so when you see a flash and then hear the thunder, count the seconds to get the distance. Fifteen seconds means the storm is three miles away." A light breeze now rippled the water around the island.

"Put potatoes and onions in here." Waawaate pointed to one of the frying pans. Bob and Bill dumped the sliced onions and potatoes into it—the sizzling started in seconds. Bob stirred the pan with his filet knife—utility items had multiple duties at a Canadian shore lunch.

Kenny started flipping the breaded filets into the other frying pan. Waawaate made sure they were body-cavity-side down to limit curling. Kenny called it "outside up." Waawaate managed the filets, which sizzled immediately and turned golden brown. Kenny smiled, it would take only a few minutes. Waawaate began singing a song, settling any debate about his Ojibway origin.

Two large cans of pork and beans started to boil; Bill had set them at the edge of the fire earlier. "Fish ready in three minutes," Kenny announced. Bill opened five cans of cold, Old Vienna beer (O.V.) and gave one to each guest.

Alluring aromas filled the air, creating a promise of unquestionable edibility. Simple food skillfully prepared. Thunder rumbled in the distance.

Waawaate jammed more birch branches into the fire to keep it going strong. The lard had to be kept hot. Quickly, he reached into the pan and turned the filets with his fingers. He didn't concern himself with the spats of hot lard that hit his hand. He was a strong, young, Indian man!

"I'm hungry, how about you guys?" Bob inquired, as he continued to stir the potatoes and onions. Everyone agreed they were hungry. "Take a plate and help yourselves," Bill instructed. "Chow's ready." The guys didn't need any additional encouragement.

They all sat around the fire on boat cushions as they ate. The talk was mostly about how great it was to be eating fresh walleyes with good friends on an island in Canada. They were supposed to be talking about business—feeding chickens, cows, and pigs—but just enough to keep the accountants satisfied. After all, this was a business trip!

"These fish are scrumptious!" Jerry announced, looking at Steve who nodded and took a large filet off his plate, held it high, took a big bite, and washed it down with a long drink of O.V.

"It's Steve's way of making a toast when he's happy with your words." Dennis chuckled. Bob, Bill and Dennis knew Steve was putting on a show for the new guys.

"With the weather changing, those walleyes will be active!" Bill asserted. Predator fish always became active feeders just ahead of a sharp change in the weather. This was when they lost their caution and hit baits with reckless abandon.

"Steve, what color jig would you use out there right now?" Carl asked—he had every color jig in every size and had been preoccupied with his tackle. He was finally eating now, showing some interest in Bill's comment.

"Any color as long as it's white!" Steve advised. The sky above was clear and blue but a change in the weather was coming; white was the secret color for such a change. Bob and Bill were predicting the weather would move east of the island, allowing them to fish to the west after lunch.

Steve took a Texas-sized bite from another, larger filet, one from a fish he knew he'd caught. "Best fish this side of the north pole," he declared.

"The black flies are biting now," Leo reported, as he put a spoonful of beans and one small filet on his plate." He had been quiet until now and was looking a little green.

"Leo! You can talk!" Dennis was surprised. Leo had been in Dennis' boat and hadn't said a thing all morning. He'd been drinking and playing poker in Dryden the previous night and didn't do so well. He was in his mid-twenties, the youngest of the party.

"Yup, I can talk," Leo said, not amused.

Bob looked at Leo, then at Bill. "Tell him that joke!" Bob asked Bill, he knew Leo had been out late and was suffering.

"Not again, you always ask me to tell that stupid joke." Steve and Dennis were laughing because they knew the joke. Bob looked at Bill again . . .

"Okay, okay, I'll do it for Leo's sake: Little Johnny was five years old and had never talked. Otherwise he was a healthy young boy. His parents had taken him to a dozen doctors who found nothing wrong.

Johnny could hear but didn't talk. Not one word. One night when he was having dinner with his parents, he suddenly blurted out, "These potatoes are too hot!" His parents were astonished. "Johnny, you can talk!" they cried out. "Why have you never talked before?" Johnny answered, "Everything has been all right until now!"

Everyone laughed, including Leo. Make some coffee for this man," Bob told Kenny, pointing to Leo.

"How long before the rain hits?" Dennis asked. Bob and Bill kept hoping it would miss them and move east. It would take a strong southwest wind to make that happen. It was possible.

"Soon," Waawaate answered. "Big rain coming." He kept frying filets for those wanting seconds and thirds, which was everyone except Leo. When the sky had green bands in it with corkscrew shaped clouds coming out of the main cloud body, it not only meant big rain but big wind too. Corkscrew clouds hovered high in the north but it was still blue and sunny above the island.

"Come and get more fish," Bob called out, then told the guides to eat hardy but no beer! They gladly obliged and only ate fish.

Bob salted another plate of filets. Bill opened the cooler and handed out more beer. The fishermen went down the hill to the shore, which was a small beach area surrounded by giant boulders and an uncountable number of smaller rocks before it became sand. They stood while they ate and watched the clouds. A cleanup crew of gray-backed gulls flew in and landed in the water just off shore, calling loudly to each other. They could see the walleye skeletons by Kenny's rock.

Suddenly, a bright flash bolted through the thunderclouds that now extended across the entire northern horizon. Then another. The clouds' mountain shapes had become distorted. The green band that ran through them had thickened and was moving southeast toward them. The sky was still blue overhead but the breeze was gone now. It was dead calm and the water looked like an endless sheet of stainless steel.

"Best time to catch walleye," Kenny said. He had walked down the hill from the fire and was standing on shore with another plate of fried walleye filets, holding it out for the fishermen that still wanted more. "Even the Great Spirit eats these fish!"

"Good time to eat them," Carl, Jerry's tackle-crazy cousin, declared. He had been down at their boat sorting lures, tying lines, sharpening hooks, and had missed getting seconds. He was first to grab a filet off Kenny's plate of extras. Carl shuddered when he looked at the clouds. "I didn't bring any rain gear, just a two-dollar plastic poncho."

Kenny knew it was the calm before the storm, and that the lodge where they were staying was north of them, getting hit right now. They were fifteen miles from the lodge and would have to go right into the storm to get back. They would need to hunker down on the island until it was over. Kenny had experienced bad storms many times.

Steve was considering what to do: go fishing or hunker down... This storm could still miss them if that southwest wind came back strong but that was unlikely.

"I doubt it will miss us," Bob said. "It's a nasty looking front, solid across the north and closer now. Just look at those clouds, black with rain! Carl, I have extra rain gear in my boat—it's under the back seat." Carl ran to get it.

"Fish go crazy now—eat everything," Waawaate said. He had come down the hill after dousing the fire and was standing on shore by the boats with everyone else.

"For how long?" Dennis asked.

"Short time," the young Indian answered, "until rain comes, then they go deep and stop eating."

"Let's go out to that big rockpile west of here; it's not too far," Steve suggested to Waawaate. "We can come back fast if it gets bad. Dennis, come with us, here's your chance to catch a monster walleye."

Waawaate didn't need any more encouragement, he hopped in his boat and started the motor. "Get in," he shouted to Steve, who dragged Dennis into the boat by his collar. "You're not too old for this," Steve insisted, instructing in a tone he would use when prescribing medicine for Denny's cattle.

"I need my fishing rod!" Dennis shouted. It was in one of the other boats.

"Get in! I've got two extras ready to go. Time is short!" Steve insisted.

"I don't advise it," Bill said loudly from behind them. But they were already off, heading out to the reef about two miles west in open water.

"Put your life jackets on!" Bob yelled out to them. "Dammit!" he didn't want anyone going out!

"Everyone else get your rain gear on and get away from the water. Go to that low brush pile at the base of the hill, it's away from the trees. Sit on something, get those coolers down from up on the hill. Sit on them, feet up. Or on seat cushions. Sit like an Indian at a pow-wow. Keep your feet off the ground!" Bob yelled like a drill sergeant. He knew lightning could travel on the ground a long distance from where it struck. The bolt you see is the discharge back to the clouds—you don't see the strike!

"It's just a rain storm," Leo said. Kenny's instant coffee hadn't revived him much. He was wearing a thin hoodless jacket and shorts. Being his first trip with the group he, like Carl, hadn't paid attention to the must bring gear list Bob had sent to everyone. Carl was wearing Bob's only spare rain gear.

"Big storm," Kenny confirmed loudly. "Be ready!" There was constant lightning and thunder across the entire northern horizon now. The sky above the island had morphed from clear blue to hazy gray-blue.

On the reef, Steve and Dennis were catching walleyes. Nothing big so far, but the small ones were hitting bare jigs on every cast. No leech, minnow or nightcrawler was required on the jig! Just a bare hook! Waawaate ran the boat slowly in reverse, closely watching the sky. It was calm but the thunder and lightning were closer now. He worried mostly about the wind. How strong would the wind be? He had a plan if it got too bad and they were unable to get back to the others—there was a protected cove on the south side of a nearby island.

Dennis got a nice hit and immediately started reeling but did not set the hook. He lost the fish at the boat. "Five-pound fish," Steve lamented. Then Steve got a strong hit and pulled back on the rod to set the hook, reeling all the time. Waawaate put the motor in neutral and grabbed the net. The small fish were just lifted into the boat, the big ones were netted. Steve had been smart and had switched to his heavier rod with eight-pound test line. He knew the walleyes would not be spooked under these pre-storm conditions. He horsed the fish to the boat and the guide netted the nice twenty-nine-incher.

"Great fishing!" Dennis exclaimed. Steve was looking up and starting to get concerned. The heavy corkscrew clouds had changed from gray to black and were moving toward them. It was still calm, so they kept fishing.

Suddenly, a brilliant lightning flash discharged high, vaulting completely across the sky—a huge branching flash with tentacles. Seconds later, a deafening explosion of thunder vibrated everything.

"That better get the boys to come in." Bob was worried.

"Where the hell did that come from? Bill asked. It's still blue above."

"Lightning can come out of the blue—literally—sometimes with no storm close. And travel miles over water." Bob reminded him. Bill had missed five of the yearly trips, so he didn't have as much time on the water as Bob.

"Twelve years ago, two men were out in one of the lodge's boats in a storm and the guy in front got hit by lightning! It ripped him apart. It hit him in the neck and came out his stomach along with his guts. He looked like a pile of hamburger when they got back to camp." Bob explained the gory facts. "Didn't I ever tell you about this?"

"No!" Bill answered. "It was before we became partners and you never told me. Wow, what happened to the guy in the back seat?"

"Never touched!" Bob replied.

"How the hell did the guy in back survive millions of volts hitting an aluminum boat?" Bill quivered.

"He had rubber boots on and was sitting on an insulated cushion. His name was Elmer, a local." Bob, remembering all of it now, became frightened by his own words.

"And the guy in front?"

"Standing up in sneakers, fishing with a graphite rod! Alive one minute, then disemboweled one second later! It could have happened to Ben Franklin when he proved lightning was electricity; remember, he held a wire tied to a kite with a metal key hanging on it in a storm. Old Ben was lucky—this guy wasn't."

"Still, that close, you'd think both would have been hit." Bill was still unsettled.

"Don't know; lightning can be like that. Sometimes it gets everything close and other times it doesn't," Bob said. "The seat cushion and rubber boots must have provided enough protection. Elmer was lucky!"

"God! How did Elmer take it?" Bill asked.

"He was an old guy, took it in stride. At least that's what the dock boy at the lodge told me. That young dock boy was Kenny!"

"How could you take something like that in stride?" Bill couldn't understand.

"Elmer was an odd duck. He told Kenny he was bringing in a dead guy with cooked guts. I guess he didn't know him that well—it was his first-time fishing with the guy. Old Vern, the lodge owner then, didn't know what to do. Kenny threw a tarp over the dead guy and Vern called the Ontario Provincial Police. It took the OPP two hours to get to the lodge; meanwhile Kenny had to gas up boats at that same dock before the OPP arrived. Some of the guests walked right past the tarp-covered guy without knowing it," Bob elaborated.

"Jesus," Bill said. "Does Kenny talk about it?"

"No. The 'hamburger-man' story is mostly a secret. Bad for business!"

"Big rain can kill!" Kenny said loudly, looking at Jerry, Carl, and Leo huddled down, sitting on coolers and seat cushions at the foot of the hill as far away from trees and the lake as they could get.

"Buckle up!" Bob yelled, right when the wind picked up. Then he, Bill and Kenny ran over and joined the other three.

The big rain came on in a torrent of wind and pelting bullets of cold water. Then it became an opaque sheet of water with knife-like edges producing a whiteout. It was almost like being underwater—unrelenting wetness. Two bolts of lightning hit trees behind the fire pit on the hill and shook everybody. Leo, overwhelmed by the stinging cold rain was curled up in a wet ball lying on two seat cushions. Bob had given him a small tarp to cover with but the first gust had blown it away. The others sat yoga-style on cushions and coolers, rain-gear hoods tied shut, heads down so they could breathe, feet off the ground as much as possible. Bob and Bill hugged a large log with their legs, riding it like a racehorse. It was too astonishing to think about being afraid; their mind's survival mode took full control—there was no reserve energy for fear.

A horrendous electrical bolt lit the sky immediately to their right, hitting a tall pine tree. A cylinder of intense, white light the diameter of a telephone pole rose above the struck tree, discharging back into the clouds. The tree split in half lengthwise in a deafening detonation, followed by blasts of echoing thunder that shook everybody again! The sweet, ethereal smell of ozone laced with cinder smells of something trying to burn filled the air. The men covered their heads. Sheets of water cut down on them. Everyone felt electricity in their hands and feet—the static-electricity Ben Franklin felt when he touched the key on his kite.

"Holy shit! Bill, are you okay?" Bob shouted between explosions of thunder. Bill was tightly holding onto the log directly behind Bob, knees bent, feet off the ground.

"I can hardly hear—my ears are ringing!" Bill shouted back.

"Mine too!" Bob yelled, as loud cracks from smaller trees snapping in half obliterated his voice.

"What?" Bill was freaking out.

"Mine too!" Bob shouted again. In all his fishing trips, he had never experienced a storm of this magnitude.

"Where did it hit?" Bill yelled, holding the hood on his rain jacket closed—the zipper had broken. It was hard for him to yell into the pelleted rain. Both Bob and Bill continued to hug the upper side of the log, pressing their knees tight against it, like riding some race to the end of the world. Jerry and Carl were sitting on separate coolers looking down at the ground—the hill at their backs providing protection. Kenny was sitting on three boat cushions with his legs crossed. The wind howled and blew broken branches around like two-by-fours in a lumber yard during a tornado. One of the huge branches just missed Kenny. Another hit Carl in the leg with a glancing blow. The wind propelled the slanted raindrops like BBs shot from a gun. Leaves and sticks spun in mini-vortexes while the sky was on fire with lightning.

"It hit here, somewhere over to the right!" Bob yelled.

Suddenly, another bolt hit something close and they all ducked again. This blue-white bolt returned, shooting upward from a tree next to where the first tree had been destroyed! The ear-shattering explosion broke the sound barrier as it reverberated back at them. Lightning had struck twice in the same place.

"Holy Jesus!" Bill screamed in pain, holding his hands over his ears. The decibels were eardrum-rupturing, well over the 120 decibels average for thunder—more than ten times louder than a jack hammer!

"Look at that boat!" Bob shouted. They could barely see it. One of the boats that was closest to them had a bundle of graphite fishing rods standing up next to the motor. Not a bolt of lightning, but something else— like static electricity streaming trillions of electrons— contacted the rods and created a fluorescent blue light that encircled the boat around its gunnel. Then the blue light brightened and lit up the entire boat. There was no sound for several moments. Everyone stared in disbelief: was this all a bad dream?

The continuous rain poured down in such amounts that nothing beyond ten feet could be seen. Kenny had helped Leo by lying him flat on two logs pushed together, then bungee corded burlap sacks and two life jackets around Leo's body.

Sitting on a water-soaked cushion didn't insulate a person—not in this total wetness. Sitting Powwow style—feet off the ground— on a plastic cooler provided the best insulation. Constant thunder and lightning—exceeding the power of any fireworks grand finale— boomed directly above them with no time between lightning bolts and horrific thunder claps. This was World War III—nature against human beings and everything else.

One hour later it was dead calm and sunshine emerged. A shift in the wind had moved the storm past the island—a surreal strangeness penetrated the stillness.

"Is everyone alive?" Bob shouted. Everyone was alive but stressed and wet through to their souls. Shocked, stunned and strangely emotionless.

"Can anyone see a boat?" Bill shouted. "Where the hell are the boys?" Nothing was in sight.

"Waawaate took them to a protective cove on the south side of another island," Kenny said.

"How do you know?" Bob asked him.

"I know," Kenny said. "Been there in many storms. It's a narrow channel between two rock cliffs, wide enough for only one boat. No trees! Just two sheer rock cliffs, one on each side. There wouldn't have been room for four boats had we all gone out fishing."

"Kenny, I sure hope you're right!" Bob was sick with concern, thinking, why did I agree to come out this far for shore lunch when there were spots closer to camp? "Bill, stay here with Jerry, Carl, and Leo while Kenny and I go out and check that cove. Stretch out in this wonderful sunshine and finish the O.V. We'll be back soon."

The sun glistened through the trees, and the warmth it brought back was welcome. The war had ended. The big rain and the wind and electricity that propelled it had moved south, beyond Eagle Lake to other lakes. Everyone was safe. Steve and Dennis, guided by Waawaate, had made it back to the lodge before the others. They had their own storm story to tell.

Everyone felt the relief of escaping unpredictable danger unharmed. Every pine needle on every pine tree held at least one drop of water at its tip. Many thousands of trees had been uprooted or damaged—good news for some wildlife, bad news for others. It was nature's way of assuring that such a storm, such a tremendous washing and uprooting, did not totally leave with the wind and rain. It was nature advancing entropy over order in the short run, but creating the opposite effect in the long run as new order came back.

Gray-backed gulls called to each other and fed ravenously on fish killed by the storm. A plethora of small animals found new opportunities in the broken trees. Beavers had more branches to build houses; moose and deer had more open spaces to graze, billions of insects would now thrive in the broken wood where birds could easily find them. Overhead, a bald eagle soared, his eyes scanning all that was going on. Offshore, the walleyes that had been feeding on the rock reef had moved to deeper water. They'd gone crazy feeding in the calm before the storm. They would not feed again today.

Postscript:

This story is based on true experience and I was in it. It was important for me to highlight the personalities of the others without overriding theirs with mine. So, I kept my name out of the action. I would have been the sixth guest.

My experience with storms while fishing Ontario lakes goes back thirty-five years. In that time span I've made over seventy fishing trips to Canada. Only twice did lightning hit close to me: Once when I was sleeping in a cabin at a fishing lodge—it literally blew me out of bed onto the floor! The second time was on the island in this story, it blew up a tree twenty-feet from me.

The story's message is this: If you're planning a fishing trip to one of Canada's big lakes, make sure you're prepared for it—for the unexpected. Proper rain gear, comfortable life vests, waterproof shoes, insect repellant, SPF-50 lotion, and basic emergency supplies are essential. Never be without a good knife, two flashlights and waterproof matches! And be prepared to stay on an island overnight if necessary! I had to twice.

Hagia Sophia in Istanbul

10

Three Days in Istanbul
Mission: Cleanse the Environment and Save My Honeymoon

$\mathcal{P}$rologue:

My first trip to Istanbul was on our honeymoon. It was my wife's first trip outside the USA and included a beautiful rough-water cruise that started in Italy and wound up in Turkey—a nice December outing on the Mediterranean Sea punctuated with pitching, yawing, and wave-percussions. The Italian cruise ship's stabilizers were ineffective; we had no choice but to sleep buckled into bunk beds and forgo any bathing. I can still vividly see our wine glasses, vibration-walking across the dinner table on our first night at sea, then spilling in our laps. And yes, decades later, Phyllis is still with me!

Fortunately, the sea calmed before we entered Istanbul harbor, permitting a fine view of Old Constantinople's domes and minarets. In January of 2001 I spent three days in Istanbul investigating the potential for reducing petroleum pollution with probiotics (beneficial bacteria) in East Asia. Some background information on Turkey is important to the story.

First, Turkey has the largest standing army in the Muslim world and is strategically located between Europe, the Middle East, and the Caucasus region of East Asia. Seven countries border Turkey: Bulgaria, Greece, Armenia, Georgia, Iraq, Iran, and Syria. Turkey controls the Bosporus Strait that links the Black Sea with the Mediterranean. Tanker ships—mostly Russian—transporting Caucasus oil must pass through Turkey.

Second, Turkey is a secularized, democratic republic with a constitution that protects freedom of religion, surprising since ninety-seven percent of Turkey's eighty million people identify as Muslims: seventy-eight percent Sunni and twenty percent Shiite [1]. There is a significant movement of Muslims in Turkey who have made adjustments to Islamic law—like allowing dancing, singing, pet dogs, and broader dietary choices.

Third, the Ottoman Empire that dominated Islam from the fourteenth century until the end of World War One was so vast at its peak in the 1570s that you could travel by land from Turkey to the Pacific Ocean only speaking Turkic! During Ottoman rule, justice was served by religious courts in a codified system that regulated every aspect of a person's life. Turkey's secularized constitution reversed this after World War One and opened the door to a wide variety of western businesses.

[1] These two major denominations within Islam differ by who they believe was the true successor of Muhammad: Ali, his cousin and son-in-law, or Abu Bakr, a friend and advisor. The Shiites believe it was Ali because he descended from Muhammad's family while the Sunnis elected Abu Bakr. Since Muhammad's death in 632 A.D., these two denominations have fought to the death over this question.

Istanbul, Turkey, January 2001

It was cold in the restaurant. The four of us could see our breaths as we talked. We were in the back of the dimly-lit establishment, the only customers so far, but it was only 7:00 p.m. I was happy I'd worn a wool sweater under a heavy tweed sport coat I'd bought in London the week before. I had learned a lesson from a similar cold dinner event in Helsinki last year.

"Order a whiskey," Robert told me. "They serve good whiskey here!" He was still wearing his heavy overcoat. Robert Kaplan was a Turkish-born financial consultant who, at age seventy-eight, had made many business connections in Turkey. He lived in New York City now but travelled frequently to East Asia and Turkey.

"Go ahead, have a drink," the two other men insisted. I understood they were Sunni Muslims and wouldn't drink alcohol.

"We don't drink in public," Yusuf, the older of the two Muslim men said. "We don't broadcast our moderate views."

"Moderate views are vital for good business relationships. The key words in Yusuf's declaration are 'in public,'" Robert said, smiling. He had known Yusuf for years. Close in age, they both had the wrinkles and gray hair confirming their wisdom and experience and both were successful businessmen. Robert ordered a Crown Royal Manhattan, straight up.

"Okay, I'll have the same." I rubbed my cold hands together while looking at Yusuf and Eymen; both had ordered black tea. They were business partners in Turkey; Eymen, twenty years younger, had a degree in chemical engineering and was Yusuf's technology arbitrator.

"Too cold for you?" Eymen asked me. It had to be around forty degrees (five Celsius) at our table.

"I'll be fine when the drinks arrive," I smiled. It appeared to me the restaurant management was under orders to limit utility costs.

"Stan's from Minnesota; it's below zero there now!" Robert asserted just as the lights brightened and a second party of four came in.

When the drinks arrived, Robert discussed the restaurant's climate situation in Turkic with the waiter, who then went into a closet behind us and came out with an old electric space heater.

"What are your thoughts about global warming?" Eymen asked me, probably prompted by the heater.

"Well, it's not happening in Istanbul today," I quipped. There was snow on the ground this morning—unusual near the Turkish coast even in January.

"Do you believe we are causing it?" Yusuf interjected.

"Not to any significant extent," I answered. "When there's warming the sun is more active, more sunspots. When there's cooling the sun is inactive, with few or no sunspots. The sun is the main cause of our weather, and many poorly-understood phenomena affect its activity."

"You mentioned to me in New York last fall something about volcanoes causing global warming?" Robert remembered.

"Yes, volcanoes are next in line as causes after the sun. If undersea, like hundreds of thousands of them are, their eruptions warm the oceans and contribute to global warming. They also cause the release of megatons of methane—a more potent greenhouse gas than carbon dioxide. It's a significant effect," I explained.

"That doesn't get much press coverage!" Robert added. "Unlike wood stoves and cow farts!"

"Of course not, politicians can't tax the sun or volcanoes. However, pollution is caused by man and should be taxed, with China and India paying the most," I didn't want to take mankind completely off the hook.

We all ordered Kuzu Tandir (slow roasted lamb) with rice and mixed vegetables at the recommendation of the waiter. The old heater glowed and vibrated but didn't throw much heat.

"Do you know much about Turkey?" Yusuf asked me.

"Some. I was here on my honeymoon years ago." After hearing this, all three wanted to hear more about it, so I elaborated until the food arrived.

As we began eating—the lamb was pre-sliced, tender, and easy to eat—Robert switched the conversation to business. "I'll let Mr. Randolf tell you about his company's pollution control technology—it's quite interesting. They use oil-eating bacteria to clean up petroleum pollution!

"Before I start, can you tell me about the dimensions of the oil pollution problem?" I looked at Yusuf and Eymen.

"The Caucasus region is a lethal mess," Eymen blurted. "Outdated Russian drilling equipment leaks everywhere!" The Caucasus Mountains between the Black Sea and Caspian Sea ran along the borders of Russia, Georgia, and Azerbaijan, a region of immense oil reserves and terrible pollution.

"And the leaked oil collects in pools that drain into rivers that supply drinking water to millions of people. Noxious methane and hydrogen sulfide gas pollute the air." Yusuf added. "Disease rates are three times higher and life expectancy five years less than in central Russia."

"Much of Azerbaijan is highly contaminated—barren wasteland caused by one hundred years of sloppy drilling. The Turkish government has threatened to close the Bosporus Strait to Russian oil tankers until something is done," Eymen added.

"Well, that confirms what I've heard and read!" I went on and explained how certain species of bacteria were able to utilize petroleum as a food source and detoxify it—producing only water and carbon dioxide as the byproducts.

"What are the stumbling blocks? It sounds too good to be true." Robert interrupted.

"The main stumbling block in America is the government's refusal to issue use permits. There's a lot of opposition from big companies that provide chemical treatments and physical cleanup services. Microbes that grow, multiply, and keep working long after you buy cultures of them are not considered an appropriate business venture—chemicals get reapplied more often."

"Where did these oil-eating bacteria come from?" Eymen asked.

"From Alaska! After the Exxon Valdez oil spill in March of 1989 it was discovered that one stretch of beach remained free of oil contamination while surrounding beaches were black and oil-soaked. Microbiologists isolated a species of Arthrobacter bacteria from the clean beaches and found they loved to dine on oil! Our lab crew figured out how to grow them in tanks and produce a liquid culture that could be sprayed onto oil spills."

We continued discussing natural pollution control using microbes. Details on how to use them were critical to achieving success.

The lamb dinner was excellent and while I continued explaining, Yousuf insisted we have all have baklava dusted with ground pistachios for dessert, along with thick Turkish coffee. Nobody argued.

The large ballroom dining area finally drew my attention. It was brighter now and somewhat warmer. Also, there was noise, more patrons. I unplugged the old heater.

Yusuf provided Robert with the names of key officials in the Turkish government who could help organize the testing of our probiotic anti-pollution technology in the Caucasus region and in Turkey. Eymen, the chemical engineer, would guide the project. The next day, thanks to Yusuf, we would meet some of those government officials. Yusuf believed in moving fast.

Before leaving the restaurant, I noticed the chandeliers suspended from the ceiling had what looked like large white eggs hanging above the light fixtures! They had to be eggs—Ostrich eggs? I kept staring at them, totally perplexed, until Eymen tapped me on the shoulder

"Ostrich eggs." he said. "They repel spiders. That's why you don't see any cobwebs on the chandeliers."

I made a mental note for our product development team: Find out how ostrich eggs inhibit spiders.

The Hyatt's complimentary breakfast on the sixth floor was brighter and warmer than last night's restaurant. Looking through the windows, Robert and I could see it had warmed outside too; the window washing crew was in shirtsleeves.

"Fine Mediterranean weather today," Robert said.

"The sun is shining on old Constantinople!" I affirmed, holding a stack of test reports I had just photocopied in the hotel's office center.

"Got what we need to convince the Turkish ministers to let us run tests?"

"I believe I do. Our pollution reduction data from Mexico's Tabasco State is amazing. Before we applied the Arthrobacter culture (oil-eating bacteria) the coastal waters were so crusted over with oil-tar I could walk on them. Then, one month after applying the microbes, I was able to take a swim."

"Did the photographs copy well?"

"Very well, they had a color printer in the office center!" Hearing this pleased Robert. Just then, Yusuf and Eymen walked in.

"Gunaydin," they said in unison.

"Dobroye utro," Robert replied. We all laughed out loud; Robert had replied to the Turkish "good morning" in Russian. If our project was to succeed we would have to work with the Russians after convincing the Turk officials.

"Take a look at this photograph," Robert instructed them. He had opened one of the reports to a picture of me walking on the tar encrusted water before applying the microbes. "Mr. Randolf can walk on water!"

Eymen grabbed the report, holding it so Yusuf could see over his shoulder. "Only Allah should be able to do this!" Eymen winked at us. My ears were red.

Yusuf had arranged meetings with governmental ministers he knew, including those in the emerging Ministry of Environment. They had come over from Ankara for a convention and would be happy to "fit us in" thanks to Yusuf.

On the way to the first meeting we crossed the Galata Bridge that took us from Europe across the Bosporus into Asia—Istanbul was a city divided by two continents! Donkey carts pulling wagons of produce mingled between cars and trucks as Eymen and I talked in the backseat. From our meeting last night, I knew I could talk candidly with him.

"I'm curious, Eymen—is it common in Turkey for Muslims to regard Muslim law with flexibility? I was born a Catholic but grew up quite flexible regarding Catholic doctrine when it diverged from Jesus and the Ten Commandments."

Eymen nodded, smiling. "It's more common in Turkey than anywhere else in the Middle East. Our constitution protects us—we're a secular democratic republic with freedom of religion—despite ninety-eight percent of the population's claim to be Muslim. Many who claim to be Muslim don't follow all the life-controlling rules. We're careful not to make our flexibility too obvious, like not having an alcoholic drink last night. But we're still Muslims and believe the good passages in the Koran."

"The government isn't a worry currently, but there are, let's say, 'deeply religious brotherhoods' that frown on Sunni Muslims who do not accept Islamic law as obligatory and unconditional—and they carry sharp knives!" Robert added.

Yusuf's car was a large, smooth-riding Volvo. As he drove on, I noticed it was less congested on this side of the Bosporus.

Eymen tapped my arm. "Istanbul is calmer and greener on the Asian side, fewer people and more serene. Yusuf lives here," he explained. "Our first meeting is with Minister Arslan at Yusuf's house. If he approves your project, the other ministers will follow!"

Yusuf's home was impressive, as was his neighborhood. Most of the homes were large two-story villas with swimming pools and gardens surrounded by green lawns. Yusuf's home reminded me of Tuscany—beautiful and quiet with lots of windows! This was a different Yusuf from the heavy-coated senior citizen I met at dinner last night. The sunshine and our conversation had enlivened him!

Yusuf led us into his home. "Make yourselves comfortable." he insisted. The large room had a dozen vertical windows looking out to the garden. We sat down in white satin armchairs and admired the view.

"The Juda trees bloom in winter!" Robert pointed to several of the red-flowered trees in the garden.

Yusuf explained how the tree got its name. "Judas reputedly hung himself from one after returning the thirty pieces of silver he got for betraying Jesus to the Roman soldiers." The nuns had never mentioned Juda trees in Sunday school when I was a kid.

"Minister Arslan will be here shortly," Eymen said, flipping his cell phone closed.

"Alina!" Yusuf called out. "Bring out the raki—the lion's milk."

A well-dressed, silver-haired lady brought out a tray containing four tall glasses filled with a milky liquid. Raki was the Turkish National Drink made from twice-distilled grapes and anise seed. It was served mixed with ice water—a cousin to Greek ouzo.

"To flexibility in Islam!" Yusuf declared while walking over to each of us buried in our chairs, then bumped the bottom of his glass with the bottoms of ours—a Turkish toast.

The meeting with the Minister of Environment went very well as did the other meetings that followed. We didn't have to move from Yusuf's villa. They all came to us. That told me something: our pollution control tests would go forward because Yusuf was involved. All the ministers drank lion's milk!

After they departed in their Mercedes, Alina, Yusuf's faithful housekeeper, made a fabulous Turkish dinner for the four of us. Robert, Eymen and I then took a taxi back to Europe, dropping Robert and me at the Hyatt and Eymen at his apartment. Yusuf had offered to drive us back, but we insisted he rest. It had been a busy day and the four of us would be together again tomorrow.

Day three arrived as another beautiful Mediterranean day; the cold front had moved east over the Black Sea. Yusuf and Eymen picked Robert and me up at the Hyatt and we headed to the Istanbul Chamber of Industry where Yusuf had friends he wanted us to meet; they had helped many American companies launch new projects. The picture of me "walking on water" got things started with good humor. The meeting went well. It was informative to watch Yusuf operate. He'd obviously had many successful business ventures over the years and was respected and admired, but most important: he was genuine and sincere. He put an exclamation mark on the adage: "Possessing knowledge is one thing, understanding how to use it is another."

After the meeting we headed back to the Hyatt taking the Kennedy Caddesi Highway with the Sea of Marmara on our right and some spectacular architecture on the left: first Hagia Sophia, then the Topkapi Palace, and finally the Blue Mosque. These were the domes and towering minarets that dominated Istanbul's skyline when you arrived by sea. Yusuf and Robert's detailed descriptions added new perspective for me.

"Did you say you didn't see the Topkapi Palace when you were here with your wife?" Yusuf asked while looking toward Robert who was nodding.

"That's correct, we missed it."

"You must see it! We have time," Yusuf insisted. "It was a pleasure haven for the sultans where they could enjoy their harems of concubines, starting with Mehmed the Conqueror in 1459. It was complete with a mint and a treasury—spending money. It will give you an idea of the adjustments they made to Muslim law—for themselves!"

"Great," I responded, smiling.

"It's a heavily guarded museum now that's full of old treasures!" Robert added.

"I saw it once in elementary school," Eymen remarked. "Happy to see it again."

"I vaguely remember a 1960s movie called Topkapi. Maximilian Schell and some gal robbed the palace—taking the famous emerald encrusted dagger by hanging from wires so not to set the floor alarms off." My memory was coming back.

"And they replaced it with a fake and almost got away. Except a bird got in from the skylight they came through. When it landed on the floor, it set the alarm off!" Robert had seen the movie too.

"You'll see the Topkapi Dagger—the real one—and the Spoonmaker's Diamond plus other jewels. The sultans took good care of their concubines; each sultan had his own 'Privy Chamber'" Eymen interjected.

The palace was a walled complex of four main courtyards filled with multiple domed pavilions and minarets—Ottoman-Baroque architecture. It had been expanded over the centuries to its current size of seven hundred thousand square meters. It easily covered four square city blocks.

Yusuf led the way through the first courtyard explaining things louder than the tour guides. Being January, tourism was light; by April it would be crowded. Inside the palace, the blues and magentas grabbed me. Artistic inlaid tiles covered walls as did Turkish rugs and other treasures. Glass chandeliers hung from ceilings, but I didn't notice any spider-repelling ostrich eggs hanging—probably replaced by spraying Raid insecticide. Outside, dozens of minarets towered over newer buildings. I couldn't imagine what it sounded like back when prayers were called five times a day from each one, Turkey's "forbidden city." As Yusuf said it would, my perspective broadened.

Back in Yusuf's Volvo, the temperature outside read 18 Celsius or 64.4 Fahrenheit. We took our jackets off as he drove to a seafront restaurant for lunch where we could summarize what our efforts had produced over the last three days. Thanks to Yusuf it was all good news, Eymen would work with our technical team and get the pollution control trials going—first in Turkey then in the Caucasus region. We agreed on a list of priorities and time targets.

"We can take lunch outside today," Eymen remarked.

"Yes, that's our plan," Yusuf replied. The restaurant was in Europe with a good view of Asia across the water where the Bosporus joins the Sea of Marmara. The sunshine felt great as we enjoyed marinated octopus for a starter—tender from pounding it before grilling. Our discussion turned to the weather again.

"This is welcome global warming!" Robert commented. "It's the Turkey of my childhood."

"How many of those underwater volcanoes did you say there were?" Yusuf asked me.

"It's estimated there are four thousand underwater volcanoes per million square kilometers in the Pacific Ocean—that extrapolates to over a million total for all the oceans. And many thousands are over a kilometer high. A big one called Mount Marsili southwest of Naples is burping millions of BTUs (heat) into the sea right now—it's a giant underwater furnace!"

"This never makes the news!" Yusuf lamented. Then, before Yusuf could continue lamenting, the waiter brought out their famous "mixed-fish" dish: deep fried cuts of three different fish species laced with bits of colored peppers, okra, and pomegranate. Marvelous!

After lunch Yusuf and Eymen had a funeral to attend and had to excuse themselves. They would meet us for breakfast in the morning; Robert and I had a noon flight to Athens.

"Back to the Hyatt?" Yusuf asked.

"Can you drop us off at the Grand Bazaar instead?" Robert suggested, looking at me. I nodded yes.

"Of course!" Yusuf said, smiling at me. "Be sure to tell Robert your honeymoon's 'rug-story.'"

"I will!" I replied before he dropped us off at one of the many entrances to the Grand Bazaar.

Robert looked puzzled. While he'd been having a deep conversation with one of the ministers at Yusuf's house yesterday, I'd had a chance to explain the rug-story to Yusuf.

Robert was walking fast, looking at me. "Did you pay too much for a Turkish rug on your honeymoon?"

"No, it was a bit more exciting than that. I'll tell you over a thick coffee later."

"Don't forget!"

The Grand Bazaar was the number-one tourist attraction in the world in 2000. More than eighty-five million visited that year! And there were about that many different things to see! As we walked into one of the entrances, Robert said, "Look up! Nobody looks up." Above us was a beautifully-inscribed domed ceiling with blue tiles inlaid in different patterns. Beyond it, in the distance were orange tiles on the ceiling engraved with robed people and then black and green arches beyond that.

"The ceilings in the large corridors are all domed and decorated," Robert explained. "There are over four thousand shops enclosed within twenty-four separate buildings that are all connected."

Truly, there was floor to ceiling merchandise all neatly organized in myriad shops—millions of things to look at and buy: all things copper, ceramic, glass, silver, wood, silk, wool, plus jewels, spices, lamps, knives, daggers, and on and on. Then there were the rugs, rugs, and more rugs! Even walking at a good pace, it would take you over eight days to stop for one minute at each shop.

We had walked through three of the domed buildings when we heard shouting—mostly women's voices—and noisy clamor, like pots and pans falling and banging.

When we got closer we could see women fighting, throwing pots and pans at each other. Women dressed in Islamic attire were fighting women in western clothing. Some of those western clothes were bikinis, worn to spite those wearing Islamic attire, which ranged from simple head scarfs to full burkas with slits for the eyes.

"They're all Sunni Muslims!" Robert declared.

I was somewhere between a state of disbelief and a desire to take photographs, when a teapot zinged by us. This was serious, the women were enraged.

Two sales clerks at the Copper Turkey shop were gathering their merchandise and trying to hide it behind some curtains: trays, kettles, pots and pans of all sizes. It wasn't working: bearded men retrieved it, pushing the sales clerks aside while rearming the Islamic-dressed women. One of the well-endowed bikini-clad women lost her top—this invigorated the Islamic attired women even more.

The fighting was all around us now, we were surrounded by a crowd of tourists mixed in with the fighting women, pushing and shoving with heavy metal flying everywhere. There was an endless supply of it now; large racks of the shop's cookware had been tipped over. Robert and I had our hands up, protecting our heads.

Just then, a large copper kettle hit a lady wearing a full burka in the face and blood gushed from her eye slits. She fell to her knees screaming as a tourist lady rushed to help her—then the tourist lady got hit in the head. Madness!

"Look out!" a man behind us yelled as a copper frying pan frisbeed over Robert's head and a kettle hit me in the left leg above the knee. It hurt! I was worried about Robert. I grabbed his arm and we elbowed our way out of the crowd and into a rug shop where clerks and patrons were hiding behind stacks of rugs.

"It's all about the head-scarf issue," Robert said. "It's illegal in Turkey for women to conceal their face and hands in public places. It's part of the secular-religious debate. All the women fighting are Sunni Muslims! That should tell you something."

The topless woman was wrestling on the ground now with a woman in a burka—trying to pull it off her. Never wear a bikini in a burka fight! I thought.

Then whistles sounded and six Turkish soldiers wearing helmets with face guards and waving batons pushed their way into the center of the bloody fight and started duct taping everyone's hands and feet, including some tourists who had gotten involved. And that was it for the excitement.

"Let's go find some thick coffee," I suggested, rubbing my leg. "Whew!"

"We got married on December 20th that year and were off to Europe three days later!" I was showing Robert a picture of Phyllis with our four children taken recently.

"She looks so young for having four children," Robert said holding the photo and sipping his coffee. We'd found a peaceful café in a different building.

"Thanks, I'll tell her you said that."

"Does she still travel with you?"

"Only to certain places, like Ireland and England, once to France and Germany."

"Not Africa or the Amazon? Or China and India?" Robert remembered some of my world travel destinations from past discussions.

"Nope, no chance; she's a stay-at-home All-Star mother."

"Tell me the rug story."

Here's the story I told Robert:

On the last day of our honeymoon we got up early and took a taxi from the cruise ship to the Grand Bazaar. The ship was docked in Istanbul's harbor and would leave at 5:00 p.m. So we had most of the day.

When we got to the Bazaar, we were overwhelmed—four thousand shops and I wanted to see them all. I hadn't learned moderation yet. We walked a lot and finally found a building devoted to rugs. Rug shops were everywhere. I don't know how many rugs we looked at—many. Finally, we found a small rug with an exquisite design we both liked, but it was expensive! The shopkeeper and I bargained, he eventually came down to 250 from 350 dollars. Phyllis and I debated and decided we couldn't afford it. As we walked away he shouted, "Two hundred dollars!" That got my attention, but Phyllis shook her head. After all, it was just a three-foot rug; too expensive to use as a rug, but we could hang it on a wall in our apartment—Turkish art. No. We took a taxi back to the ship.

It was 1:30 p.m. when we got back to the ship and had lunch. All I could think about was that Turkish rug! The shopkeeper had come down to two hundred dollars. It was 3:00 p.m. when I decided to go back. Phyllis stayed on the ship. I would rush in, buy the rug, and rush back before 5:00 p.m. when the ship would depart. It was a 30-minute taxi ride.

The taxi dropped me off and I hurried in; it was crowded now. I started to walk fast, looking around, but didn't recognize anything. The taxi had brought me to a different entrance! I had been smart enough to jot down the shop's name and location number on one of my business cards. I showed it to a lady shopkeeper who spoke English. She showed me on a map of the bazaar where it was—four buildings away. It was 3:40 p.m.

I ran to the rug building trying my best not to run into anybody; some bumping was unavoidable. There was no way to avoid the busy congestion in a labyrinth of shops. I got to the rug shop at 4:00 p.m. and quickly found the rug on top of the pile where we left it three hours ago. I grabbed it and ran over to the shopkeeper who was busy selling a rug to a woman, explaining the weaving process to her. He smiled, recognizing me, and raised a finger for me to wait. I had no time to wait. I took two U.S. hundred-dollar bills out of my wallet and waved them at him, pointing to my watch. He understood, excused himself, accepted the money, and offered to wrap the rug. I shook my head, rolled it up quickly, and ran out of the shop.

It was 4:10 p.m. and I had to get out of the maze of shops and find a taxi. I had no idea where an exit was, and no one I asked spoke English. I ran straight ahead and saw a door in the distance, when I got to it and went outside, I found myself in an encampment of the bazaar's employees, frying fish for dinner—they lived here in tents! Wrong door! It was 4:20 p.m. I could feel my heart pounding. The ship departed at 5:00 p.m. and it was at least a 30-minute taxi ride to get to it.

I went back into the bazaar and ran past more shops—I could see an entrance in the distance. When I got outside on a main road there were no taxis in a queue as I had expected. It was 4:30 p.m. and I was frantic. This could mean an end to a very short marriage.

I stepped up on the curb and waved with both arms, not at all confident I would hail a taxi soon enough. Just then one pulled up and unloaded four people. I threw myself into the backseat and showed the driver a picture of the ship on a folded brochure, then pointed to the number five on my watch. It was 4:40 p.m. He shook his head no.

"Not possible!" He gestured. I immediately pulled out my last hundred-dollar bill and held it up. His eyes lit up, it translated to twenty average taxi fares. He floored the accelerator, jolting me against the backseat. He had morphed into Mario Andretti! We headed north on Oruculer Caddesi toward the Galata Bridge—fast.

"What's your name?" I shouted.

"Kerem," he shouted back, sounding the horn constantly while swerving through traffic. Other cars and trucks sounded their horns back with a prominent doppler effect—sounds blurring and quickly fading as we rushed past all the vehicles.

It was too dangerous to be scared—all for a three-foot rug. The Taxi vibrated when he went off the road for a short distance. Then we made a sharp right on some road and a quick left. It was 4:45 p.m.

I could see the Galata Bridge ahead which would take us to the Karakoy passenger terminal and the ship—and hopefully my wife. Kerem never let up on the horn. There was a mixed bag of traffic on the bridge, we almost destroyed a donkey cart full of oranges that had stopped; we swerved just in time, squashing only a few oranges. I could see the ship up ahead in the water, past the bridge. It was 4:55 p.m.

The gangplank was being raised when we pulled up to the ship— my wife was standing next to the Captain at the bow. The ship's deafening horn growled just as I grabbed the rug and jumped out, waving. I could see the gangplank reverse and come back down. I gave Kerem the victory sign and one hundred dollars. It was 5:01 on my watch.

Postscript:

Our pollution control tests worked out well. We had a photograph of Eymen "walking on water" on a lake in Azerbaijan that had been crusted over with tar before being cleared with our probiotic microbes.

The business developed slowly, mostly due to Russian interference. They came out with competitive microbes that didn't work— casting a shadow on pollution control with probiotic microbes. This caused us to have to prove our technology in each and every different location before making a sale.

Yusuf and Robert stayed active for several years then retired; but their advice was always welcome.

I had gained a new perspective on Islam: There are Muslims and there are Muslims. A diversity of thought and behavior was emerging within Islam. Much like it had in Christianity and Judaism. The Source allowed for that.

The rug lives in my office in Minnesota along with fossils, minerals, seashells, woodcarvings, paintings, and photographs from around the world.

Castro, Chile—unloading wood from sailboats into horse carts

11

Frozen in Peru
Humanity's Future is Preserved Here!

$\mathcal{P}$eru, April 1992

There are over four-hundred square miles of Peruvian desert southeast of Lima. I was excited to get a chance to fly over this area of South America in Pepe's twin-engine Beechcraft on the way to Santiago, Chile. We left Lima early to make sure the sun would be at a low angle when it rose over the Andes. At an altitude of five thousand feet we could see the Nazca lines clearly. The animal shapes they formed could not be seen from the ground, only from the air. They were Peru's mysterious geoglyphs.

"Those line carvings were made by the Nazca Indians between 500 B.C. and 500 A.D.," Pepe said, looking like quite the aviator in his yellow headphones.

I could see the image of a giant hummingbird below us as Pepe dipped the plane's wing. It could have filled a football field! "I read they were made by digging narrow trenches ten to fifteen centimeters deep exposing light-colored clay underneath the darker surface stones."

"That's right, there's about three hundred geoglyphs out here." Pepe noted. "This desert is unique; ancient volcanic eruptions in the Andes spewed iron-rich stones that rusted and became reddish brown—they blanketed the yellow desert."

After passing the hummingbird, we flew over the condor and monkey glyphs. "They're bigger than I expected from what I saw in the guidebook." I had read that some of the images on the sloping Nazca terrain were deep enough to walk through. But on foot there was no perception of animal forms, just paths in the desert.

"Notice how the monkey's tail swirls into seven concentric circles." Pepe pointed to them. "A Major-Brigadier in the Brazilian Airforce told me those circles served as antennas!"

"In 500 B.C.!" I quipped. "Who were they listening to?"

"Or broadcasting to?" Pepe countered. "It's a mystery. There are other spirals east of here that we won't see today. But what's coming up is quite interesting."

We stayed on a southeast heading at five thousand feet. I was using binoculars and looking ahead. "See it?" Pepe asked.

"Not yet."

He backed off the throttle and banked the plane left. "It will be lying roughly east-west with its head to the east and legs pointing west, toward the ocean." Pepe pointed where to look.

"I see it! On a hillside facing the Pacific. You can't miss the round, space-bubble head with big, bulging eyes—perfectly round eyes. One arm is pointing to the sky, the other at the ground."

"Now you've seen our 'ancient astronaut,'" Pepe declared. "All two hundred feet of him."

"Yup, just like in the guidebook." I had the book on my lap.

"Some say it's a fisherman holding a fish with his right hand, and the space bubble is a net standing behind him," Pepe claimed.

"Another Nazca mystery. I never saw a fisherman with eyes so big they covered most of his face; maybe he's an alien fisherman." I joked. The fact that the image was ambiguous stayed with me.

"At least he doesn't look like a bipedal lizard! Not to me anyway," Pepe remarked as he increased the engines' RPMs to cruise speed, leaving the geoglyphs. We had twelve hundred miles to go to Santiago, about five and a half hours. I watched the Pacific Ocean and its 321-million cubic miles of water glide by on the right. I was serving as Pepe's copilot but had never flown a twin-engine plane. So all I had to do was flip switches and press buttons on his command.

I had met Pepe Lopez in Salinas, Ecuador, five years earlier. By sheer coincidence we were both looking to hire a charter boat to go marlin fishing when we literally bumped into each other. It took only a few sentences of conversation to get us to agree on sharing a charter. Big marlin swam off the coasts of Ecuador and Peru! Pepe was a Peruvian businessman who had investments in aquaculture farms—shrimp in Ecuador, salmon in Chile. As a scientist, I was involved with probiotic products (beneficial bacteria) that reduced disease and improved yields in aquaculture—shrimp in Ecuador, salmon in Chile. We were destined to meet.

"Jon Robinson will meet us when we arrive in Santiago," Pepe reaffirmed. "Don't tell him you skunked me again marlin fishing last September!" It had been a long, hot boat ride that day requiring SPF-100 sunscreen and wet towels around our necks. We fished for eight hours without any action before a white marlin slammed my bait at 4:30 p.m. It weighed in at two-hundred fifty pounds and put up a tough fight for over an hour.

"I would never do that to you. Skunks are kept secret." I assured him.

"I'm just kidding; Jon already knows. I told him." Pepe laughed.

"How long have you and Jon been partners?" I asked, knowing he had just trapped me.

"Three years now. Jon's a good man—he knows how to farm salmon in ocean cages. It's a business that will help feed the world and reduce the danger of overfishing the oceans. The problem with cage aquaculture, as you know, is water pollution. He hopes you can help reduce it!"

"I can!" Pepe knew I could—our probiotic water treatments were already working on a salmon farm in New Zealand and on many shrimp farms in Southeast Asia. They stimulated the ratio animal plankton (zooplankton) to algae (phytoplankton) which enhanced the food chain and reduced pollution. Pepe was a hands-on partner in several businesses and traveled as much as I did. This was our first trip to Chile together.

"I'm anxious to meet Jon!"

"And he's anxious to meet you; he has a red-tide problem right now and needs your advice. We'll spend the night in Santiago and fly to Castro tomorrow; you'll get to try his salmon at dinner. Chile is a long, narrow country—twenty-six hundred and fifty miles long and only one hundred and ten miles wide. Locals say their country is a man that always has his head in summer and his feet in winter. Santiago, at halfway, is his belly—where great Chilean cuisine is found." Pepe's description inspired my appetite.

The buzz of the twin engines pushing us with nine-hundred horsepower was hypnotic. This Model-18 Twin Beech had been custom reinforced for military duty and had extra fuel capacity—only its civilian paint job of yellow, blue, and white was not military grade. "She's a mean machine," Pepe asserted, proud of his customized airplane. He told me to flip the APX switch on and then took his hands off the wheel. "We're on autopilot now"—he said, and began whistling a Peruvian army tune.

I allowed him to finish the tune before interrupting: "Pepe, are you still involved with that group of businessmen in Lima—the one that sponsors archeological projects?" He had mentioned them when we were together last September.

"I'm glad you remembered, yes, I am. In fact, I have an assignment that may overlap our aquaculture mission on this trip. We may need your help—it shouldn't take more than one afternoon."

"Of course!" I replied. Pepe was a friend and had helped me understand the aquaculture business in South America.

"I recall you told me you collect mineral and fossil specimens."

"That's right, I got started in Morocco on a student tour back in undergraduate school. I had been thinking about making geology a second major."

"Your fossil knowledge may come in handy."

We devoured a bag of trail mix and a sack of Argentine pistachios, washing them down with Orangina sodas. I made sure all the hulls got collected. Pepe gave me some basic instructions, then let me fly the Twin Beech with the APX off. "Keep her even and steady at eight thousand feet," he instructed. It was trickier with two engines than flying my brother-in-law's single-engine Cessna. But I held her steady—no tricks—for an hour. Then he took control again and three hours buzzed by.

We had been following the towering Cordillera on our left—the Andes Mountains. They rose well above our wingtips, paralleling the Pacific Coast while dazzling flamingo-pink in the afternoon sun. With snow still covering the peaks, the highest, Mount Tupungato, soared to 21,555 feet east of Santiago. We could see it in the distance on our left.

"On our right, offshore a hundred miles, is the Peru-Chilean Trench," Pepe remarked. "It's twenty-six thousand, four hundred feet deep, one of the Pacific's deepest canyons."

"Deeper than Tupungato is high," I said, humbled by the realization.

"You need to give that some deep thought." Pepe grinned.

"How many monster-size black marlin swim in that trench? Give that some deep thought," I replied.

"TNTC," he exclaimed without a pause! I knew he didn't like hypothetical questions—it was his old military training coming through. TNTC meant "Too Numerous to Count." I laughed because he had heard me use that acronym whenever there were too many bacterial colonies to count on a Petri dish!

"We'll be landing soon—at sea level!" Pepe affirmed, still grinning. My brother-in-law, who flew small planes, once told me that landing was the most stressful time for a pilot; it could be thought of as a controlled crash. Landing in a cross-wind was always a challenge, but today the windsocks were limp and hanging straight down. It had been a smooth ride all the way from Lima.

Pepe used the flaps to reduce airspeed as we started to descend, a controller at Santiago International gave him landing instructions in Spanish. Pepe knew where to go; he'd been here and done this before. We deplaned with our luggage and headed for the door that led to customs. It was a warm April afternoon.

"Pepe! Pepe!" Jon Robinson was waving as we came out from customs. He gave Pepe a firm handshake and said some words in Spanish. Then he turned to me.

"Buenos tardes, Stanley! Finally, we meet face-to-face." Jon and I shook hands. We had spoken on the phone several times.

"A van is waiting for us outside," he declared, grabbing both our suitcases and pulling them toward the door, refusing my attempt to help. Jon was about my age—mid-forties and medium build with a mop of brown hair. He had a master's degree in ichthyology—fish science—and was born in Quito, Ecuador but grew up in Texas. He spoke Spanish and English with a Texas accent. Pepe, one hundred percent Peruvian, stood out in contrast to Jon and me; he was older and more distinguished, with dark eyebrows and a mustache that complemented his slightly graying hair.

The forty-five-minute drive to the hotel gave Jon time to update us regarding Ocean's Best Aquafarms; the company he and Pepe owned. There were many potential problems, most related to different infections that could kill the salmon. A red-tide disaster was now occurring, seriously affecting one of their two farms. We would take a boat tour of both farms to evaluate the situation. I had brought a small microscope, various test strips, agar tubes, and Petri dishes for running analyses.

The van dropped us off at the hotel which was just south of the Plaza Italia—near the center of Santiago.

"Let's go to our rooms and freshen up, then meet on the balcony for a coffee," Jon suggested.

"Sounds good," I replied. Pepe nodded. Our rooms were on the eighth floor, and when we got off the elevator I could see the city of Santiago spread out in front of the white-capped Andes—quite a spectacular view!

"Some say it's the most dazzling view and backdrop for a capital city!" Jon remarked.

"I agree," Pepe said. "What do you say Mr. Randolf? You've been around the world many times! Anything come close to this?"

"I do believe this view is Number One in the capital-city category!" I had to scan my memory: Hong Kong, Rio de Janeiro, Cape Town, Istanbul, Sydney, San Francisco, Naples, Venice, Salzburg, and Shanghai all had spectacular views, but I didn't recall any were capitals. I had to agree, Santiago's view was the winner.

I showered and changed shirts and went to take a quick look out my window. It faced the back side of the hotel so there were no mountains, just city. I noticed a large army bus painted in green camouflage parked at one of the intersections and another one several blocks away. An armed guard dressed in camo stood outside the door of the closer bus. I watched as he checked a bag of groceries an older woman was carrying. He made her take out the groceries one by one—bread, broccoli, lettuce, carrots, plus other foods—and lay them on the sidewalk. When they were laid out, he nudged a few with his gun barrel and then allowed her to pick them up and leave. How strange and scary, I thought . . .

Pepe and Jon were talking and having espressos when I walked into the hotel's balcony restaurant. "Looks like you took a shower," Pepe observed.

"He does look cleaner!" Jon said. I smiled and ordered a mocha. It was obvious Jon had a sense of humor like Pepe.

"Hey Jon, I've got a question for you." I explained what I'd just observed from my window and asked him if this was normal. I was concerned.

"It's normal for Santiago and some of the other bigger cities," Jon lamented. "You won't see it in Castro tomorrow."

"What could an old woman have had in a bag of groceries that would concern the military?" I asked, restating my concern.

"Nothing," Pepe interjected before Jon could speak. "The inspection had nothing to do with groceries, it was about creating fear of the military! Welcome to South America. It's like this in Peru, too, but not quite as obvious."

"It's Augusto Pinochet—our president," Jon added. "He's paranoid about being assassinated; he took control of Chile in a military coup d'état in 1973 and has been president ever since. He's been good for business but bad for people who oppose him. The opposition says tens of thousands have disappeared under his rule."

"He probably exiled them to labor camps in Antarctica," Pepe said half-jokingly.

I knew about these things before this trip; I had been to South America several times and a military presence could always be felt. Soldiers guarded banks, airports and train stations, also large department stores. But stark, blatant street searches of locals jolted me.

The three of us talked for two hours over several coffees, alternating between Chilean politics and Jon's problems at their aquafarms in Castro. We'd decided it would be more productive to focus on solvable problems—like controlling microbes that harm salmon. It's crazy how politics can suddenly emerge and take charge in a conversation; this tendency must be genetically ingrained in people worldwide.

It was 5:00 p.m. and we needed to eat something. It had been over eight hours since breakfast in Lima, so Pepe and I were hungry; the trail-mix and pistachios had been our only a snack. There was a seafood restaurant nearby that Jon and Pepe had vetted several times—meaning it was safe to eat there!

I thought I was in China when we entered the front door of the restaurant! In the lobby, there were large tanks containing fish, crabs, lobsters, and other denizens of the deep. Just like in downtown Shanghai but without any fish odor. You could pick the ones you wanted to eat while a chef-in-white stood ready with a net.

"Ocean's Best designed and installed the water filtration system. There's no odor!" Jon announced proudly. "Those are our salmon in the big tank."

I looked at the system, pleased to see it utilized rotating biofilters. All the fish and crustaceans were a picture of health.

"How do the tanks and filters look to a scientist?" Pepe asked me.

"I can see the tanks are well-constructed and the filters have excellent capacity and flow; that's my quick assessment."

Pepe smiled, looking at Jon. It was no surprise that the three of us selected salmon for dinner. Jon picked up another net and helped the chef catch them—two nets were better than one! I let Jon and Pepe specify the preparation details.

We started out with the house special; salmon ceviche: chilled chunks of salmon (netted yesterday) marinated overnight in lime juice and a secret sauce made from fermented chili peppers. It was the perfect appetizer. When it was time to eat the ones Jon and the chef had netted, grilled Chilean style, we were ready.

After dining on the "red meat"—low-cholesterol variety—we decided to take a walk. Jon led us beyond the Plaza Italia, north to a park bordering the Rio Mapocho that bisected Santiago. We walked narrow side streets filled with kiosks and sellers of all things cloth, ceramic, and copper. There was no shortage of gymnasts performing, musicians playing, and magicians pulling doves out of hats—all for tips, of course. It was vibrant.

One of the merchants got my full attention; he had a table covered with amethyst crystals—single, hexagonal, violet crystals—some the size of large apples. These were rare! I haggled with the seller, getting help from Pepe and Jon, and bought two for twenty dollars each. These transparent crystals had formed during Precambrian times— over five-hundred million years ago! I have a room at home in Minnesota that contains natural artifacts and specimens from around the world; that's where these two amethysts would soon reside. Shamans claimed they had special power.

As we headed toward the River Park, Parque Forestal, we could smell the eucalyptus trees and see that the hedges and bushes had been perfectly manicured. But even in this sizable park, there was no leaving the vibrant hum of the city.

"The trees clean the air," Jon remarked as we walked on, finding a bench by the river. After we sat down, Pepe wanted to see the amethyst crystals.

"Are these really over five-hundred million years old?" He asked me, handing one to Jon.

"Yes, they are; they're from Brazil's minas gerais, the general mines. Their age is well understood."

"These exact crystals were here when Tyrannosaurus Rex ran around—all the dinosaurs for that matter," Jon deduced while holding up the larger of the two amethysts.

"T. Rex! That tyrant lizard ran around here only sixty-five million years ago." Pepe added a time perspective.

I was humbled by the thought of how such perfection—these stunning purple hexagons with their internal reflections and inclusions—could remain unchanged for over half a billion years. Continents had separated and moved, mountains had formed and eroded, seas had relocated, and all current life forms had evolved, all while these crystals hid deep in a cave in the earth exactly as you see them now. Comparing them to the sliver in time it took modern humans to evolve—three-hundred thousand years—made holding these crystals a spiritual experience.

Pepe couldn't get Jon's reference to tyrant lizards out of his mind. He knew they walked on two legs and had hands. "Who knows what they might have evolved into if they'd had vocal cords!" he wondered. Jon figured his partner must have studied reptile evolution at some point.

When I woke the next morning my first thought was to check out the sunrise over the Andes from the hall window by the elevators. Instead, something told me to look out my room's window. The camouflaged bus was still there, but no guard was standing outside it. There weren't many people on the street this early, so maybe the guard was taking a break. Just then, a back door on the bus opened and two young ladies in short skirts stepped out while combing their hair. Shortly, the guard came out the front door carrying his rifle; presumably ready to inspect old ladies. Along with the crystals, a few other things never change . . .

I met Jon for breakfast. Pepe was already at the airport getting the Twin Beech fueled and ready for our four-hour flight to Castro. Jon and I took a taxi from the hotel and met him on the tarmac—he was ready to go.

Castro is a fishing town in the Chiloe Archipelago of islands in southern Chile—750 miles south of Santiago. The flight to Castro gave us plenty of time to discuss salmon farming and aquatic probiotics (beneficial bacteria). Pepe asked Jon to review their current situation again.

Jon explained: "Our salmon are raised in floating cages in the ocean. The cages can be round or square and typically hold fifty-thousand fish each; we have two separate farms and both have ten cages. The cages are stocked with smolts (five-inch salmon) which are harvested in eighteen months at a target weight of ten pounds. Feed pellets are automatically dispensed over the surface of the cages. Feed that is not eaten falls through the bottom of the cage onto the ocean floor, causing pollution. Pelleted salmon feed can vary in quality—poor quality feed creates more pollution. Most problems are associated with infectious microbes: algae, bacteria, parasites, fungi, and viruses—that's where we need your advice!"

"The Big-Five Bug Worries!" Pepe summarized as the pitch of the engines changed when he banked to avoid a thunder cloud.

I had told Pepe that microbiologists like to call microbes "bugs," so the word was now part of his vernacular, like TNTC. Staying healthy on planet earth was largely about controlling bad bugs with good bugs (probiotics). Pepe asked me to review how probiotics work in aquaculture.

I had plenty of time—Chile was a long country: "The basic principle of using probiotics involves their ability to powerfully dominate the ecozones where harmful microbes live. This could be in the water, on the ocean floor under the cages, on the salmon, in the salmon, or all the above. We accomplish this by adding live, probiotic Bacillus bacteria to the feed. I paused to let Jon ask questions.

"How involved will it be to culture Bacillus probiotics on the aquafarm?" Jon expressed some concern; he knew the economics required it.

"It's quite simple. I'm going to teach you how to do it using ingredients from our company—it will not be expensive. Culturing (or brewing) probiotics onsite is the only way you'll afford the trillions of them required to dominate the bad microbes (bugs). And it has to be done with specific controls that prevent contamination!"

"We need trillions of good bugs that are TNTC," Pepe recapped. His mind was a steel trap. "Jon! Are you ready to become a probiotic farmer too?"

"Absolutely!" Jon was satisfied now. I continued explaining details for the remainder of the flight.

Pepe landed the Twin-Beech at a regional airport on Isla Grande, Chile's largest island. Jon went to get the Ocean's Best van.

The Chiloe Archipelago is an expanse of several dozen islands in the Gulf of Corcovado—a big body of water. The gulf runs along the east coast of Isla Grande before joining the Pacific Ocean. Castro is in the middle, facing the archipelago.

"It's Stanley's first time down here," Pepe told Jon.

"Aha. I figured that," Jon replied. "Then we need to show him some things. Jon turned off the Pan-American Highway which ran down the center of Isla Grande and took the scenic route to Castro. After he turned onto Pedro Montt road, dozens of quaint wooden houses on stilts appeared, multicolored and nestled together, suspended half on land and half in the Gulf. Behind them was rural forest.

"These are the palafitos, fishermen's houses," Jon pointed out. "We call them postcard houses." There was a spectrum of colors: bright yellow, magenta, shades of blue, and white. They made perfect reflections in the calm water and radiated a picturesque charm. Looking at them was a bit like listening to Mozart.

"I'll show you the best view of the islands before we go into Castro." Jon turned back on the Pan-American Highway and went a short distance north to the town of Dalchue.

We drove up a hill before crossing a bridge between two islands and came into a small harbor with wooden boats on shore, colorful like the palafitos. My pragmatic father would have called it, "a great place to be a paint salesman." But then I saw something truly unique: Out in the harbor in shallow water were two eighteenth century sailing boats—sails furled—unloading fish into carts pulled by horses standing in the water! This even surprised Pepe.

"They live like the Amish in Texas, but they're ethnic natives," Jon explained. "They live without cars or electricity." It was remarkable to watch them; the clock had just turned back a hundred years.

My customized tour included several large islands of the archipelago that were connected by bridges. I could see beyond these to the outer islands. It was easy to appreciate the potential for salmon aquaculture since the islands provided many sheltered shorelines. A huge circular basin had been cut into the middle of Isla Grande during the last ice age. Volcanic activity in the Andes then created the islands, along with many underwater reefs. Castro was on the west shore of the basin facing toward Argentina; fish business dominated the town.

"These can be treacherous waters with hidden reefs and strong currents," Jon warned. "Spanish sailors in the sixteenth century respected how the native Chonos Indians could safely navigate the area in their small wooden boats. Many Spanish ghost ships haunt the bottom of the gulf—those that didn't navigate safely!" We were standing at the end of the road on the Isla Quinchao looking east into the Gulf of Corcovado. Jon pointed south in the direction of Ocean's Best aquafarms, their pride and joy.

"Let's get to Castro and our guesthouse," Pepe said. "Maria will have lunch ready. We'll change into seaworthy clothes after eating and take the Boston Whaler out to the farms!" Ocean's Best owned and operated the guesthouse for occasions like this and for entertaining buyers from large grocery chains. It was next to their office building and warehouse, walking distance from the boat docks.

Maria, the house manager, gave Pepe a big hug when he greeted her. He introduced me and I got one too. She waved off Jon, "I see him every day!" she said in Spanish.

Maria had made pastel de choclo, a traditional Chilean meat pie. Her special version was stuffed with chunks of Argentine beef, chicken and local vegetables. Along with a cold brew—a Kross Stout; it was great. We checked lunch off our "to do" list and went to our rooms to put on rubber-soled shoes with good traction and insulated rain jackets equipped with emergency CO2 inflation.

I was glad to see that Jon and Pepe were safety conscious. It was difficult to predict the weather and the strength of the wind in southern Chile; treacherous conditions could develop quickly on an otherwise perfect day. We weren't that far from Cabo de Hornos—Cape Horn. The southern end of South America.

We walked to the dock and the boat—a twenty-seven-foot Boston Whaler Cuddy powered with two, 200-horsepower, Mercury outboards. It was impossible to miss their logo of two salmon jumping over a rainbow embossed on the hull. Whalers are fast and unsinkable; this one was well equipped for the aquafarm. Jon drove as Pepe and I stood on each side of him holding onto the amid-ship steering console. It was overcast and calm; we cruised at forty miles an hour.

It felt like I was in Canada on a strange lake where I didn't know the rocks, the ones just below the surface; but I knew the guide knew them. Here, I knew Jon knew them. I thought about the Spanish ghost ships that didn't known them.

"It's dangerous in these islands if you don't know what's below the boat," Pepe stressed. The sonar on the console read the depth at sixty feet, but that could change in seconds. The rocky reefs out here were lava piles from ancient volcanic eruptions.

"These reefs come up fast and look like miniature volcanos or Christmas trees on the sonar screen," Jon explained. "Pointed, triangular rock piles—if we hit one we'll be hanging onto sections of a broken Whaler in the water."

"Jon's not joking. A Boston Whaler advertisement shows several fishermen holding onto floating sections of a Whaler that had hit a submerged oil rig!" Pepe added.

"I get the point!" I remarked.

"There is an old legend out here," Pepe announced as we cut smoothly through the water heading southeast. "There's a goddess called Pincoya that all the old fishermen know. She has exceptional beauty and is in touch with the soul of the sea! She can order fish to be abundant or scarce depending on her mood. Jon can finish the story." I was enjoying this.

Jon cleared his throat. "When she's in a good mood, she dances half-naked draped in kelp. She does this standing on shallow reefs between the islands or on beaches at night. Sometimes she's seen surfing the waves totally naked. It's the obligation of all fishermen to keep her in a good mood!"

As visions of Pincoya faded, we arrived at the first aquafarm, the one with square pens. The salmon I saw were around two pounds each and had ten months to go to get to the ten-pound harvest weight. The foreman, Alejandro Perez, was expecting us; he was short and stout with a fuzzy black beard. He greeted us dressed in waterproof boots and a black apron.

"Buenas tardes señores!" Alejandro shouted over the idling outboards. He helped me tie up the Whaler, then gave Pepe a hand getting up on the cage deck. Pepe spoke with him in Spanish for a couple minutes before Jon joined in. It had been almost a year since Pepe had seen Alejandro; he was the man who knew everything salmon.

Alejandro then came over to me and delivered a big, wet hug. He had been netting runts. He told me in Spanish he was very happy to meet an American scientist. "Alejandro can understand English but he's afraid to speak it," Pepe clarified.

Without wasting any time, we all got into discussing how the current red-tide infection was affecting salmon farms in the area, including theirs. Its acronym was HAB for Harmful Algal Bloom; I had dealt with HAB in New Zealand on salmon farms. It's caused by warmer-than-normal water temperatures that activate a type of algae that colors the water red and produces a lethal neurotoxin that kills fish—losses can exceed fifty percent. If farmed salmon are overfed, uneaten feed accumulates on the ocean floor beneath the cages and exacerbates the problem.

"This is another El Niño year so we have higher than normal water temperatures in southern Chile," Jon explained.

"How bad is the situation here?" I asked as I looked at the fish in the cage behind me. The floating stainless-steel cages were bolted together and anchored to the bottom.

"Not too bad. We do not overfeed." Alejandro had found his English.

Jon explained their secret: "We have installed underwater cameras at the bottom of each cage. When a camera detects uneaten feed falling under a cage, it sends a signal to the automatic feeder to shut off—indicating the salmon have stopped feeding. We can regulate feed consumption perfectly; not too much, not too little. This was Alejandro's idea."

"Brilliant. Alejandro, you're the man!" I declared. Alejandro smiled and took a bow.

"But it's bad at our other location where neighboring farms are closer!" Jon lamented. "The neighbors overfeed their salmon with poor quality feed and it affects us."

"It's why we need your probiotic technology," Pepe interjected. "We can't control our neighbors."

I let the three of them keep talking while I walked around the cages and ran tests for water quality and microbial profiles. I netted and sacrificed two of the fish and removed their gills for microscopic examination. I was ready for the second farm.

The other Ocean's Best farm was a thirty-minute run to a different island, farther out; Alejandro went with us. I explained on the way that we have a Bacillus probiotic that inhibits red-tide algae. "The application is simple: a small pump sprays a metered amount of liquid probiotic onto the feed every time it's dispensed," I continued discussing details. This was mainly for Alejandro's sake—Jon and Pepe knew it from our airborne seminar.

When we arrived at their second aquafarm I could tell immediately things were different; there was a putrid, dead-fish odor for starters. One of their transport boats with a crane was hauling in a cage of dead fish that had been collected from the farm.

"There's over fifty-thousand dead salmon being taken away for incineration," Jon said, pointing to the cage being lifted out of the water. Pepe shook his head.

Rat—Tat—Tat! Rat—Tat—Tat! The sound of an AK-47 was unmistakable. It came from islands east of us. *Rat—Tat—Tat* again. Pepe quickly glanced at the long PVC tube that was bungee-corded at the base of the Whaler's transom. Instinct told him to check and make sure it was still there.

"Someone is shooting at sea lions!" Jon declared, not surprised. "It's common now that the water is warming up." I was somewhat relieved to hear that.

"Probably," Pepe answered. "Marauding sea lions can rip open salmon cages and eat themselves silly. But there are competing drug smugglers who shoot at each other, too. And rogue Russians who steal boats and sell them in Argentina! A twenty-seven-foot Boston Whaler with twin 200-horsepower Mercs is worth big money."

Pepe walked around the cage deck slowly, looking out at the gulf with binoculars, checking the time on his Rolex. He had the binoculars focused on a large trawler that appeared to be anchored about a mile away. While Pepe scrutinized the ship, I repeated my testing and sampling. While I was busy, Jon and Alejandro spoke to the farm's young foreman regarding the probiotic project and what it would involve.

After Pepe had made his way back to us, he reinforced the probiotic message with urgency. "Stan, Jon, and I have discussed the costs, they are reasonable. We will use probiotics at both locations." I knew Pepe's tone of voice well enough to recognize he now had more than salmon farming on his mind.

Alejandro had a few more pointers for the young foreman before leaving him to his job; workers were waiting in line for their assignments. The four of us got into the Whaler and headed back to the first farm. On the way, I asked Pepe if he saw anything with the binoculars.

"It's a Russian trawler," he told me. He was driving the Whaler now, and I was standing next to him holding onto the steering console. Alejandro and Jon were sitting in back, talking. The water was mostly calm, and the Whaler's hull cut through it smoothly.

Pepe had invited Alejandro to have dinner with us. The restaurant was outside Castro in the direction of the airport. It was busy with quite a mix of people—a Chilean barbeque modeled after the Brazilian version. All types of meats, including Ocean's Best salmon, were sizzling on a large grill that was half inside and half outside the building. There was no menu except a card identifying all the meats available. Male waiters pushed carts of different meats—all were savory and tempting; great food for carnivores. Female servers carried trays of side dishes. When you saw something you wanted, you turned a small wooden cylinder red-end up and the server would stop. If the green end was up, he just passed by.

We sat down at a table in a far corner so we could talk. Pepe excused himself to make a phone call right when Alejandro turned his cylinder red end up, stopping a lamb-chop cart. "Three of them," Pepe yelled back to Alejandro as he headed to the phone booth. Alejandro put three lamb chops on Pepe's plate and took three himself. Jon and I red-ended an Argentine beef cart, then a salmon cart. There is a restaurant called The Carnivore outside Nairobi, Kenya—they have every meat available including lion steaks. For an instant, I was there again.

Talking and eating, Jon and Alejandro discussed the changes they would make on the automatic feeders to accommodate probiotics. They were drawing equipment sketches on dinner napkins. When Pepe came back they stopped talking and drawing.

"Important phone call with The Group!" Pepe explained in a serious tone. "The Russian Trawler is the rogue fishing vessel that was taken over by Russian army deserters. But it has arrived two days early!" The three of us listened intently, I was obviously the odd man out. My briefing regarding The Group on the flight to Santiago was just that—brief!

"That trawler did come from Antarctica! I confirmed the flags." Pepe said before taking a bite out of a lamb chop. He rechecked the time on his Rolex, both local and Greenwich Mean Time. "Its early arrival changes things for us; we are responsible for coordination and proper delivery of its pre-purchased cargo. The trawler has a military Zodiac suspended from a crane—a large, high-powered raft in brown camouflage. They will use it to deliver the cargo."

"Like those semi-rigid inflatables used in Navy Seal commando operations?" I presumed.

"Affirmative," Pepe replied. "It's 19:00 (7:00 p.m.) local time now. The Zodiac will leave the ship at 22:00 (10:00 p.m.). We've got to be there and be invisible!"

"I must make the critical phone calls now," Alejandro declared. He got up and headed to the phone booth.

"Jon and I are going out 'fishing' in the Whaler to get behind the trawler before the Russians leave in the Zodiac for shore. We must insure they absolutely get to the right place! Alejandro has a separate mission. Are you okay to go with us?" He asked me. "We know you're a good fishermen."

"Absolutely, I'm happy to go fishing." Pepe was morphing into someone I didn't know. But I had to admit there was an excitement about it and, after knowing him for five years, I trusted him implicitly.

"Can you shoot a Browning Automatic Rifle (BAR) chambered in 30-06 caliber?" Pepe asked me.

"Yes, I have a BAR chambered in a three hundred Winchester magnum. I use it for elk in Colorado."

"Very good! There's a 30-06 BAR in that large PVC tube on the Whaler. It's set for full auto and has long distance laser sights," Pepe confirmed. "And there's plenty of extra ammo in the cubby."

"Just in case we get attacked by sea lions?" I joked, grinning.

"Affirmative." He grinned back.

Jon turned the wood cylinder red-end up as the waiter carrying a tray of roasted cabrito came by. We ate the goat meat for dessert and put some on Alejandro's plate. He was still on the phone.

After eating all we could, Jon paid the bill and went to get the van. Alejandro had made the critical calls; he said they went well. We got into the van and drove directly to the dock and the Whaler. Pepe gave the security guard a U.S. hundred-dollar bill and thanked him for watching the boat. "Tips are important in South America," he emphasized. Pepe always carried a roll of US hundred-dollar bills in one pocket and local money in another.

The Whaler's white hull stood out in the moonlight. My excitement level was increasing—what the hell was this all about; what kind of merchandise had been pre-purchased? Jon drove the boat while Pepe discussed the situation with Alejandro who agreed to stay at the farm until needed.

When we got to the farm both Alejandro and Pepe went up the ladder to the deck. Pepe still had something to say to Alejandro who kept nodding and repeating, "I'll confirm it again." That's all I could decipher.

The watchman smiled when Alejandro told him he would have company for a few hours—playing carioca, a cousin to Gin Rummy. It was my thinking that Alejandro was a backup for whatever we were going to do. They were spoon-feeding me information. So far, I had survived significant episodes of adventure on other trips—unplanned and out of the blue—why not again?

Jon hit the throttle and the Whaler leaped forward like a Mako shark—cutting through the water at fifty miles an hour. We headed out east of the Russian trawler. It was obvious Jon knew what Pepe had in mind. Everything was happening fast—two days ahead of time.

Pepe asked me to rig two fishing lines with marlin lures, one on each side of the boat, such that they would be easy to reel in fast when we had to move. A mile northeast of the Russian trawler with the lights of Castro behind us, we started trolling. "The fishing decoy is operational!" I declared.

"A little night fishing for those big, black marlin," Pepe confirmed. Knowing they rarely fed at night.

"Well, we're not over the trench yet where it's twenty-six-thousand feet deep!" I remarked. Pepe and Jon laughed.

"I estimate twenty thousand," Pepe said.

"Meaning what?" I asked.

"The number of giant marlin swimming in the trench. Remember your question on the plane?"

He got me again; the excitement had shut my memory down.

Jon told me to take the wheel and keep the boat heading 170 degrees south at seven miles per hour, parallel to the trawler. That put Castro's lights west of us, off the starboard bow.

Neurons were firing in my gray matter! I knew we were involved in something big—a plan to deliver merchandise from a Russian trawler that had just come from Antarctica. Our job was to prevent bad things from happening: Like being double crossed by the Russians in the Zodiac, interception by drug runners, or rogues in the Chilean Military, Pincoya's jealous boyfriends, or whatever. We were supposed to remain invisible. I kept the Whaler steady on the 170 heading.

Jon went into the cubby at the bow of the Whaler and brought out a large spotting scope and fastened it to the starboard gunnel. Then he and Pepe took turns studying what the Russians were doing. I kept the boat trolling for black marlin, figuring the best decoy of all would be to catch one.

"Not much is going on right now," Pepe observed. "They got the Zodiac in the water tied to the Trawler's anchor chain with a rope going up to the deck. Two men are standing near the ship's crane—both are smoking. It doesn't appear they can see us." It was dark and we had all our lights off, but moonlight appeared and disappeared with the clouds. I could see the Southern Cross on and off. I imagined it was four and a half times longer, then dropped a mental line perpendicular to the horizon from the end of the longer cross—that was due south or 180 degrees, ten degrees to the right of our heading.

With me comfortably at the helm, Pepe opened a large map of Antarctica and spread it out on the floor. He turned on a small fluorescent light at the base of the steering console that was not visible above the gunnel. Now my excitement was peaking!

"Here she is, all five-point-four million square miles of her," Pepe pointed to the map. "The coldest, driest, and windiest continent on the planet—total population of humans: less than two thousand. Penguins: more than five million. The South Pole is here, not quite in the middle—any direction you go from it is north! At the top of the map is Queen Maud Land which is closest to South Africa. To my right, about a quarter of the way around the continent is the Antarctic Peninsula—closest to Argentina and Chile (us). And at the bottom is the Ross Ice Shelf and Victoria Land— closest to New Zealand."

Pepe took a breath then continued: "Here is where the Russian trawler has been." He pointed to the Ross Ice Shelf near New Zealand's Scott Base and the US McMurdo Base. "All I know right now is when the Russians examined truck-sized chunks of ice —and other icebergs that had recently broken off the glacier—there was an interesting biological specimen in one of them."

It was obvious Jon knew some of this; he and Pepe were more than just aquafarm partners! The two of them gave me time to cogitate and troll for marlin. Shivering, I zipped up my jacket. No fish had been interested in the two white lures so far.

Jon stepped behind me to check the spotting scope. I throttled back to slow down for him.

"Pepe, come see this," Jon said in a low voice. Pepe kneeled on two seat cushions and took a long, deliberate look through the scope as he zoomed it to sixty-power.

"Full stop!" He ordered. I slammed the throttle into neutral.

"They're lowering a large rectangular box into the Zodiac, it looks like a large coffin. That's what The Group told us to watch for," Pepe confirmed, keeping his voice down.

"The headquarters in Lima?" Jon responded.

"Yes," Pepe replied. "They intercepted a telegraph message sent to the Chilean military from the trawler the day it left Antarctica. Our mole, the chief of Chile's military communications, received the message. The Group responded to the trawler posing as the Chilean military— providing delivery instructions. Thank God for old technology! Neither the Kremlin nor Washington know anything about this. Our job is to make sure the specimen gets delivered to the right place—frozen! The Russians on the trawler don't know we're here. The Group had difficulties communicating with the trawler when it was at sea, so they decided to keep our presence secret. We're the insurance policy." That confirmed it for me, I was now in the insurance business.

We were directly east of the Russian ship, a half mile away now. Jon had told me to angle toward the trawler at a heading of 220-degrees. Clouds still allowed some moonlight through. Pepe checked the time on his Rolex. Noticing it reflected moonlight; he took it off and put it in his pocket. My black Casio with non-reflective glass didn't reflect anything. "Gotta get me one of those!" he said.

Finally, it became totally dark when clouds completely blocked the moon and the wind picked up.

Pepe took over the wheel and told me to get the BAR out of its tube.

Jon kept watching the Russians who were manning the crane. "There are two men dressed like Navy Seals sliding down the rope into the Zodiac! The coffin is frosted on top and streaming vapors, obviously, much colder than the surrounding air. They've started the outboard on the Zodiac—a one hundred fifteen-horse Yamaha. They're heading into the archipelago!" Jon exclaimed.

I had already reeled in the two fishing lines before picking up the BAR. Pepe turned the boat and accelerated until he could see the Zodiac's wake, then slowed and followed behind it—attempting to stay out of sight where their wake dispersed.

"With that one-fifteen -Yamaha hammering in their ears they won't hear us." I said.

Pepe told us that their destination, if everything had been communicated clearly, was the palafitos, those charming houses on stilts. But there were serious navigation issues coming up. The wind and dark magnified the dangers of the infamous archipelago. Pepe motioned for Jon to take the wheel—he knew the hazards best! We pulled the cord on our jackets inflating them with CO2.

The Zodiac must have seen us because it accelerated after passing a small island; the tracks of our wake were dimly illuminated by Castro's distant lights. Jon accelerated to keep up with them knowing there were shallow volcanic rocks ahead.

"They're heading in the direction of the palafitos, that's good news!" Pepe shouted, he'd had nightmares the Chilean military had discovered their plan.

The Zodiac was swerving, probably trying to get a better look at us. They turned sharply, going around a large island that Jon knew well.

"There's a shallow, rocky ridge just under the surface on the back side of that island!" Jon shouted as he turned to go around its opposite side. Neither boat was able to see the other now.

It took about ten minutes before we could see each other again coming from opposite ends of the long island. Directly ahead of the Zodiac was the invisible rocky ridge. "They're going to hit those damn rocks head-on!" Jon shouted. He slowed down and kept the Whaler clear of the rocks, which extended out over fifty yards.

Then came three rock-smashing thunks, seconds apart. The Zodiac hit the rocks and stopped abruptly. Its outboard motor flew up, and everything loose hurled forward the moment it crashed on the rocks. We saw the coffin bust several Bungee cords and shoot up along with a seal-man on top of it. With substantial momentum, it flew forward from the middle of the Zodiac and landed on the rubber bow — teetering precariously before sliding back into the Zodiac. One seal-man rolled off the coffin and sat up, apparently unharmed. The other seal-man driving somehow managed to hang on to the motor's throttle and stay in the back of the Zodiac.

Jon stayed away and made a big circle around them. We were in open water between several islands. The Russians knew we were part of this now, but had no idea whether friend or foe! The driver started the Zodiac's motor, surprisingly on the first pull. It rattled and clamored like a washing machine filled with nuts and bolts when shifted into forward.

I was holding the BAR under the rim of the gunnel, so they couldn't see it. We could see two AK-47s bungeed in the Zodiac. In the distance, to the northwest, were the dim lights of the palafitos. I was kneeling, ready to duck behind the gunnel if they started shooting. Shooting back at them would deflate the Zodiac and sink the coffin and the specimen.

Pepe gave the orders: "Jon, kneel and keep circling around them at this distance — fifty yards. Stan, lie down flat and hold that BAR on your chest, pull the slide back and put one in the chamber; put the safety on. Be ready to kneel and shoot if I tell you! Aim at the water in front of them, not at the Zodiac. They don't know we're armed yet."

Reaching around Jon, Pepe uncoiled a megaphone from under the steering console. Then he stood up and spoke into it: *"We Are Friends! Coffin Reception Team."* He said this in Russian that he had memorized. The Zodiac's mechanical clamor was loud; did they hear and understand? He repeated the message.

Rat-Tat-Tat! Rat-Tat-Tat! One of the seal-men fired two bursts at our bow, hitting where the stainless-steel railing joined the fiberglass hull. They could see we were in the middle and back of the boat. These were clearly warning shots!

"Hand me the BAR," Pepe commanded. "Stay down!" He clicked the safety off, and aimed the red laser beam two yards in front of the Zodiac and shot two bursts, ka-boom-boom-boom, ka-boom-boom-boom! Then he ducked down behind the gunnel. The 30-06 cartridges were hot-loaded and much louder than the AK-47 rounds.

Now the Russians realized we were heavily armed and not in a rubber boat! Pepe stood back up and barked into the megaphone: *"Throw Guns In Water!"* in memorized Russian. And repeated: *"Throw Guns In Water!"*

The Russians did exactly that. They stood with their hands up as we approached the Zodiac. Jon gave the wheel to me and went forward to get a rope. He signaled me to steer the Whaler in front of the Zodiac and then he threw the rope to them. Pepe signaled the Russians to tie the rope and sit down. Jon took the wheel back and started towing the Zodiac toward the palafitos.

I don't know who the Russians thought we were—certainly not the military, maybe the coast guard. When the houses were in sight we could see a paramedic van with blue strobe lights flashing.

"That's our pickup vehicle," Pepe said with relief. He put a spotlight on the Zodiac and then on Alejandro, who was standing on shore with two men disguised as paramedics—and a couple of old fishermen who woke up early because of the 'ruido fuerte.' I was surprised to see Alejandro at first, then my left brain started to make sense of it all; he was a vital cog in the wheel, not simply a back-up. Jon ran the Whaler up on the sand as there was no dock close. Then he and Pepe got out and helped the "paramedics" deal with the Russians while I stayed in the Whaler with the BAR. Pepe told the Russians to climb out of the Zodiac which had started to deflate, then he frisked them for small arms and ordered them into Alejandro's truck. Pepe promised them in Russian they would be taken back to their trawler. Alejandro gave each one a Cuban cigar and a cold beer. Then, under Pepe's strict orders, the heavy coffin was lifted onto a gurney and slid into the van.

The two paramedics, hands cold from helping lift the coffin, drove away with the Russians in Alejandro's truck. Pepe and Jon got into the van and, according to Alejandro, drove to the regional airport and Pepe's plane.

Alejandro drove the Whaler back to the aquafarm with me. He drove slowly, avoiding any hittable rock reefs. It was a relief to see the farm. I grabbed the rope and tied the bow to the deck support.

"Listen," he said. We could hear the automatic feeders turn on and fifty thousand fish splash as they began to feed. Alejandro laughed at the coincidental timing and pointed to underwater lights under the cage and the rotating camera. After about five minutes the feeder got a signal from the camera to shut off. "No pollution," he said to me. My mind had to refocus on aquaculture, a safer place for it to be.

"Can you find the guesthouse?" Alejandro asked before climbing up the ladder to the farm's deck. There's no rocks from here to there."

"After what we've been through, with my eyes closed."

It was clear now that the Boston Whaler operation was necessary insurance and security for the mission. No, there wasn't any military or drug-gang interference. Yes, the Russians had been headed toward the agreed upon drop off at the palafitos. But, there were the rocks! And, without us, without a fast tow in, the coffin would never have made it. The Zodiac was deflating and our fast towing of it was an imperative. Otherwise, the specimen might be surfing the waves with the Goddess Pincoya.

I hit the throttle on the Whaler, thankful there were no rocks from here to the guesthouse. A king -sized bed was waiting for me.

I had to be content until breakfast to get more information. I was having coffee with Maria when Jon came down from his room. It was 10:00 a.m.

"Buenos Dias," he announced. "Looks like we've got sunshine today!"

"Good morning," Maria and I responded together, which got a smile out of him. She poured Jon a cup of coffee and refilled mine. She told us the cook was making huevos rancheros Chilean style. I was starved. After serving breakfast, she excused herself, seeing that Jon and I needed to talk.

Jon looked at me, smiling. "Thanks for helping us last night! It was much appreciated. It turned out very well, but there were other gremlins besides the rocks that could have interfered."

"I presume Pepe took the coffin someplace safe," I commented, digging into a spicy huevo on a tortilla.

"He did!" Jon said. "Let me tell what happened after we left you and Alejandro last night: First, we pulled over and I took the lights and decals off the van; turning it back into a plain white van—we certainly didn't want to encourage a police escort! Then we drove straight to the airport. Pepe and I found two tarmac attendants to help lift the coffin into the plane. They had commented that the hombre in the box was pesado and mucho frio; but stopped wondering about it when Pepe gave each one a hundred bucks."

He knew the flight to Lima would be a grueling twelve hours with a need to refuel in northern Chile. Pepe insisted he had to do it alone. I asked him if he knew whether there was enough ice in the coffin. He told me it was well insulated, vacuum-sealed, and would stay frozen for at least another day, four-hundred pounds of ice went along as backup."

Jon paused and took a drink of coffee. I was excited to hear more.

"Pepe started both engines and began to taxi. I could see the determination in his eyes. He told me he would be back early the following morning, flying commercial. Until then we should get the lab outfitted to test and brew probiotics." Jon smiled.

I appreciated what Jon had shared with me—what I had missed while asleep in the guesthouse. After breakfast, he and I walked over to the laboratory and got started on the probiotic project.

Later that afternoon, Pepe telephoned Jon from Lima. "It's safely locked in a deep freeze in Mira Flores right now," Pepe's voice blared over the phone—Jon held the receiver away from his ear, so I could hear. Mira Flores was an upscale suburb of Lima—a place frequented by international businessmen. Pepe told Jon he had a meeting scheduled with The Group and couldn't talk long—what an energy reserve this man had!

"All this secrecy over a frozen mermaid? Walt Disney should be here," I tested Jon.

"You'll find out; just don't tell your wife if the mermaid's naked!" Jon warned. "It could be one of Pincoya's ancestors. I'm as mystified as you are, we'll be told when the time is right. I'm not ruling out an infant T. Rex."

I could sense there were some latent concerns bothering Jon that were partly neutralized by a little comic-book humor.

Pepe called Jon from the regional airport at 2:00 a.m. It had been a long day—plus some—but he was back in Castro and still fully energized. The specimen was in excellent shape, frozen in Peru. He wanted to meet with us at the company office in sixty minutes—3:00 a.m. sharp!

Jon, Alejandro, and I waited in the company's conference room; nobody was sleepy or tired. I was astonished when Pepe walked in; I wouldn't have recognized him on the street. He was wearing a black leather jacket and an officer's hat with four stars. A sparkling patch on his jacket was embossed with the letters "TG." We stood up, but he motioned us to sit down.

Jon had told me more about The Group when we were working in the lab. It was organized like a military command. The highest rank was a general, the lowest a lieutenant. Both Alejandro and Jon were captains; Pepe was one of three generals. It was no kid's game! Big money from around the world was involved. Everyone had other business activities in addition to their membership in The Group. All sponsored activities were altruistic—for the advancement of mankind. Everything was decentralized and coded.

It was obvious Pepe was prepared to tell us something: "For Stan's understanding as our newest associate, I have some news about The Group, 'TG' as we like to call it. As Jon and Alejandro know, we are a fraternity of private businessmen and scientists who support the disclosure of vital historical information that the public is not aware of—Information that can change the way we look at the world and the way we live! What 'TG' now has in its possession, thanks to us, will enervate this process." Pepe paused for a few moments then pulled a photograph out of his jacket and handed it to Jon first. "I took this photo when we opened the coffin. It took some effort to open it—the Russians definitely had it hermetically sealed."

Jon took a long look at it, then turned the photograph sideways and kept looking. His face turned red. "This is jolting me—I'm confused between wonderment and anger!"

"Yell it out, Jon—I know what you're feeling!" Pepe shouted.

"Augusto Pinochet is not getting this one! Not this perfect one!" Jon shouted, holding the photograph while pounding his fist on the table. "That murdering dictator has already tried to extort half the world's ruling class by threatening to reveal the bones of twenty-foot humanoids dug up in the Andes! It would have worked for him except the Smithsonian Institute had their secret basement full of giant humanoid bones dug up from Indian mounds in the USA—ones they had certified as 'fakes'—so they called Pinochet's bluff. They would have certified his giants as fakes too. The elite doesn't reveal these things, they hide them—it was an act of God that allowed us to intercept this specimen. Pinochet would have used it like he tried to use the giant bones—to extort and distort the world!"

Jon, calm after his emotional release, filled only with wonderment now, handed the photograph to Alejandro who had already put his glasses on. What he saw opened his eyes wide! He looked at the specimen for a full minute, shaking his head in disbelief. I was convinced before looking that it wasn't an infant T. Rex or a mermaid. Even knowing what the specimen must be, I was still astounded when I looked at it. I stared, eyes wide open, then turned the photograph sideways and kept staring, studying the details. Amazing! There was a silent air of astonishment between the three of us. Jon picked up the photograph again.

"Look like anybody you know?" Pepe asked me.

"Yes, it does: It's the Nazca Astronaut in the flesh." I said softly, clearly visualizing the geoglyph in my mind, but still overtaken by the amazement of seeing the real thing. The alien was in perfect condition, frozen in a clear block of ice. About five feet tall, it had huge round eyes! Not snake or reptilian eyes, or black slanted almond eyes, but big black, round eyes. His mouth was open, the size of a silver dollar in diameter. Perfectly circular, like he was trying to blow out birthday candles, his last expression before being flash frozen. He must not have had any time to experience fear, just a few conscious seconds, then the piercing cold.

The ice was a little cloudy near its hands. It looked like there were just three fingers. His arms and legs were long and thin and his belly bloated. The skin was more golden than green, maybe olive green—and blotched with small scales—no hair anywhere. He did have some reptilian character but looked more curious than fearsome; the head was round, not cone shaped. I wish I could have seen it in person, but Pepe's photograph was quite clear. The alien had some of the characteristics of those featured in comic books and movies, but this one was real and there were differences from what I had perceived. This was not a skeleton or a fossil. It was a perfectly preserved Extraterrestrial—a real ET.

"Have any idea of his age?" I asked Pepe. I was still enveloped in amazement.

"Now? Or when he froze?" Jon interjected some humor.

"Around twelve-thousand years, toward the end of the last ice-age," Pepe answered. "When the Ross Ice Shelf formed in Antarctica. We'll have to do some scans and x-rays to estimate his age before he froze. He looks like a young 'guy.'"

"Wow, seven thousand years before recorded history—and here he is in perfect condition," I said.

"Kind of like your amethyst crystals!" Pepe remarked. "At some point The Group will show this ancient astronaut to the world. The timing will be critical! Then, in a history-making event, this alien entity, this authentic, hard evidence will finally prove that we are not alone! Until then it will secretly remain...frozen in Peru."

Postscript:

This story is based on true experience. I did not see the actual alien, only its photograph. I believe it was real; the experience of delivering a coffin brought in by a Russian trawler was real. Names have been changed to protect those involved. The men represented by Pepe and Alejandro are no longer with us. I have no information regarding the status of The Group—but I believe it is still around and can only imagine why it hasn't disclosed the ancient astronaut yet, if indeed, it was an astronaut. Maybe we are the astronauts!

I kept in touch with the man I called Jon for about ten years. He left Chile and moved back to Texas in the mid-1990's. I don't know where he is today—he often mentioned New Zealand.

The Ocean's Best aquafarm was sold and subsequently misman-aged. The probiotics worked amazingly well when produced and used properly, but that changed with the new owners. In Southeast Asia, many shrimp farms now brew probiotics on site—resulting in increased yields and reduced pollution.

Author at the Golden Triangle with two Thai ladies

12

The Golden Triangle
Thailand, Laos, and Burma—Three Countries, One Scare

Prologue:

Thailand, Laos, and Burma (Myanmar) meet at Thailand's northern border where the Mekong River joins the Ruak River—the junction is called the Sop Ruak by locals. The two rivers form a natural boundary: Laos being east of the Mekong, Thailand west of it, and Burma north of the Ruak. The overlapping border area of about 950,000 square kilometers is called The Golden Triangle—named by the CIA in the 1960s—because gold was used by Chinese traders to pay for opium cultivated there, bringing renown to the region during the Viet Nam War. It's an intersection laced with history.

The countryside is hilly, and the river water flows opaque with mud through scenery that is not notably attractive. But you can visit all three countries on the same day by taking a cruise on a wooden long-boat.

There's a ubiquitous presence of Buddhist monks and their many temples, or wats, in The Golden Triangle. They stand in defiance to unlawful and immoral activity.

Bangkok, Thailand, June 2001

After a week of inspecting prawn farms around the Gulf of Thailand, I had the weekend free before heading to Kuala Lumpur, Malaysia and more prawn farms. I hadn't been up to northern Thailand, the Chiang Mai-Chiang Rai area, so I hired a car and driver, checked out of the Hilton in Bangkok on a Saturday, and headed north with Chai. His name meant a lively person filled with joy. He had a college education and spoke English well.

"Mr. Stan, I'm happy you hired me, I drive you good," Chai said joyfully as he navigated Bangkok's stifling traffic. He was short with alert brown eyes and braided hair.

"The concierge at the Hilton recommended you; he said you were a good guide, too—a smart one."

"Thank you, thank you, Mr. Stan. I'm very happy he recommended me to take you north in our country. The air will be clean, not like in Bangkok."

"That's reason enough for going north." I'd been to Bangkok several times and the air pollution was usually bad. The drive to Chiang Mai was seven hundred kilometers and would take a good nine hours. Chai and I had plenty of time to talk.

Once out of Bangkok we were able to move faster. At the first substantial town we came to, a dogcatcher turned in front of us. In the back of his pickup truck was a large cage filled with yelping, crying dogs. Yes, crying. Somehow, they knew their fate: the dog butcher. As in China and Viet Nam, and in some parts of Thailand—mostly rural towns—dog meat was considered good table fare. Pet-loving Thais were against it in the cities and often protested butcher shops. The times were changing.

"I don't eat dogs," Chai assured me.

"Neither do I, knowingly." I was thinking of the time in China when I'd eaten chow zits, square noodles stuffed with mystery meat, then found out later it was dog.

"The dog catchers only catch stray dogs," Chai insisted.

He drove around and passed the truck with the dogs. None were fat. We then passed seven Buddhist monks dressed in bright orange, all carrying shoulder bags, also orange. Some were buying fruit from local vendors.

"City monks," Chai said. "They can have watches and phones." The monks were clean shaven, barefoot young men with short hair. They walked in line along the road. "They follow the Ten Precepts (training rules) of Thai Buddhism. The first is to refrain from harming living creatures."

"What about the Forest monks?" I asked, knowing they were more constrained.

"They use nothing modern, wear dark robes, and rarely leave the temple; once ordained, they follow two hundred and twenty-seven precepts. Lots of rules!"

"But both types practice Dharma, right? Buddha's teachings."

"Yes, but there's a third type too, like me," Chai said. "I'm a Lay Buddhist guided by five precepts—not so strict." This was fascinating—options in Buddhism.

"Tell me what Lay Buddhists believe," I asked him.

"We believe it's important to live an ethical life, but we must not harm anyone. We enjoy this life with a wife, music, dancing, and celebrations—and seek to create good Karma."

"How is Karma different from Dharma? I've heard different explanations."

"Dharma, called Dhamma in Thailand, is the religion of the Buddha, the path you take when heading toward your destiny. Karma is the actions you perform while on that path.

"Buddha taught that nothing in this world is permanent, everything must end. And that truth comes gradually and awakening to it requires sustained practice. I pray every day to find truth."

"You're a good man, Chai!"

We drove on, the road was good. It was hot and humid outside but comfortable in Chai's air-conditioned taxi.

"Do you want to ride an elephant?" Chai asked as we passed six elephants carrying a group of Japanese tourists. They looked nervous sitting in chairs strapped to the pachyderms.

"No thanks, I did in Sumatra."

"For fun?"

"For work. It was the only way to inspect flooded banana plantations for fungal infections. In my business we use probiotics—beneficial bacteria—to fight infections like the Fusarium fungus that kills banana plants. I had to ride the elephant bareback with my legs spread as wide as they would go, now I'm bowlegged!"

Chai laughed. "Did you stop the fungus?"

"We did, by spraying it with the right probiotic bacteria."

"Did the elephant like you?"

"Yes. He couldn't help that he had such a wide back; there were no skinny elephants available. So I whispered to him, promising a bunch of bananas when were done if he walked slow and straight. He understood—he loved bananas!"

"Here they give trail elephants watermelon for a treat," Chai said. I smiled, remembering the story of a boy who did that in Africa.

We passed various small towns and villages alive with rikshaws, three-wheel tuk tuks, and mopeds. Chai was a very alert driver, and I appreciated the mostly-smooth roads. When we came to another group of orange-robed Buddhist monks, these being followed by a troop of macaques, Chai slowed down.

"Those are Assamese macaques. They live in the same temple as the monks; they're heading home together," Chai explained.

Two of the female monkeys had babies clinging to their stomachs and were scampering to keep up with the fast-walking monks; these were thick-set, rust-colored, short-tailed macaques, unlike the roadblock crews of grey, long-tailed macaques that stopped traffic in Java, Indonesia—but that's another story.

The monks totally ignored the short-tailed macaques. I wondered if there was a precept for not regarding them.

"I know a clean restaurant in this town," Chai said.

"Tourist restaurant?" I asked him.

"Yes, but Thais eat there too. Very safe, well-cooked food."

"Will they customize Pad Thai for me? I don't want any fish sauce used in mine."

"I will tell them not to use fish sauce in yours."

Let's go then." I realized I was hungry. Opportunities to eat safely were important in Southeast Asia and didn't always correlate with being exceptionally hungry—particularly on a road trip.

Thai fish sauce is made from bony milk-fish fermented outside in tubs of sea water, stirred occasionally for a month or so, then the smelly mush is filtered through an old tee shirt stretched over a plastic bucket, yielding fish sauce. Enough said.

Pad Thai is Thailand's national dish: rice noodles stir-fried with chunks of tofu and tamarind pulp with fish sauce, shallots, red pepper sauce and typically, dried shrimp. At some point, near the end of the stir-frying, palm sugar, lime juice, and ground peanuts are added. It must be served hot!

My customized version: No fish sauce, only fresh shrimp, and one-half the amount of red pepper sauce.

Chai let me order in English, then he explained my requests in Thai. Respecting Chai's Lay Buddhism, I ordered a coke without rum—following one of the precepts. After lunch, we hit the road; we were five hours south of Chiang Mai.

Driving in rural Thailand was more civilized than in Africa, India or Indonesia: smoother and faster with less congestion, but you still had to watch carefully for bicycles without lights, donkey carts, slow moving tuk tuks, and people in dark clothes walking the road at night. Thailand's fifty-five million Homo sapiens lived in a space about the size of Texas; some measurable percentage of them walked the roads at night.

"I saw a bus kill two women last year, not far from here," Chai exclaimed. "It never stopped. The women were Muslims dressed in black."

"My God, that's terrible! What did you do?" Chai proceeded to tell me the horrible details. He had no phone along and had stayed with the bodies until morning, when a provincial patrol just happened to come by.

"It was the biggest challenge of my life, sitting with those poor dead women. I kept reciting verses from The King of Prayers. Verses that exclaimed worlds of ten directions and infinite oceans, of

Buddhas as numerous as all the atoms in the universe, and of guides that help with self-reckoning of one's past and future lives… I asked the stars to please guide these two women forward."

We were both quiet as we approached the location of the accident, I was humbled by my feelings for two women I'd never known, souls that were hopefully creating positive Karma in a different place . . .

"We Thais don't like big government ruling our lives, but there should be a law against walking the road at night dressed in black." I had to agree with Chai. There were no laws in Thailand for other potentially lethal infractions either—like drunk driving or driving without lights. Parts of Asia had a lot of catching up to do without going overboard with too many rules.

"You have many rules in America," Chai remarked.

"Yes, we do. The Republicans believe in fewer rules than the Democrats, but since we only have two parties, usually an equitable compromise results. Historically, the parties alternate power and our constitution provides protections that help assure their mutual survival.

"That's hard to do in Thailand—we have over forty political parties! It's very hard for them to compromise on anything," Chai lamented.

"It's a worldwide problem!" I added.

We arrived in Chiang Mai late due to several unplanned stops and a slower drive after dark. Chai dropped me off at a guesthouse where I had reservations and would pick me up at 8:00 a.m. for our drive to Chiang Rai and The Golden Triangle. I knew more about Buddhism after a day with Chai, and he knew more about probiotics after a day with me. He was quite interested in how probiotics helped prawn farmers grow more prawns on less feed with less pollution.

Chai arrived on time the next morning to find me sitting in the garden of the guesthouse talking to a couple of graduate students from Denmark. They were studying enzymes that digest plastics—a technology with potential for cleaning up the distressingly monstrous, plastic dump in the Pacific Ocean between Hawaii and California. I suggested they focus on using live cultures of enzyme-producing bacteria rather than enzymes, per se. The bacteria would be more cost- effective because they multiply in number, where just enzymes would require more frequent applications. They were interested in what my company was doing with probiotics; we exchanged contact information. I could see Chai was restless; it was Sunday and he wanted to show me Chiang Mai's famous Sunday Market.

The market started at The Phae Gate and ran up to Ratchadamnoen Road—a good distance but well worth it. You can walk it or hire a rikshaw. Handcrafted art was everywhere: carvings, brass temple bells, paintings, glass blown ornaments, authentic artifacts, Thai clothing, you name it—a welcome relief from common tourist fare. And all the while, you're surrounded by Buddhist wats, five of them, for when you need a break from materialism.

After a quick Thai snack of a banana on a stick dipped in chocolate, we had to travel further north, two hundred kilometers to Chiang Rai where two legendary rivers joined in The Golden Triangle.

I supplemented the banana snack with a large alphonso mango that I ate in the backseat of the taxi on our way to the Triangle—cut with my Swiss Army Knife such that all the pulp broke away from the peelings in little squares. When done right it's easy to bite off the squares without making a mess. The pit was for the birds, literally.

Chai made a quick pass through Chiang Rai, leaving the supra-normal Wat Rong Khun (White Temple) for another time. The White Temple was stunning as we drove by it—ivory spires covered with marble swirls and squiggles— but it was more of a sci-fi tourist attraction than a church. I had made reservations for a boat tour of the Golden Triangle; the wat didn't fit our schedule.

When you stand in front of the gate to The Golden Triangle, with its sculptured interpretations of elephants and tigers, and maybe have your picture taken with two young girls in colorful traditional Thai dresses, you will find yourself standing in Thailand with Burma

(Myanmar) across the river to your left, Laos across the river to your right, and the vastness of China behind them in the distance. This is when you realize you're not in Kansas anymore!

Chai drove us to the dock where the longboats departed for the river tour. I bought him a ticket to go along with me just as a dozen European tourists arrived and bought tickets.

"They provide a guide," he said. "You don't need me."

"I know," I replied. "But I want you because you pray for the truth, and that's what I want to hear, not tourist commentaries in four different languages."

"You honor me, Mr. Stan."

"It's my pleasure to do so." Chai had majored in math at Bangkok University and was one smart lad.

The boat crew (captain and a mate) had to switch boats to the extra-long model to accommodate fourteen of us. It was a long, flat tour boat with twelve rows of bench seats and a flat roof that somewhat shielded from sun and rain, but otherwise was open all around. It was what I had expected.

We all boarded and quickly were off, splashing into the notorious Mekong River heading toward Laos. In short order we were following the Laotian shore line, watching the wildlife—locals washing clothes and bathing naked. Their clothes were drying on rocks. Several of the European ladies on the boat had a hand over their open mouths, not believing the nakedness.

"Laos is very poor," Chai said. "These people live in a primitive village behind the tree line. You can see their thatched houses if you look carefully," he pointed.

We saw an older woman frying something in a pan over a wood fire; two men were eating whatever was in the pan, breaking it apart, and eating certain pieces.

"What are they eating?" I asked Chai.

"Fried bugs—maeng da,"

"Big ones." I could see. "They must be giant water bugs." The men were breaking off the wings and heads and eating the contents of the thorax and abdomen. Much like eating an oyster out of its shell.

"Yes, I forget their American name."

"They're huge and full of viruses, but frying sterilizes them! I got bit by one in the Philippines last year," I remembered vividly.

"Ever eat one?"

"Part of one in Indonesia—it was mushy and had a strong black-licorice taste."

"In Bangkok, we dip them in spicy soy sauce after deep frying."

"It's hard for me to wrap my mind around eating bugs," I said. "So, these people are poor but self-sustaining?"

"Yes, you could say that," Chai answered. "They only need rice to supplement the catfish and bugs they catch in the river."

"Do they grow rice?"

"No, they grow poppies and trade the seed pods for rice."

"Opium poppies!" I assumed. "A bushel of seed pods must translate to a mountain of rice."

"It does," Chai replied.

"I'm sure that you already know what the mate is explaining to the Europeans. When you scratch an opium poppy's seed pod, a white latex containing twelve percent morphine leaks out and dries. When you dissolve the dry latex in hot water and add calcium carbonate (chalk), crude heroin precipitates. It's ancient chemistry," I said, but Chai knew this.

"Yes . . . very simple chemistry," Chai lamented. "Nobody bothers these river people. They trade with other locals who process crude heroin for local use." I nodded. This was why I needed Chai to be along.

The muddy river was still opaque, and as we moved along we could see two teenage boys standing on the beach wearing conical Chinese hats—otherwise naked. They waved while holding their genitals. Chai and I only waved back. This got all six of the European ladies to gasp. When one of the ladies looked at me for my reaction I shrugged my shoulders, "This is Southeast Asia. Life happens."

The sign read "Welcome to Don Sao, Laos." We had docked at an island in the Mekong that belonged to Laos. No passport or visa was required. Chai and I politely waited for the Europeans to disembark.

"Don't get too excited," Chai said. "It's just souvenir shops and a beer bar."

I figured that out while stepping out of the boat and into Laos for the first time. The beer bar part of Chai's sentence sounded civilized.

Any liquid would be better than discarded Evian bottles refilled with local tap water—you always had to remember where you were! In Bangkok the other night I'd seen a cook behind a food stand refilling Evian water bottles with a hose. I could sense Montezuma wanting to expand the range of his revenge.

The beer was almost cold; hard to believe. Beerlao, brewed by the Lao Brewery Company, Ltd. was a bitter-tasting lager probably stored too long in the sun. Chai drank an orange soda from a bottle.

"The Longneck Tribe is going to dance," Chai raised his eyebrows several times. "Local actors!"

He was spot on. A bunch of amateur Laotian locals poorly acted out a silly dance to drum music, trying to get the European women to participate. Two of them did, marginally surviving the embarrassment. The singing was now worse than the dancing. Chai consulted the captain of our boat who checked his watch, then said something to Chai in Thai.

"Let's take a walk around the island," Chai said to me. "We have time."

After leaving Laos, some real excitement developed. Once we entered Burmese waters we were facing the sharp-pointed peninsula where the Ruak River joined the Mekong. A military patrol boat flying the Myanmar flag came along our port side and discharged three horn blasts. Our mate put the boat's outboard motor in idle. Chai's facial expression was enough cause for alarm.

Two Burmese soldiers in green camo tied their patrol boat to ours, then leaped aboard. The two boats were now drifting toward Burma's deserted shore. The patrol boat was half the length of our tour boat but twice as wide with a 50-caliber machine gun mounted amid ship.

"Ninengankuulaatmhaat!" The taller soldier barked in Burmese.

"He wants to our passports," Chai told me. Hmm, this was interesting. These were obviously soldiers of the military junta, not border cops.

The captain of our boat came out from up front and instructed everyone to show their passports. I could see concern in his face.

The taller soldier started collecting passports. The Europeans were aghast, fumbling through their purses and shoulder bags. I pulled an expired passport out of my pocket, an extra for such a situation—I had been through this drill before. I had learned not to argue and to pay them what they demanded.

"Twenty-five thousand kyat," the shorter soldier said in gobbledygook. The Burmese language was a distant cousin to ancient Chinese; you could sing parts of it. This soldier couldn't sing!

"Twenty-five dollars each," Chai translated. "Touring charge."

"Bull roar!" I said. But, realizing no options existed, I pulled a fifty-dollar bill out to cover Chai and me. The shorter soldier immediately took my money and waved off any need to take my passport or Chai's Thai identification pass. He had to help his tall comrade deal with the Europeans. Our boat's captain and mate were white-faced—they mostly kept quiet.

It took almost an hour for the soldiers to sort out the Europeans who apparently were on a group tour and didn't know each other well. They fumbled with traveler's checks and a smorgasbord of different currency not wanting to pay in Euros, but they couldn't convince the soldiers to take Thai baht or Malaysian ringgits.

"They will accept only dollars or Euros!" Our captain said in German, then English.

Two of the German men had a calculator and were attempting to convert dollars to Euros which were about six cents apart. This infuriated the soldiers.

"Twenty-five Euros each!" Our captain shouted.

The two soldiers were red-faced now, I could see their patience had expired. I was nervous; both had side arms and a third soldier was manning the machine gun in the patrol boat.

"This is not an official operation!" Chai whispered to me. I had deduced that it was rogue.

Chai continued, "They should just pay, then the soldiers will leave. They know the Thai military won't respond to tourist claims of being robbed for twenty-five Euros."

The tall soldier—his face crimson-red now—unholstered his 9mm pistol and pointed it at the European tourists. There were two empty bench seats separating the group from Chai and me.

Booff! Booff! Booff! He put three shots in the water. The open air and water muffled the 9mm. Chai and I hit the floor. The European women screamed. Instantly, the European men organized the payment of three-hundred Euros—twenty-five for each person. The soldiers grabbed the money, threw the passports on the floor, untied their patrol boat, jumped in, and sped away. I put my expired passport back in my pocket next to the valid one and breathed a sigh of relief.

A stopover in Burma would not take place on this cruise. Paying the unofficial "touring charge" took time—it was 5:30 p.m. and the Burmese border closed at 6:00 p.m.

I was relieved to make it back to shore in Thailand minus only sixty dollars: the "touring fees" plus ten dollars for beer in Laos. It could have been worse. Chai filed a complaint with the tour's management in Chiang Rai who seemed surprised; the last time this had happened was over a year ago.

The Burmese military denied it occurred. No refunds were offered by the tour company. When Chai and I drove away we could see the Europeans arguing with tour officials for a refund.

I spent the night at a small motel outside Chiang Rai that reminded me of many disquieting, small motels I'd spent one-nighters at in Southeast Asia. Chai stayed with friends.

There were crickets in covert locations in my room, but at least the air conditioning worked. I always brought ear plugs on trips, usually to silence someone snoring on a plane, but these crickets were on steroids and required suppression.

The next morning, Chai drove me to the Thai river town of Mae Sai opposite the Burmese town of Tachileik, forty-five minutes south of Chiang Rai. It was easy to organize a VIP Pass and visa in Mae Sai for the day in Myanmar. My passport (the valid one) would be held in Thailand until I returned. I preferred this to the passport being held at the border in Myanmar, the other option. That said, I always kept a color photocopy of my valid passport's photo page as backup. If you ever needed a replacement from a U.S. Consulate—having a copy expedited the process.

Chai would spend the day with his friends in Chiang Rai and pick me up at the border at 6:00 p.m.

After crossing the bridge over the river, a sign read: Republic of the Union of Myanmar. The name of the country was changed from Burma to Myanmar by the ruling military junta in 1989—the year after thousands were killed in an uprising. The capital, Rangoon, became Yangon and the government had begun promoting tourism in 1992.

I considered taking one of the green tourist buses into Tachileik, but after seeing three guides with their motodops (carriage pulled by a motorbike) idling, ready to transport and guide me for the day, I decided to choose one of them. This being my first time in Burma and time being short, I had to quickly sort them out.

"Good morning," I greeted the three of them. Two replied in English with Thai accents. Chai had told me most of the guides spoke Thai with some English.

"Who speaks the best English?" I asked loudly.

"Of the two who had said, "Good morning," the youngest lad yelled, "I do," while the middle-aged guide said, "Me do." The oldest of the three men, who could have doubled for a professor I knew in Beijing, just pointed to himself.

I went over to the older man and asked, "Why should I choose you?"

"My name is Shway, I can help you find gold today," he replied.

All three had asked the same price for the day: twenty dollars. I didn't argue. My experience with guides was to pay what they asked, within reason, if you wanted the best service. I got in the backseat of Shway's motodop carriage and we headed into Tachileik.

Shway had fought with American GIs against the Japanese in 1945 to reopen the Burma Road. This allowed the Allies to resupply Chiang Kai-shek with supplies flown into Rangoon and Mandalay and then by the Burma Road into China.

"I know American English," he told me. He was eighty years young. We had a good talk enroute to his first recommended stop, the Tachileik Shwedagon Pagoda, a smaller version of the original in Yangon. Both were gold-plated stupas that "blazed in the sun." A conical design that was neither a Muslim dome nor a Hindu temple, but unique to Burmese Buddhism.

"Locals sell flowers, candles, and incense to tourists and worshippers," Shway explained. "It's their only income." We stopped to look inside, and I donated five dollars.

Our next stop was a hiking trail west of town, designated only for local use, but when guided by Shway an exception was allowed. The trail went up a hill that overlooked the town and the golden pagoda. It was refreshing to see local people in their element. I had made the right decision in selecting Shway.

The Burmese town of Tachilek had welcomed tourists for nine years but they were funneled into certain areas—like the town's main marketplace, our next stop.

Stalls in open areas between buildings were covered by large umbrellas of assorted colors. The first thing I noticed was the preponderance of contraband merchandise—even more than in Thailand. Guns, watches, porno tapes, python skins, pirated music and movie tapes, switch blade knives, and then, in certain shops, hidden away in old dusty buildings: rhino horns, ivory carvings, endangered animal pelts, counterfeit currencies, diamonds, and gems.

Also, knock-off drugs were readily available, like in Mexico. I was sure some were diluted with chalk to ineffective strengths. Others were repackaged, expired drugs with new expiration dates. I knew China supplied many of the knock-offs.

Shway's concise advice was, "Don't buy any drugs."

There was one old basement Shway took me into next that I'll never forget. It was in a nondescript building adjacent to a street in the marketplace filled with food stands covered by large umbrellas. We entered a dimly-lit room through strings of beads—very oriental. The smell of Jasmine incense relaxed me. A gray-haired man with a white triangular beard was sitting in a leather chair watching a small television. When he saw us, he reached for a switch that brightened the lights.

I was stunned, then horrified by what I saw: Numerous Siberian, Bengal, Malayan, and Sumatran tiger pelts hung on the walls. I counted forty-six of them with prices ranging from 3,500 to 9,500 U.S. dollars. I was unsettled and could feel my pulse rate increase. Neither Shway or the bearded man said anything.

Sweating now, I touched several, thinking of what they had been. They were alarmingly smooth. I thought about Doctor Robert Weaver's research to preserve the Sumatran tiger's habitat and dissuade poaching—a devoted scientist who I had the honor to visit in Sumatra five years ago. And the game wardens I had met in Delhi who were planning an expedition to save India's Bengal tigers. Now, all around me on the walls were four of the world's most endangered tiger species.

"None of these tigers were poached," the bearded oriental man finally spoke. "Or killed in the wild."

His words gave me pause. Knowing I could become gullible when emotionally unsettled, I just kept looking and didn't say anything.

"They are raised on game ranches south of here on the peninsula and north of Mandalay," Shway explained in a subdued voice. The bearded man nodded and showed me photos of the ranches.

I started a conversation with them about how valuable and how magnificent it would have been to release these tigers into the wild in areas that were still habitat rich for them. The bearded man didn't seem to understand. "Nobody can see or touch them in the wild," he said, while rubbing the shoulders of a Siberian tiger pelt.

Shway seemed sorry he'd brought me here, I believe he understood my position. He hit me with something to consider: "If tiger-rearing ranches didn't exist, wild tigers would be in greater danger of extinction."

I had trained my mind to shift gears at times like this when faced with something unfortunately logical to many, but the opposite of what I believed. Then I shift back to it later, after my subconscious has had time to cogitate. There was still more to see in Tachileik's marketplace.

The saleswomen laid out a black satin cloth on the counter and then, slowly and carefully, dispensed the red crystals onto it. I stared at the uncut gems; some were perfect hexagons; some were fractured, partial hexagons. She handed me a ten-power magnifying lens and I confirmed they were uncut and in the trigonal crystal system.

I took a clear quartz crystal out of my pocket and showed it to her. She nodded, understanding. I picked up one of the fractured hexagons and attempted to scratch the quartz with it—a deep, clear scratch resulted.

She smiled, knowing I had confirmed the hardness of the red crystals. The mineral corundum had a hardness of nine on the Mohs scale, quartz tested seven. A nine would scratch a seven.

"Aluminum oxide infused with chromium—corundum," I said to her.

"Yes," she said smiling. "A very special corundum."

"Indeed," I remarked. These crystals were blood-red with a bluish hue—mystical Burmese rubies that had formed hundreds of millions of years ago in tectonically-pressured orogenic belts, miles underground in the "Valley of Rubies," two hundred kilometers north of Mandalay.

I bought two of the hexagons the size of half-dollars that were hazy- red, great specimens but not gem quality. Affordable additions to my mineral collection. I felt good about the purchase.

Shway was happy I'd bought something. He was sorry for taking time to show me the tiger pelts. I told him not to be—it was important for me to see them. It got me thinking about possible solutions.

We snacked our way through the food stalls as we headed to where Shway had parked his motodop. I was careful to only eat hot cooked food where I could observe its preparation. Deep fried "stuff" was safe. Rice stir fried with turmeric and prawns was one of my choices, Shway had it with fish.

Shway's motodop didn't encounter much traffic in Tachileik, mostly motorbikes and three-wheel vehicles modified to carry goods. Most of the streets were paved but, beyond the marketplace, were largely empty.

I was happy to see Chai and retrieve my passport after crossing the bridge back into Thailand. The next day he and I spent more time in Chiang Mai.

Postscript:

Tachileik's westernization was a work-in-progress in 2001. The people were friendly and well dressed, at least in town. It was obvious to me they understood that they would grow in direct proportion to the growth of tourism. And that would require the authorities to lighten up on tourist restrictions while cracking down on blatantly illegal activities. The people were ready for it.

Hopefully this story about the Golden Triangle region will not dissuade you from visiting but will open the door to some cautions and preparations you should consider. Adventure is everywhere when you know how to find it. Many times it just finds you!

Two Brothers Hill in Rio

13

Big Surprise in Rio
Strange Visitors

When I first flew into Rio, sitting in back on the left side of the aircraft, the renowned thirteen-hundred-foot hump called Sugarloaf Mountain emerged from an island at the mouth of Guanabara Bay. Then, magically, four of Rio's famous beaches came into view: Flamingo, Copacabana, Ipanema, and Leblon. In the background, the Twin Brother Peaks stood guarding the glistening beaches. When the captain banked the aircraft over the center of the city, I could see the widespread arms of Christ the Redeemer on top of Corcovado Mountain.

Brazilians call it Cidade Maravilhosa—the Marvelous City. It's also a mystery metropolis where unexpected adventure can emerge out of the blue!

Rio de Janeiro, 1995

Marcello and I walked ankle-deep in the ocean on Copacabana Beach. In many places we would have attracted attention, but not in Rio—even though we were in business suits with our shoes on. Since I had come to expect the unexpected from Marcello, this extemporaneous event was no surprise.

Somehow, I'd had the foresight to wear soft-soled running shoes with my suit that morning; they were unobtrusive, comfortable, and sloshed well in the ocean. Marcello, well-heeled in his high-backed Bruno Maglis, had to exert extra oomph to move in the water, but he did it with vigor. This trim and fit, middle-aged Italian businessman spoke Italian, English, German, and Portuguese fluently. He was somewhat eccentric, but for that matter, so was I.

"Don't worry, the people don't see us," he asserted, kicking at the sea. The late afternoon sun was casting long shadows on male surfers, warming the hearts of observant young females in string bikinis on the beach. The beach, white and wide, was mostly populated by local Brazilians.

"I believe you're right," I agreed, looking around. Nobody paid any attention to us. It was a young crowd.

"Put your wallet in your front pocket!" Marcello instructed after two teenage boys splashed past us. "Many are well-practiced pickpockets. One runs into you while the other grabs your wallet."

"And then they run away at Olympic speed, not possible to catch." I had already sequestered my wallet in a front pocket, always a necessary precaution in South America. Beautiful Rio was especially notorious for aggressive pickpockets.

"Voce compreende," Marcello blurted in Portuguese, confirming that I understood.

By the time we were thoroughly wet from the knees down, Marcello wanted to get back to the business conversation we'd been having at dinner, prior to charging across Atlantica Avenue onto Copacabana beach.

"So, how much will it cost to build a starter-culture factory down here?" He asked me as we sloshed along.

"Using fermentation and processing equipment from the USA in an existing dairy facility in Brazil, three million U.S. dollars."

"Hmm, so much?"

"The freeze drier, centrifuge, and ultra-sterilizer will cost half of that, leaving the other half for fermentation tanks and hookup." I explained.

"You need to tell that to Carlo tomorrow—discuss the details." Carlo Ricci was Marcello Lotti's business partner in Milan, Italy but they also had businesses in Brazil and Argentina. Both men had discussed splitting the investment.

A starter-culture production factory makes the inoculum or "starter" that initiates the production of cheese, yogurt, and other fermented foods. The factory we were discussing could also produce probiotics for animals and humans—beneficial bacteria that keep their guts healthy. Marcello and I were prepping for the meeting with Carlo while plowing water in the Atlantic Ocean.

After we had traversed Copacabana beach, coming to the rocks that separated it from Ipanema Beach, Marcello was ready to sit down somewhere and dry off. We found a café that accepted two businessmen wet from their knees down. Here we did get looks from some of the elderly patrons—we just smiled and waved to them.

I ordered a Campari and tonic; Marcello had hot chocolate with cookies— a delayed dessert. He lived with his wife and two young daughters in New York City but travelled to Europe and South America frequently, always watching over the Lotti family's money. He had a nervous curiosity about technology and always wanted the "full details."

"Tell me again about the Cochineal bugs that color Campari," he asked me as I took a drink of the red bittersweet, highball.

"There is a species of scale insect that lives in the tropics—more of a fly than a beetle. In Mexico it feeds on the prickly pear cactus, only the females produce color. The insects are dried, crushed, and boiled in water; the resulting dull-red solution is then filtered to remove the insect bodies. When alum is added, bright red carmine forms. It takes seventy-thousand insects to make one pound of carmine—or carminic acid—a natural, red food color."

"Amazing," Marcello said, then took a bite out of a cookie.

I had another Campari and tonic while Marcello followed his hot chocolate with a bottle of water. He wanted to talk about water purification next and had many questions about how my company used microbes to purify water. I finished the red-bug-juice cocktail while we discussed it.

"Let's walk while we talk," he suggested. "We can walk to the hotel—it's not that far."

"Sure, it's a fine evening," I agreed, checking my wallet's location. We were staying at the Marina Hotel on Leblon beach, beyond Ipanema in the shadow of the Twin Brothers—a healthy walk.

When we arrived at the hotel it was dark, but Marcello was still full of energy and so was I. His questions were catalytic. Marcello was not a scientist but asked questions more cutting-edge than many from PhD scientists I knew. Our discussion had turned to Carl Sagan and cosmology.

"Let's go up on the roof and look at the galaxy," he insisted. The sky was clear, and the hotel was quiet compared to those near Copacabana beach.

The elevator to the roof was slow and sounded like it needed an overhaul; we could hear cables straining. Not being a fan of elevators, I was relieved when the doors opened to the observation deck on the roof. We were not alone. Two couples were looking out at the sky over the Atlantic Ocean—away from the lights of Rio. The older couple, hearing the elevator open, turned, stared for a moment, then motioned for us to come over. The man, wearing a look of astonishment, pointed to several lights in the sky and said something in Portuguese to Marcello.

There were three circular, white lights that formed a large triangle suspended over the ocean. When I looked carefully, I could see they were connected to a massive dark object. Suddenly, a fourth light came on, much brighter; emanating from underneath the object, illuminating the water.

Whatever we were looking at was huge. A monstrous, triangular something suspended over the ocean—at least a thousand feet in length. I was shaking—somewhere between excited and disbelieving. Remembering what a brilliant chemist, Mr. Fred Portz, would say when mentoring me years ago: "Don't believe what anybody tells you and only half of what you see." Fred, a true genius, had an IQ estimated at 180.

Marcello was talking to the older man in Portuguese. The man's wife remained silent. She was older too, and I just assumed she was his wife. Then the younger couple came over, not looking astonished or even surprised.

"Grande!" The young lady said pointing at it. "Muito grande."

The young man with her shrugged his shoulders. "Estrangeiros," he mumbled matter-of-factly, not looking very concerned. Translation: Aliens.

Marcello translated what the older man had explained: "We were watching it for thirty minutes before you two arrived. Two fishing boats were out there when the triangular craft first appeared. Now they're gone!"

We kept watching . . . I could feel my heart beating. Was this an evolved version of what the Germans developed during World War II? Or was it truly alien—extraterrestrial? I'd seen mystery lights in the sky on other trips, but none that were attached to anything the size of an aircraft carrier that could fly.

The massive craft suspended motionless for another ten minutes, scanning the surface of the ocean with its spotlight, which had turned blue. The light made the dark craft glow—creating an indigo shine. Listening carefully, I could hear a faint, low frequency thumping sound. When the sound stopped, as we all watched, it tilted toward us and slid into the ocean.

"This is incredible," Marcello mumbled, totally astonished. My brain resonated inside my head—its hippocampus had been activated. I would never forget this.

Marcello couldn't take his eyes off where the craft had entered the ocean. A minute passed before a massive wave—as wide as the craft—rolled onto the beach well beyond the high-tide mark, presumably equaling the volume of water the UFO had displaced. But now it was a USO—an Unidentified Submersible Object.

My mind was in search mode for an explanation based on what I'd learned from my astrophysicist buddies. Intellectual jam sessions with them had helped me sort out many scientific "mysteries." I recalled seeing reports describing how the Nazis had reverse-engineered crashed alien saucers and produced working prototypes—but nothing as massive as what we'd just seen. However, that was over fifty years ago. Had the Nazis made improvements somewhere? Or, was this truly an alien craft—possibly a mothership? And what happened to the two fishing boats? Haunting questions!

Carlo met us for breakfast at the hotel the next morning. He was tall, very Italian, and reminded me of Salvatore Tessio in The Godfather. His long face and penetrating eyes were guarded by dark eyebrows above a powerful nose that partly hid a faint mustache. A serious-looking man who unexpectedly came with a charming demeanor, he hugged and backslapped Marcello then introduced himself to me.

"Tell me about the aliens!" he insisted. Marcello had called him last night and explained what we'd seen. "I would appreciate an assessment from the world-traveling scientist."

"Well, what I saw was daunting and disquieting to say the least. It kept me up most of the night making notes. Six of us witnessed the sight; it was no apparition. A formidable wave hit the beach shortly after it submerged."

"But we didn't see any little green men with scales and lizard eyes come out of it," Marcello said, raising his hand for a server to come over with a large tray of Brazilian pastries. Many of the customized sweet rolls were too exotic to resist. I was taken in by a large Danish pastry covered with sliced red peaches. A second server brought us three espressos.

I recounted as many of the craft's details as I could remember. Carlo was fascinated; the size of it surprised him the most.

"Marcello and I talked late last night, probably while you were up writing your notes. I have some questions about building the culture factory that we can talk about later—but I want to stay on this UFO thing right now. Is there any chance what you saw is part of an American black project, above top secret and not acknowledged?"

"There is that chance," I answered.

"What kind of technology are we talking about?" Carlo asked. Marcello was busy consuming a sweet roll stuffed with some local jam concoction, listening intently. I got the impression Carlo was testing me.

"Anti-gravity technology for sure, possibly employing monopolar, highly-magnetic liquid metals in cylinders that rotate around each other. These could propel the craft by isolating it from earth's gravity. And frequency-modulated, high-strength alloys for the craft's exterior construction, like magnesium layered with bismuth." I stopped there, but could have said more, recalling details from a lecture I attended last year in Palo Alto, California.

"If it was from a U.S. black project—when and where did it start?" Marcello asked.

"The Nazis got the secret from the aliens, then built prototypes (flying saucers) and hid them in Antarctica, allegedly." I said.

"When would this have happened?" Marcello asked, wiping the mystery jam off his cheek.

"In the 1930s and during World War II," Carlo was quick to answer. "One year after the war ended, the U.S. sent a major naval force to Antarctica in 1946." Carlo was animated now, surprising me with his knowledge. "The operation involved five thousand men and was called Operation High Jump. I'd read about it in the newspapers in Milano—in my younger days."

I shouldn't have been surprised by Carlo's knowledge—he was twenty years senior to Marcello and me and had grown up in Italy during WW II.

"Admiral Richard Byrd commanded the operation, twenty-six aircraft and thirteen warships, one an aircraft carrier," I added. "Not a minor campaign!"

"Never heard about this," Marcello said, holding three fingers up for the waitress to see. Then he pointed to our espressos, assuring this would stay a highly-caffeinated discussion.

"You were in diapers in 1946!" Carlo quipped, smiling at Marcello.

"How did the Americans explain such postwar activity?" Marcello wondered.

"Officially at first—in the newspapers: to explore Antarctica for coal and claim land for the United States. Unofficially—highly classified: to look for the Nazis and their flying saucers," Carlo certified. He remembered a lot from those newspapers fifty years ago!

"So, what happened? Were there casualties? Did the U.S. win?" Marcello asked, sipping a fresh espresso.

"Here's where the mystery comes in," I explained. "The massive operation's secret mission was hurriedly ordered by President Truman. At first, he even kept the Joint Chiefs of Staff out of the loop. Later, intentional leaks explained the classified mission's 'true purpose' as a training exercise for fighting the Russians in the arctic if they tried to attack the U.S. by crossing the North Pole. Bad weather in Canada was blamed for having to redirect the training mission to Antarctica—just a mere 12,430-mile detour. Why should that make the average person question anything? We had just won World War II."

"Keep going; I'm anxious to hear more," Carlo insisted.

I continued explaining: "Allegedly, the Germans ambushed the American fleet after it entered the Weddel Sea in Antarctica. Large disc-shaped Nazi aircraft propelled by anti-gravity engines and armed with laser-beam weapons emerged from the sea. U.S. P-51 Mustangs were no match for them; several P-51s were shot down and the pilots killed. Some of the ships including the aircraft carrier, The Philippine Sea, suffered damage. Deathbed testimonies later revealed that the Nazi saucers had attained speeds over four thousand miles per hour and were able to make sudden stops and turns at that speed.

The overwhelmed American fleet was escorted out of Antarctic waters by the Nazis and sent home months early. Bad weather was reported as the cause for the early curtailment of the mission." I paused and drank some espresso. My mind was still trying resolve what the Nazis developed with what Marcello and I had witnessed last night.

"In his last speech shortly before he died mysteriously, Admiral Byrd warned that the United States was in danger of 'being attacked by fighters that are able to fly from one pole to the other with incredible speed,'" I added. Carlo nodded and sipped his espresso, Marcello stared at his cup in disbelief.

I could see Marcello was overflowing with questions. "When and how did the U.S. get reconnected to this incredulous story?" He asked me. Carlo was smiling like he knew but wanted me to answer.

"It's not clear to me when the U.S. got in on the Nazi's critical technical secrets—probably in Truman's second term between 1948 and 1952 when food and fuel stopped being resupplied to the Germans in Antarctica. Neither is it clear to me what became of the Nazi operatives in Antarctica. I would guess they were brought to the U.S. as part of "Operation Paperclip" which sent many of the German rocket scientists to the U.S. directly from Germany. The translated reports summarized by my physicist buddies didn't cover this. The important takeaway fact for me is that many UFO sightings are of the home-grown variety, mostly of U.S. origin now. But not all of them!"

After the lively UFO discussion, it was obvious that Marcello was strongly affected. The information had hit him like a kick in the head. For the first time in his life—fifty years on planet earth—Marcello knew that both aliens and UFOs—and USOs—are for real.

Carlo's driver was talking with the concierge when the three of us exited the hotel's breakfast restaurant and entered the lobby. Lucas immediately came to attention and saluted Carlo who told him, "o escritorio," indicating he wanted to go to the office. It only took Lucas a few minutes to bring Carlo's BMW around to the front door.

The drive through Rio's environs was always interesting. Lucas took us past the Jardim Botanico and onto the Rua Sao Clemente which lead to the office complex; Corcovado Mountain was off to our left.

Carlo's large office was filled with futebol (soccer) memorabilia including a framed picture of him standing with Brazil's 1994 World Cup winning team. Next to several autographed soccer balls were several skiing photos of Carlo with Marcello. I recognized the mountains.

"Cortina?" I asked, pointing to the skiing photos.

"Did he punish you in that place too?" Carlo questioned. The ski slopes in the Italian Alps were beautiful but challenging. What's called a blue slope in the Alps is a Black Diamond in Colorado. On my best days, I'm an average skier; Marcello could have skied in the Olympics!

"Yup," I replied to Carlo. "He would race down at light speed and dare me to keep up. Once I lost sight of him and took a wrong turn that ended up in a snow-filled valley with no lift. He had to send a snow machine to come get me."

Carlo laughed. "He did that to me in Switzerland!" Marcello just smiled. He was reading the signatures on the soccer balls.

After one of the secretaries rounded up Carlo's engineering team, I started a slide presentation showing photographs and diagrams of a starter-culture factory I had designed in Wisconsin. His engineers spoke English and followed everything I said. Three hours went by fast. I was happy the Italian slide projector behaved itself.

"I don't see any reason why we shouldn't make the investment," Carlo declared, looking at Marcello who nodded. Everyone was excited to get started. I was pleased.

"We better take lunch, it looks like Marcello's blood sugar needs a boost," Carlo deduced. We both knew Marcello was hypoglycemic and often needed to be resupplied with carbs to prevent a low blood sugar attack.

"If you ate more protein and less carbs as your normal diet you could eliminate your attacks." Carlo advised him. I nodded.

"Whenever my blood sugar goes below seventy mg/dl I need something sweet fast," Marcello replied.

"Try phasing out the sweets and eat more protein before that happens." I recommended. "But keep glucose pills handy just in case." Marcello nodded. He knew all this, it was the right thing for all the other hypoglycemics to do.

Lucas had the BMW idling with the air conditioner on high when we exited the office building. Carlo gave him instructions and we were off to the Churrascaria Palace restaurant in Copacabana.

The restaurant was a meat lovers' paradise, a truly authentic Brazilian barbeque experience. A cart with an assortment of grilled meats was brought to our table and meat was sliced off from sword-length skewers. An assortment of vegetables was brought out by other servers. The atmosphere was straight out of Lisbon—quaint with old-world traditions.

Marcello and Carlo were true red-meat lovers, I was too, but over the last couple of years I'd skewed my diet toward more seafood. But Marcello and Carlo insisted I start with Brazil's famous grilled picanha—the beef-sirloin cap grilled over a wood fire. Butchers in the U.S. break the sirloin cap into smaller cuts which changes the dynamics of how the fat melds with the meat during grilling. When done right and sliced thinly, the outer quarter inch of a slice is well done while the inner portion is rare or medium rare, resembling lightly grilled Ahi tuna. It was excellent!

"Have you ever been to the top of Corcovado?" Carlo asked me.

"No, the one other time I was in Rio everything was a big rush; no time for sightseeing," I said.

"Come on, let's change that." Carlo announced. Marcello agreed.

The red, electric Rack Railway took us to the top of Corcovado Mountain (Monte Cristo) in twenty minutes—2,330 feet. It's a solid granite dome that is literally the center of attraction in Rio de Janeiro. Then, thanks to elevators and escalators, we avoided walking the 223 steps to the observation deck at the foot of the statue of Jesus: Christ the Redeemer, 125 feet tall, with arms spread wide. The view of central Rio, its parks, beaches, and Sugarloaf Mountain with the blue Atlantic in the background was spectacular enough to even impress Albert Einstein.

"Do you think he knows about the aliens?" Marcello asked Carlo, looking up at the commanding statue of Jesus. Both Marcello and Carlo were Roman Catholics.

"How would your physics experts answer that?" Carlo cleverly diverted the question to me.

"The ones I associate with know the universe is more complex than we ever imagined and possesses undiscovered forces and dimensions that wrap around and through our perceived reality—where the microcosm of subatomic complexity parallels that of the galactic macrocosm. Their conclusion: statistical sigma values of multiple cosmic parameters overwhelmingly indicate that sentient life is not an aberration—it requires an intelligent creation process—from The Source." What I find amusing is how many scientists dismiss this while accepting that once-upon-a-time all the hundreds of billions of galaxies in the universe were stuffed into an object smaller than a pinhead—that just happened to explode one day creating everything without any help (The Big Bang).

"Interesting, but you didn't answer Marcello's question," Carlo replied.

"I'll try harder. There are myriad forms of sentient life in the universe. Human beings, Homo sapiens, exist here on Earth in a restricted reality—one where the laws of physics operate within four dimensions (three spatial, plus time). The human mission is to thrive within these restrictions and constraints. Some do, some don't—much depends on how a person exercises free will, but 'luck' is also involved. Our souls agreed to this in advance of coming here.

"Jesus is from a group of avatars that represent The Source. They have the power to redeem humanity from the restrictions, constraints, and sins of this world. These avatars are immortal, intrinsically benevolent allies of humanity. Most exist only as spirits and have never lived in human form, like the Holy Spirit. Jesus is an exception. You can call them gods or angels instead; it doesn't matter—don't let semantics cloud your thinking.

"Humans, with their limitations and emotional intelligence, represent an exceptional way to exist in this world of restricted reality. We crave the challenges of mortal life and have souls. This is not true for hybrid androids and robotic droids and other artificial intelligences that crave nothing, have no souls, and simply follow programs—ultimately winding up obsolete in the junkyards of the universe."

"Bravo!" Carlo clapped as he hugged two women he didn't know. They had heard what I said and were crying.

"This makes perfect sense," Marcello said. "An android or robot wouldn't enjoy skiing, they would be programmed not to fall; and every kick in a soccer game would be a score or predictable miss."

"And you wouldn't find one interested in catching a thousand-pound Marlin. Or hiking in the mountains just because they're there. Or playing a guitar, experiencing the satisfaction of making fewer and fewer mistakes the more you played. Or any of the thousands of other activities humans do for joy, happiness, and love," I elaborated.

"Simply stated: Authentic joy, happiness, and love can't be programmed; they must come from living a mortal life." Marcello asserted.

"This tells me Jesus knows all about the aliens; the fact that they exist is proof enough for me that he exists. Where there is advanced strangeness there must also be perfect divinity," Carlo affirmed. "Meaningful evolution stopped with Homo sapiens. Christ is our redeemer!"

After returning to sea level on Corcovado's Red Railway, I could see that Carlo and Marcello were deep in thought. We walked without talking to the parking lot where Carlo signaled Lucas to start the BMW.

"I wonder how much the Vatican knows about all this?" Carlo asked, breaking the silence, looking northeast.

"They must know." Marcello shrugged his shoulders.

"They have an advanced telescope on a mountain in Arizona," I said.

"Really?" Carlo raised his eyebrows.

"Yes! It's called the Vatican Advanced Technology Telescope— VATT for short; it has a variety of capabilities including viewing in infrared."

Marcello looked at Carlo, then they both looked at me. Several quiet moments passed.

"You've seen it?" Carlo asked me.

"Yes sir, it's on Mount Graham not far from Mexico."

"This calls for a walk in the ocean," Marcello declared, stepping into the BMW.

Carlo nodded, and looked at me. I pointed to my ocean-proven shoes.

"Para a praia," he told Lucas. "Take us to the beach."

Postscript:

Between the sixth and eighth of March in 1981, a certain meeting was allegedly held at Camp David, Maryland. William Casey, then director of the CIA, and a team of four advisors and one special officer, the Caretaker, briefed President Ronald Reagan and Vice President George H.W. Bush on a subject classified as Above Top Secret (ATS). A tape recording of the briefing was transcribed into a written document. I believe this briefing occurred, so I'm including a shortened version of it here in this postscript; it has about an equal number of believers versus skeptics. This is not surprising considering the revolutionary information it contains—if true, it will rewrite the history of mankind. The topic of the alleged presidential briefing: Unidentified Flying Objects and Extraterrestrial Visitation of Earth.

The full transcript of this "Reagan Briefing" can be found on the Internet on Lynda Moulton Howe's comprehensive website www. earthfiles.com and in other places. What follows is my excerpted version, a "brief of the briefing." For brevity, I have removed introductions, most procedural formalities, redundancies, and superfluous details. Actual excerpts of the alleged briefing are in quote marks. Text paraphrased or summarized by me is not quoted but preceded by my first name, "Stanley."

I put this in the postscript in an effort to add perspective to the alien (ET) issue which is as hot a topic today as it was in March of 1981. The validity of the briefing is up to you, the reader, to decide. Obviously, it has not been confirmed by the United States Government.

A Brief of the Alleged Reagan Briefing:

THE CARETAKER: "The United States of America has been visited by Extraterrestrial Visitors since 1947. We have proof of that. However, we also have some proof that Earth has been visited for many thousands of years by various races of Extraterrestrial Visitors."

STANLEY: The Caretaker also refers to them as ETs. He mentions that during a storm two ET spacecraft crashed in New Mexico in July of 1947, and the U.S. recovered the debris and one live alien designated EBE-1.

PRESIDENT REAGAN: "What does that mean? Do we have codes or a special terminology for this?"

STANLEY: The Caretaker answers and then explains that five dead aliens along with the one living alien were recovered with the first craft (the Roswell Incident). The second craft wasn't discovered until 1949. Four additional alien bodies were found with it—they were mutilated and decomposed.

PRESIDENT REAGAN: "Can we classify them? I mean can we . . . well, connect them with anything Earthly?"

CARETAKER: "No, Mr. President. They don't have any similar characteristics of a human, with the exception of their eyes, ears, and a mouth. Their internal body organs are different."

STANLEY: The Caretaker goes on to explain that their breathing is different, their blood isn't red, their skin is nothing like human skin, and they have two eyelids (suggesting a bright home planet).

PRESIDENT REAGAN: Maybe I'm getting ahead, but do we know where they came from? Mars, our system, or where?"

CARETAKER: "Yes, Mr. President, we do know where they come from. I can do this now, or I can wait until it comes up in the briefing."

STANLEY: The President agrees to wait for the answer. The Caretaker explains that EBE-1 died of natural causes in 1952. In the five years he lived on Earth, we learned a great deal from him. Yes, these ETs or EBENs have males and females. U.S. military personnel were responsible for the safety and care of EBE-1.

A communication device that survived the crash was repaired by EBE-1 and used to contact his home planet in the star system Zeta Reticuli—forty light-years from earth. If a spaceship traveled at light-speed (186,000 miles per second—not possible according to Einstein), it would take forty years to get to Earth. Obviously, there is a hole somewhere in our physics—like a space tunnel (or large wormhole) shortcut! And, obviously, the communication device had to have supernatural properties.

Reagan has other questions that the Caretaker wants to postpone answering for a separate briefing due to compartmentalization of the information.

PRESIDENT REAGAN: "As the President of the United States, I should know everything, right, or shouldn't I? If I was to assume this was a briefing of substance, then I should hear it all. This is more important than some other things on my calendar."

STANLEY: Around this time William Casey has to settle Reagan down, explaining that the Caretaker and the advisers have to follow a particular sequence for the briefing— that there are many levels of compartmentalization. And, yes, he could hear it all, now or later.

PRESIDENT REAGAN: "Advisor #1, what do you think? "Do you know about all this?"

ADVISOR #1: "Mr. President, yes, I was briefed many times on this subject matter. As Director Casey stated, this is a very, very complicated subject. I think it took me about one year to be fully briefed into all aspects of this matter. There are different areas. The initial crash, an investigative period, some attempt to contact, a disinformation operation to protect this matter, and several other levels."

PRESIDENT REAGAN: "Oh, wow, I didn't realize how complicated it was."

STANLEY: I cut Reagan's commentary short at this point and didn't include Casey's; both were apologetic and non-substantive. The briefing continues.

CARETAKER: "It took the ET spaceship nine of our months to travel forty light-years. It was estimated that they were hundreds if not thousands of Earth-years ahead of us technically."

STANLEY: Here is where the Caretaker discusses space-tunnel technology and Regan gets confused and brings in black holes. Several people are speaking at once, probably including George H. W. Bush which would have been his first comments. It must have been hard to transcribe the tape at this point.

Next, the briefing gets into the Truman and Eisenhower administrations and what they knew about a secret group Truman had formed: Majority 12 (also known as Majestic 12 and MJ 12)—composed mainly of top scientists and generals who would analyze and advise on ET matters. In 1953 the Eisenhower administration formed Project Gleem displacing MJ 12, and in 1966 it became Project Aquarius under the Johnson administration. Its name changed, but the mission stayed the same: Keep up with what is going on with the alien presence and focus on what dangers they might present to our existence. The air force "officially" closed its Project Bluebook in 1969. It had collected a plethora of mostly bogus UFO and/or ET incidents that served to disorient the masses. Thinking any of these were real branded you a nutcase. Once that was established they could hide many things in plain sight.

This is all explained to Reagan who apparently was unaware of most of it—in March of 1981 he had only been president for forty-five days! Russia and the cold war had been mostly on his mind before the briefing started.

STANLEY: So far everything I've summarized about the Reagan briefing can be verified by other authenticated sources. But from this point on, the story gets somewhat harder to verify using separate sources. Purportedly, there have been incidents in Russia that parallel saucer crashes in the U.S. and elsewhere.

Facts obtained from EBE-1 regarding his home planet are interesting. What follows is some of that dialogue; what is reported in quotes is direct from the alleged transcript.

PRESIDENT REAGAN: "I have a lot of questions, so let me ask a few and then we can move on. I guess the first question I have is their lifespan. How old is EBE-1?"

CARETAKER: "Mr. President, their life span is between three hundred and fifty to four hundred years, but that is Earth years."

PRESIDENT REAGAN: "Is time the same on their planet as on ours?"

CARETAKER: "No Mr. President, time is very different on the Eben planet, which, by the way, we call Serpo. Their day is approximately forty hours. That is measured by the movement of their two suns."

PRESIDENT REAGAN: "Oh, well, your answer creates more questions. Okay, as I understand it, their planet has two suns. Wouldn't that mean the planet was hot? I guess that explains their eyes having two eyelids."

WILLIAM CASEY: "Yes, Mr. President, I think we are getting way ahead of ourselves. We have all that information about the visitor's planet, but we would have to present that information in a different briefing."

STANLEY: Reagan concedes, but it's clear he's irritated. Casey wants to move the briefing along.

WILLIAM CASEY: "Mr. President, the Soviet Union has had their contacts with aliens. We have a great deal of intelligence that would indicate the Soviets had their 'Roswell,' so to speak. What they know is about the same as we know. They had some bodies back in the late fifties, but our intelligence would indicate the species of aliens were different."

PRESIDENT REAGAN: "Okay, well, then Bill, that presents a very disturbing feeling for me. Are you telling me there are different races or species, as you said, visiting Earth at the same time?"

STANLEY: Casey diverts the question to the Caretaker who hesitates to answer it, because it involves a different classification of information requiring a different briefing session. That horse didn't ride well for Reagan.

PRESIDENT REAGAN: "Just answer the simple question of how many different species, don't go into details."

CARETAKER: "Mr. Director?" he asks, looking at Casey for permission.

WILLIAM CASEY: "Go ahead Caretaker, answer the President's question."

CARETAKER: "At least five."

PRESIDENT REAGAN: "Are they all friendly?"

CARETAKER: "Mr. Director?" Again, asking for permission.

WILLIAM CASEY: "Advisor #1, would you like to step in here?"

ADVISOR #1: "That is a very difficult question to answer."

STANLEY: Advisor #1 answers in a long paragraph with a disclaimer that admits they have little information on four of the five alien species, and what they do have they got from the friendly Ebens (EBE-1 et al). He ended with these alarming words:

ADVISOR #1: "Mr. President, and please don't misunderstand my words, but we think one of the species is very hostile."

PRESIDENT REAGAN: "For Christ sakes. I'm President of the United States. I should know if we are endangered by some threat from outer space. If you have something to say about a threat posed by this one species of aliens, then I want to hear it."

WILLIAM CASEY: "Mr. President, we have intelligence that would indicate this one species of aliens have abducted people from earth. They have performed scientific and medical tests on these humans. To the best of our knowledge no humans have been killed. We have captured one of these hostile aliens."

STANLEY: At this stage Casey recommends that they move on with the briefing and that Reagan hold questions about the hostile alien for later. Reagan agrees.

PRESIDENT REAGAN: Okay, let us continue. How many other presidents received this briefing?"

284

CARETAKER: Mr. President, I have briefed President Nixon, Ford, and you. President Carter was never given the entire briefing.

PRESIDENT REAGAN: "Well, knowing that guy, he probably couldn't understand it being from Georgia! (laughter heard in the room)."

ADVISOR #1: "Mr. President, I can give you some details on an incident that occurred inside the Soviet Union in 1970."

WILLIAM CASEY: "Do we want to go there?"

ADVISOR #4: "May I say something, Mr. Director?"

WILLIAM CASEY: "Go ahead, Advisor #4, step in."

ADVISOR #4: "I think this particular incident inside the Soviet Union will give the president an example of what the world has and will experience in the future."

STANLEY: A detailed explanation and dialogue ensues. U.S. intelligence had picked up voice transmissions between Soviet Air Defense pilots and ground controllers as a number of UFOs were being chased by Soviet pilots. It started over Siberia and ended over the Black Sea. Literally thousands of witnesses saw twenty different fighter planes chasing UFOs. The whole episode happened over the course of a week, and it's believed the hostile aliens were involved.

The briefing continues, and it is explained that only nuclear weapons would have any effect on the aliens in a fight. Apparently nuclear detonations punch holes in space-time when matter is converted to energy by Einstein's equation, $E = mc^2$. This could create cause misalignment of the space tunnels, time fluctuations, and other bad things.

To the surprise of the president, the Caretaker provides the names of the five races of aliens that had been assigned by the U.S. intelligence community: The Ebens (friendly), Archquloids, Quadloids, Heplaloids, and Trantaloids (hostile). Casey informs the president that we had a Trantaloid. It was captured it in 1961 in Canada and it lived in captivity until 1962, when it died. They would provide a photograph in a separate meeting. They were able to get the location of the Trantaloid's home planet—the third planet out from the star Epsilon Eridani in the constellation Eridanus, 10.5 light-years from Earth.

The briefing continues: Casey and the Caretaker explained the difficulties they had in communicating with the Ebens. It took five years to learn their language, which was tonal—they communicated in tones, not words. EBE-1 helped, but he was a mechanic, not a linguist or a scientist. It was easier for him to learn English than for us to learn his language. The briefing of the president is now thick with details regarding the communication process, which had to subvert the forty-light-year hurdle just as their spacecraft did. The repaired (by EBE-1) communication device from the crashed saucer was the only reason we could communicate with the Ebens on planet Serpo. After EBE-1 died, our technicians had learned enough to use the device. The last message received suggested a meeting in New Mexico near the coordinates of the crash site, coordinates the Ebens knew. The message mentioned an exchange program! Recall the 1977 movie Close Encounters of the Third Kind starring Richard Dreyfuss. Hmm . . . what did Steven Spielberg know back then?

This is a lot for the president to absorb, but he insists they continue after excusing himself to take a phone call.

WILLIAM CASEY: "Mr. President, this is where things get very interesting."

PRESIDENT REAGAN: "Okay, I'm waiting . . . (next comment not understood).

CARETAKER: "Our government, specifically MJ-12, met in secret to plan the exchange event. We had just about twenty-five months from the time we received their message to prepare for their arrival. Several months into the planning, President Kennedy decided to approve a plan to exchange a special military team. The USAF (United States Air Force) was tasked as the lead agency.

"The USAF officials picked special civilian scientists to assist in the planning and crew selection. It took months for the planners to decide on the selection criteria for each team member. They decided that each team member must be military, single, no children, and a career member. They had to be trained in different skills."

STANLEY: There is then an exchange between Casey and the President regarding how deep into detail they should go, their time available, etc. The Caretaker is allowed to continue.

CARETAKER: "Mr. President, a team of twelve men were selected. However, during this time period, President Kennedy died. The nation was shocked as you know."

STANLEY: This could put new light on why he was assassinated.

PRESIDENT REAGAN: "Yes, everyone was shocked. I can guess what must have happened during the project when John died."

CARETAKER: "President Johnson continued the program. When it came time for the meeting we were ready. The landing occurred in New Mexico and we greeted the Ebens. However, a mix-up happened. They were not prepared to accept our exchange personnel. Everything was placed on hold. Finally, in 1965, the Ebens landed in Nevada, and we exchanged twelve of our men for one of theirs."

PRESIDENT REAGAN: "One, why just one? Was he their ambassador?"

WILLIAM CASEY: "Well, something like that. We just called it EBE-2. We'll discuss that later."

CARETAKER: "Mr. President. Our team of twelve went to the Eben planet Serpo for thirteen years. The original mission called for a ten-year stay. However, because of the strange time periods on their planet, the team stayed three additional years. Eight (seven alive) returned in 1978. Two died on the planet, and two decided to stay."

I recommend that interested readers search the Internet for the complete briefing. Reagan alluded to it in his personal notes after he left the presidency and, cleverly, in some of his speeches. Purportedly, he also discussed it with Mikhail Gorbachev.

La tour Eiffel in Paree

14

Remembering Paris
As a Child, College Student, and Professional Scientist

Prologue:

Petite Beauregard was a housing project outside Paris built for U.S. Military families stationed in France after World War II. My Aunt Jeanette, Cousin Ed, and Uncle, Major Donald Fallin, called it home for three years in the 1950s. As the oldest of three siblings, I got the nod to join my parents to visit the Fallins in December of 1956.

It was to be an exceptional vacation for an eleven-year-old. "The trip of a lifetime," to quote my mother who reminded me often of this before we left Milwaukee. Mom had never been out of Wisconsin and had to explain to our neighbors that it was indeed, Paris, France, where we were going, not Paris, Illinois.

My father's annual salary of six thousand dollars as a policeman in the West Allis Police Department hardly provided extra funds for European vacations. No credit cards were around in those good old days—we were the talk of the neighborhood! Little did I know then that Paris, France would become a frequent destination for me in future years.

Years later, while sitting outside at the Café de la Paix on Place de l' Opéra enjoying a Campari and tonic, I recalled my first memories of Paris, amazed by how indelible they still were. Lucid awareness of subtleties the mind wouldn't preserve when experienced as an adult, had imprinted distinctly as a child.

Paris, December 1956

The window was filled with Dinky toys—model cars, trucks, and airplanes. They were expensive, so we could each pick only one. I pointed to the small Citroën coupe, a toy car that matched a real one parked on the street. My cousin Ed pointed to a gray Mercedes replica which was twice the size of the Citroen and cost twice as much. My uncle nodded, opened the door and we went inside the toy store.

Ed and I showed the shopkeeper our selections. Then, after collecting thirty francs from the Major, he retrieved our selected toy cars from the window.

Ed and I rushed out the door with our cars, spinning their wheels with our hands, testing rotation. They were not painted in bright colors but in shades of gray, like real cars outside. They were made of metal that didn't bend, even if you pressed hard. I remember the smell of the paint the toymakers used. The roof of my Citroen was black, pretending to be a canvas top that could open; Ed's Mercedes had shining silver bumpers. Both had hard rubber wheels that spun fast!

We hurried to race them on the sidewalk outside the store, but a command from Major Fallin stopped us: "Let's go, boys; you can play with them by the boat locks."

"Yes, sir," we both replied, knowing to not dispute an order from the Major! Ed's upbringing was ingrained with strict military manners, and I was told to abide by them when visiting—by a policeman (my dad)!

Ed and I sat in the back seat wide-eyed and excited waiting to see the locks that lifted boats. I had no idea what a lock was, but I loved boats.

"What's the river's name Stanley?" My uncle asked, testing me. We were on a road following it.

"It's the Seine, sir."

"Affirmative!" He replied. "We're going to Bougival where there's a lock that lifts boats. The Seine in Paris is higher than the ocean, so boats coming from the sea must be lifted up."

"How do they do that?" I asked.

"You'll see!" my uncle answered, driving on as Eddie and I, goofing around, drove our model cars over, under, and around each other in the back seat. Ed was gleeful that he had the bigger vehicle.

When we got to the locks, my uncle parked the car and told us to get out and go up to the fence and watch. At the fence overlooking the water, he pointed to a small cruise ship and said it was being lifted, but to me, it looked like it was just floating in the water in a long cement channel—going nowhere.

"See those giant gates on each end of the lock?" My uncle pointed left then right. I understood now that the channel was a lock, and the gates were solid steel doors. "Paris is eighty feet above sea level; the gate on the right will open when the cruise ship floats to that height from river water filling the lock."

I'd never seen this before. Apparently, Ed had, because he'd quit watching the cruise ship and had begun racing his Mercedes into a dozen pigeons that were pecking earthworms off the wet walkway next to the fence. Instantly, the birds took flight in all directions. Some flew into each other and feathers came off. I could see my uncle hiding a smile as he disciplined Edward, who was two years my junior at nine years old. The Major didn't call him Eddie, mostly just Ed or Son, Edward if he was mad. My aunt called him Eddie. I called him whatever came out of my mouth first without thinking about it.

We watched until the gate on the right opened, first with a loud, laboring creak, then a steady sloshing sound like a rotating cement truck makes. When the gate was fully open, the cruise ship's high-pitched horns vibrated the fence—then the ship moved on in the direction of Paris.

When it started to rain, I could smell the unmistakable odor of earthworms stranded on concrete pavement. An old man on a bicycle rode past us with an unwrapped loaf of bread in the bike's basket, its fat tires spattered muddy water on the bread while crushing worms the pigeons had missed. The man wore a flat, black hat and

291

an old black coat with brown patches on the elbows—he didn't seem to mind the rain.

We were the only ones watching the cruise ship leave the lock when my uncle ordered us back in the car. Everything was gray and smelled wet as we drove away.

"After lunch, I'll be taking you boys on the Metro to a place that sells everything. Maybe we can find some second-hand Dinkies— better than your new ones for chasing pigeons!" There must have been a gene in parents back then that coded for taking care of one's new toys—my mother would have said the same thing!

"Stanley! We're going to the big flea market." Ed, the fourth-grader grinned—wider and bigger than the sixth-grader (me). "They sell old guns there too!"

Paris, May 7, 1968—eleven years later:

"Zummmm . . . click, click, click. Zummmm . . . click, click, click" approximated the mesmerizing sound of Le Metro. Sometimes the "clicks" were "clacks" where the track was older. We got on it at Les Halles and were heading north under Paris to Porte de Clignancourt. I was with my fraternity brother, Jim Trebatsky (nicknamed Treb), and geology professor, Norman Catell (affectionately known as: "Normal Norman"), on a three-week customized student tour that began in London and would finish in Morocco. We were "Pointers" from the University of Wisconsin at Stevens Point.

Norman was dressed like a professor on vacation in Paris should dress; in a new pink shirt and a blue sport coat he'd bought yesterday at the Printemps department store in Place d' Italie. He looked good—approachable. Treb and I wore UWSP sweatshirts and Pointer baseball caps, branding us as unapproachable Americans from an unknown place in the Wild West where all men were cowboys.

A genetics professor had told me that age twenty-three was magic because it corresponded with a person's twenty-three pairs of chromosomes and provided particularly good luck on one's birthday. I had just turned twenty-three and was clicking and clacking through the bowels of "la Ville Lumiere" on its famous Metro subway. I felt great and was ready for another day in Paris—day three of four.

"You've been on this Metro route before?" Norm confirmed what I had mentioned yesterday.

"Yup, as an eleven-year-old kid. I'm not sure where we got on it, but Porte de Clignancourt was where we got off. Just beyond the Paris city limits."

"Stupid name; impossible to pronounce," Treb declared looking up from his Berlitz Language Guide. "Why didn't they just call it 'Port de Flea Market?' Nobody comes here for any other reason."

Norman looked at Treb and politely pronounced Clignancourt for him: "Clee-non-cor." That got a good-looking French woman to smile at Norm; she paid no attention to Treb. Zummmm . . . click, click, click. Zummmm, clack, clack, clack . . . The train moved on as Norman conversed with the mademoiselle.

After five stops, Porte de Clignancourt was next. This was one Metro stop I would not forget! It was the launching pad for Les Puces (the fleas)—the oldest and largest flea market in Paris dating back to 1888, a place that began as a junk collecting village filled with discarded and stolen merchandise from nineteenth-century Paris. Then, over eight decades, it grew into a complex bazaar that, in the words of my Uncle Don, "sold everything."

Norman ignored Treb and me, then continued his conversation with the mademoiselle. He had apologized to her four Metro-stops ago for Treb's bad manners. She looked at Treb and smiled.

"Looks like Norman has a new girlfriend," Treb said, not very quietly as the train jolted to a stop and we all stood up.

"Try not to be so ostentatious," I told him as we crowded off the the train. Once we climbed up the Metro's double-tiered stairway and into the misty daylight, Norm introduced us to Catherine. I guessed she was in her mid-forties like Norman. She was pleasant looking with her hair up in a bun that complimented her round face— smartly dressed in a beige pantsuit for a day in Les Puces.

The first thing I noticed was a weathered inscription on a building declaring it a Brasserie. A dozen tables and chairs lined the sidewalk in front of it—all the umbrellas were folded, and everything was wet. Catherine opened her umbrella to hold off the mist.

Steaming expresso vapors emanated from inside, where the customers stayed warm, except for one old Frenchman in a gray raincoat

293

who sat outside at one of the tables. He wore a black beret at an angle that hid his face. There was a different type of oldness here compared to central Paris or even Paris' medieval Left Bank, a more faded and worn working-class oldness.

It was an easy decision for us to go inside the Brasserie and order something to drink. Norman invited Catherine to join us and she seemed happy to do so.

"Napoleon drank here!" The old guy outside grumbled in French as we walked in, adjusting his beret to look at Catherine.

"Two café crème," Norman ordered. He was fond of the white coffee that was twenty percent cream and, apparently, Catherine wanted the same. I ordered a double espresso. Treb played with the idea of ordering a beer but he was on a tight budget. "Order one!" I said, giving him ten Francs.

We stood at the crowded bar infusing ourselves with caffeine, Treb getting his from aromatherapy. We discussed a plan for attacking the flea market. It was obvious Catherine would be with us and I was happy to see that Norm could be interested in something other than rocks and minerals—and correcting Treb.

It was a big place, not your average garage sale. We had to be attentive not to get distracted by local swap meets or sideshows. Treb and I followed Norm and Catherine, who had a map listing the various marches (markets). The list ran the gamut from those selling rare antiques and starving-artist paintings to everything army surplus, Renaissance clothing and weapons, assorted hardware specializing in unknown tools, antique toys, bottle caps, coins from Napoleon's era, Russian jewelry, war memorabilia, fishing lures, postage stamps, military metals, musical instruments, furniture, and knickknacks. Thousands of knickknacks—those things with no other name that you set around the house to look at. What I saw activated my memories from 1956.

The Rue des Rosiers was the main street running through Les Puces. I didn't remember its name from my visit as a kid but vividly recalled the bomb damage and bullet holes in the surrounding buildings. Back then, only eleven years after the war, you could go up to a brick building, reach into a bullet hole with a finger, and sometimes wiggle out a bullet. The Marshall Plan that America launched to repair Europe after World War II did not fix every bullet hole.

Paris proper had been largely spared during the war, but areas beyond the city limits were fair game for both the Allies and Germans — both had shot up and bombed the environs of Paris. What saved the city was its quick surrender to the Nazis — who had threatened to have French prisoners hacksaw down the Eiffel Tower. In fact, Hitler had given the order; fortunately, it was disobeyed.

By 1968, rubble from bombed-out buildings had been cleared and burning tires were gone. Smells were different too, it was not as musty or moldy or moth- infested as in 1956. Moth-eaten wool garments, like Nazi uniforms, had a sickening dead-insect odor not counteracted by naphthalene (moth balls) applied after the fact — these olfactory signatures, imprinted in my memory, were gone now with the uniforms of that brutal era. Not surprising; it was now twenty-three years after the war.

Also, there was a change in the authenticity of certain merchandise: When my uncle heard me blowing on a dented World War II bugle at a stand selling musical instruments, he'd bought it for me — captivated by my renditions of Reveille and Taps. Copycat versions of bugles and French horns were what I saw in 1968 — appearing authentic but unable to produce the deep-throated sound of the real thing.

Several stands selling second-hand Dinky cars and trucks were still around — back in 1956 they'd made the day for Ed and me. My uncle had told us to call them old toys when at the flea market — allowing him to negotiate a discount. Not possible anymore; they were now certified antiques!

After several hours of looking and shopping, we sat down at an empty table in no man's land and compared our purchases. Norm and I had bought several sheets of German stamps, most in mint condition. They were from 1942, some commemorated despicable successes of the Wehrmacht while others showed Hitler's profile in different colors. Catherine had found some unusual Russian costume jewelry, and Treb had purchased a Napoleon hat large enough to fit over his Pointer baseball cap—he was wearing both. It appeared we all felt that somewhat happy feeling you get when you buy things you don't really need but understand they prove you went some-where and did something.

We bought roasted chestnuts from a kiosk with propane heaters above its outside tables and sat down again. A man pushing a beer cart sold us four bottles of Heineken. The sun had made its debut for the day, and it was fun for the four of us to just talk. The propane heat felt good.

Treb wanted to talk about Napoleon. We had seen his tomb the day before at Les Invalides: a giant, maroon-colored marble sarcophagus containing six caskets displayed in a circular rotunda. Battle flags hung everywhere—a serious dedication. Presumably Napoleon's ashes were either in one casket or spread evenly in all six—there was debate about this.

"When was he in charge here?" Treb asked.

"He was Emperor of France for ten years, 1804-1814," Norm in-structed. I had to laugh when Treb refitted his hat(s).

"And then for another one hundred days in 1815," Catherine add-ed, "before he was forced to abdicate the throne. It's complicated. He promoted France's populous policies throughout Europe, like private property ownership, religious rights, equality before the law, secular education, and legal systems protecting taxation and public finance." Catherine was one smart lady when it came to all things French!

Her comments pushed Norm's enthusiasm button! "Most of Europe was against Napoleon! Finally, his Grande Armee lost the fight against seven countries, including Russia, at Waterloo and he was exiled. In France he's a hero; not so much in the rest of Europe where the elite edit history."

It was easy to see the synergy developing between Catherine and Norm. She was from Normandy and visiting Paris. Norm was happy Treb couldn't pronounce Clignancourt or they might not have met.

Treb took a drink of his Heineken, pulled down on his Napoleon hat snugging it tighter, then declared, "But before Waterloo Napoleon built the Arc de Triomphe on the Champs Elysees—under it is the tomb of the unknown soldier."

"Yes, Treb," I chimed in, "and he did it with just a touch of ego: The sun sets through it on his birthday!" I recalled a painting of Napoleon riding a white horse through the Arc de Triomphe at sunset on his birthday.

"Essentially, he dictated to the ruling blood of Europe what the U.S. Constitution did for all Americans," Norm added, "and, ultimately, got beaten down for it!"

"He's our hero!" Catherine said with a tear.

"Beethoven originally intended to dedicate a symphony to Napoleon, but then had second thoughts," I remarked, "largely because Napoleon had elected himself emperor."

"But he did change his mind and finally call his third symphony 'Sinfonia Eroica'— composed to celebrate the memory of a great man,'" Catherine explained.

"Napoleon did sell Tommy Jefferson a bunch of land for a good price," Treb interjected, impressing Norm.

"In the end it can be difficult to weigh good versus bad when judging a president or emperor. They all play the game of Risk! I guess I'll side with Beethoven on Napoleon… It's interesting to ponder where a real election would have taken France!" I added.

Norm made sure to inform Treb that our discussion pertained to Napoleon Bonaparte and not the two other Napoleons that followed him. Treb looked at Norm, confused, apparently unaware there had been three Napoleons.

The sunshine felt good, and the hot chestnuts went well with the cold Heineken.

The four of us took the Metro back into central Paris and found a small bistro in an alley off Place St. Michel that Catherine knew. Treb and I left Norm and Catherine to advance their synergy while we explored the depths of the Left Bank.

There was so much more to explore in Paris with only one day left. The influence of WW II that was strong in 1956 was largely gone in 1968. But Paris was still Paris, and it seemed to exist in a protected aura that insured its immortality. It made me recall a short story written by Ezra Pound: "There is Never Any End to Paris."

Paris, September 1980—twelve years later

I couldn't stop staring at the painting of the two men playing cards—an oil painting by Paul Cezanne from 1895—The Card Players. When it first impressed Ernest Hemingway, it hung in the palace in the Luxembourg Gardens, but now lived in the Musee d'Orsay with many other Impressionist masterpieces. Hemingway's challenge was to write what he called "true sentences"—sentences that had no ambiguity and described what a painting expressed visually. It was very difficult to do it in short declarative prose using ordinary words—which was his style. He concluded that he needed to keep words tight and integral, so they would read well out loud while creating a visual image, giving both "ear and eye" to his writing.

I kept looking at the two men playing cards, a masterpiece, worth millions. Two working-class Frenchmen sitting across from each other at a wooden table staring at their cards, one smoking a cigarette. There was no talking or gesturing going on between them, and they appeared to be alone in the back of some bistro or bar. There was a corked bottle of wine on the table, but they had no glasses and were not drinking.

Twelve years ago, I would have given it a quick glance and walked by—"two old guys playing cards" would have been the long and short of my assessment. Since that last visit in 1968, my attitude toward art had changed as had my desire to write about such things. Even a cursory study of the painting revealed how it was an amazing re-creation of the reality within the depth of an ordinary experience. The varied color and worn utility of the smoking man's jacket alone, presented a serious challenge for a writer to describe. As a scientist, I was accustomed to using tables of data and graphs when words failed. This was not an option when describing art.

To me, Impressionist art uniquely captured moments in time—moments that could be as still as a tray of apples or two men transfixed in a card game, or as dynamic as a dozen stampeding wild horses, or a harbor filled with sailing ships bouncing in the wind. I moved on and attempted to apply "Hemingway's challenge" to Monet's flowers and then other Impressionist paintings. I made notes, kicking myself for skipping so many 7:45 a.m. art history lectures during my undergraduate days, having been totally immersed in science then. Perspective takes time to evolve in some of us.

I was alone in Paris on this trip. The Danish food-ingredient company I worked for at the time produced and sold starter cultures (starter) and enzymes (Rennet) for making cheese. France was the world's cheese capital, so starter and enzymes were always in demand and continually being upgraded. I was the scientist in charge of the upgrading.

I was there to help supervise the expansion of a fermentation facility that produced Lactococcus bacteria for use in starter cultures. The facility was in Arpajon, thirty kilometers southwest of Paris. During the week, I stayed in an apartment onsite at the facility, then on weekends took the train into Paris. I got to know Paris well.

Paris belonged to the world, but it hated to speak anything but French. This forced me to remember those hours spent in "French Lab" years ago; they provided survival when off the beaten path. Whenever the indigenous French misunderstood me, I smiled at their indignation, pulled out my English-French pocket dictionary, and wrote them a note in French which included a smiling face. This usually neutralized concerns over my poor grammar and mispronunciations; like never knowing when to finish saying the word beurre . . . (butter).

Although I loved to revisit many sights like Montmartre, Jardin des Tuileries, Jardin du Luxembourg, and of course the Louvre and Orsay museums, and Notre Dame cathedral, but after plural weekend trips into the city, I began to avoid many of the monuments and tourist spots putting them on the "been there, done that" list. There was so much more of Paris to see and experience.

One sharp memory I often renewed on warm days was one of watching dozens of toy motorboats and sailboats on the circular and octagonal ponds in the beautiful Tuileries Gardens. The toy boats were steered remotely and mostly avoided collisions, lots of father and son teams operated them. It was done mainly for fun, but they did have competitions.

A most memorable toy-boating event happened on this trip. I was watching an eight-inch "finger monkey" steering a two-foot boat, intentionally grazing other boats, then turning just in time to avoid disaster... Everything was happening in miniature!

"He belongs to the lady over there," a sporty woman wearing a Galeries Lafayette sun hat said to me, pointing to a well-dressed woman wearing sunglasses, a Spanish poblano hat, and a white, long-sleeved dress. "This is Paris—expect the unexpected! She's signaling the monkey what to do."

"It's a pigmy marmoset!" I replied. "I've seen them in Kenya. One like that would sell for a thousand dollars in Nairobi, twice as much in Paris."

"She's got the money and then some; her family owns the Lotti Hotel! I'm Joyce Andersen, who are you?" She looked me up and down.

"Pleased to meet you, Joyce. I'm Stanley Randolf." I shook her hand. "How do you know all this?"

"She lives in the Lotti hotel—most of the top floor—and I work in the flower shop downstairs." The Lotti hotel was south of the Ritz near Place Vendome, two blocks north of the Tuileries.

"She's instructing the finger monkey to come toward her. They're very intelligent."

I was amazed. The monkey, about the size of a juvenile weasel, was standing straight up; it had settled down to steering the boat in a circle in the center of the pond. Cute for observers but a challenge for the sailboats that had to steer clear of him. They wouldn't challenge the Lotti lady's smart pet. When she turned her head and noticed Joyce talking with me, she repositioned her poblano to see us better.

Then she walked closer to the pond and gave the monkey a firm hand signal. The pigmy marmoset responded and steered the boat straight to her. When it reached the cement rim of the pond, she reached down with her hand and picked up the marmoset. Not something you'd find mentioned in Frommer's guide to Paris!

The monkey curled its tail around her hand as she lifted him up. He was wearing a green ribbon with a nametag. When she started walking toward us, a park employee picked up the boat and put it in a wooden box marked Lotti Hotel. A public service?

It was one of those curious moments that seem to find me. When she got to us, I automatically reached out to pet the male marmoset. He grabbed my little finger but also held tight to her, then he bent his head back, looking at her, making sure she could see him holding my finger.

I recalled a pet finger monkey in Arusha, Tanzania doing something similar, it was trying to grab the pen I was using to sign a hotel register. Finally, the desk clerk had to give me a different pen. "We have orders to keep the owner's pet happy," the clerk clarified. Strangely, I had completely forgotten that encounter—the mind has a way of holding certain memories in reserve until needed.

"His name is Joey—Captain Joey," the lady said. "He approves of you!" She looked at Joyce and nodded as Joey released my finger. "Have a fine day in Paree!" She said to us, then walked out of the gardens and onto the Rue de Rivoli.

"I have to get back to the flower shop," Joyce said. "Stop in and visit sometime."

"I'll do that," I said.

I headed through the Tuileries in the direction of the Louvre museum, passing men playing chess—a game I cherish—at public tables. I stopped and watched along with other onlookers. Two of the men reminded me of Cezanne's card players! The one smoking waited patiently for the other man to make his move. Time didn't seem to matter. They formed a perfect still-life pose for the right artist, I thought.

I walked on. Spring was well underway in the Tuileries, city gardeners were busy pruning some two thousand trees, including the stunning purple Judas. A man had his SLR camera on a tripod focused on rows of white tulips where each petal had a thin, 360-degree, crimson-red edge, producing an eloquent visual effect. There were some red-petaled tulips too, on separate plants. I could envision a plant geneticist dabbing pollen from a red flower's stamen onto a white flower's stigma—assisting flower sex—plant after plant until, after thousands of attempts, a tulip plant that only produced white flowers with thin red-edges emerged. How many people passing by think about this? I wondered.

I walked the Right Bank of the Seine to Notre-Dame Cathedral on the island called Isle de la Cite'. I had been to it several times before; the magnificent French-Gothic church had a magnetic pull on me. It took 182 years to build it from groundbreaking in 1163 to completion in 1345. Facing it, two mighty 226-foot high, square, parallel towers dominated the view. There are 387 steps in the spiral staircase that goes to the top of the south tower, but the best view of Paris is from the Grand Gallery balcony between the towers, only 240 steps. The trek begins through a doorway around the corner and to the left of the cathedral's main entrance. When you stand in the center of the Grand Gallery balcony looking out from left to right, you'll easily recognize the Montparnasse Tower, the Eiffel Tower, Hotel Invalides, Arc de Triumph, Louvre Museum, and Sacre'-Coeur. Like many times in the past, I stood out there again. Several people from a student tour group were feeding popcorn to pigeons; there were no earthworms this high.

"Remember that ugly elf, the one Hans Solo blasted in that bar in Star Wars?" A guy in a M.I.T. jacket asked another guy wearing a Princeton Athletics sweatshirt. I assumed they both were part of the student tour.

"That was in the Mos Eisley Cantina on the planet Tatooine, his name was Greedo." The Princeton student responded. He must have known George Lucas personally.

"Yeah, that guy! Looks like his kin are here," the M.I.T. student replied.

"They do resemble Greedo, don't they? Look at those eerie eyes and pointed ears!" A female student chimed in. "Those reptoid-looking, hunchback sculptures are scary."

"They're called gargoyles," I interjected. Couldn't help myself, had to butt in.

"They're medieval rain gutters!" Sandra Johnson spoke up. She had a name tag on her jacket and appeared to be in charge of the students. "They keep rainwater from dripping down and staining the cathedral's marble walls."

"They are that," I agreed. "But don't discount Victor Hugo's descriptions of them. He claimed they were put here to scare away evil demons by resembling monsters that lurked in the underworld."

"Yeah, I agree with that," the M.I.T. student blurted. "Didn't Shakespeare say: 'There are no demons in hell, they're all here?'"

"Something like that," Ms. Johnson answered, looking a bit fatigued.

The gargoyles extended beyond the ones we could see on the balcony. These creatures were carved into more of the cathedral's facades: between flying buttresses, around pinnacles, and in crypts. Some are said to be hidden in secret places. Those that don't serve as rain gutters are called chimeras—they're equally ugly.

"They look like mutant hyenas with broken backs that survived a miscarriage," another student contributed, catalyzing laughter from the group while accidentally spilling his popcorn. This seriously activated the pigeons.

"No, it's not funny, they look like Chupacabras!" A young Hispanic woman named Maria claimed. "Those dwarf aliens that run around the jungle in Puerto Rico and Mexico. The CIA has incontrovertible evidence they exist!"

"I've been to Puerto Rico, and you're right; small 'ETs' in the bush are taken seriously." I spared them any deeper analysis of Extraterrestrials, for now, at least.

The conversation continued until all the students had their say. It was interesting for sure. Sandra invited me to join them for dinner later and continue the discussion. I was happy to accept the invitation. "Expect the unexpected," I mumbled to myself. It's Paris!

Before leaving Notre-Dame I went downstairs in the cathedral to look, as I have before, at the incredible north-facing Rose Window—a giant stained-glass circle concentric with two inner circles composed of multicolored designs that turn sunshine a deep blue-violet. A stunning masterpiece where color, symmetry, and harmony meet.

Paris, December 1992—12-years later

I had just come out of a good, warm restaurant called Bistrot des Campagnes on 6 Rue Leopold Robert—a short walk from the cold and windy Boulevard Montparnasse. It was a small restaurant, one of fifteen-thousand in Paris, with the distinction of being unknown to most tourists. The poached Chilean sea bass had melted in my mouth. It came with two different species of white beans sautéed with long-grain rice in a mushroom sauce—a secret sauce. But the real secret was to wash it down with a full-bodied Montrachet white from the Montrachet vineyard in Burgundy. I'm no wine connoisseur, but I learned the magic of what a good Montrachet can do to perfectly punctuate a meal. My cousin Ed Fallin taught me this at elk-hunting camp in Colorado!

I had been working hard on a formal presentation I would give at the Pasteur Institute the following day. It focused on using Lactobacillus probiotics to improve intestinal health—a natural concept that was beginning to grow in acceptance. The challenge was to teach the many benefits of consuming live, friendly bacteria (like Lactobacillus acidophilus) to doctors, then to the public. The ultimate mission was to get a person's intestinal tract dominated by beneficial microbes and allow them to competitively exclude pathogenic germs like E. coli. Accomplishing that required consuming billions of probiotic bacteria daily!

Pasteur's close associate, Eli Metchnikoff, honored by a building named for him at the Pasteur Institute, is regarded as the grandfather of modern probiotic theory; he connected the consumption of yogurt (a type of probiotic) to longevity in eastern Europe in the early 1900s.

Hundreds of doctors from around the world would be listening to my presentation. I had the rest of the day to practice and refine it. The Pasteur Institute (Institut Pasteur) was known and respected world-wide as a major center for microbiological research—I was honored to have the chance to review the status and future potential for probiotics.

After the superb lunch, my strategy was to walk Montparnasse Boulevard to Rue de Vaugirard and then head south to Rue de Doctor and the Pasteur Institute. I wanted to see Louis Pasteur's laboratory where germs were discovered, now a museum. Then look around the famous institute to make sure I knew where to be at 8:00 a.m. the next morning. I was excited!

Pasteur's laboratory was perfectly preserved, seemingly ready for the Father of Bacteriology to arrive at any time and start transferring bacterial cultures from one flask to another, flaming the necks with a Bunsen burner, then plugging them with sterile cotton, then into an incubator—a proven technique for growing pure cultures of bacteria that hadn't changed in 150 years.

Above me on the roof was where Pasteur had proved that air always contained bacteria, which could infect a flask of sterile broth if the cotton plug was pulled out, even momentarily. His simple experiment confirmed the ubiquity of bacteria in the environment and that "spontaneous generation" (infection without a source microbe), a commonly believed theory, was wrong.

I left the institute primed, needing to find some of that special ambiance Paris provides where I could study my notes and 35mm slides in preparation for the next day. I hailed a taxi and took it to "A Good Café on the Place St.-Michel."

The café was a favorite place for journalists and writers to hang out between the two World Wars and before. Especially Gertrude Stein's crew: The likes of Ford Madox Ford, James Joyce, Henry James, John Quinn, and, of course, Ernest Hemingway. When they couldn't get an issue resolved there, they would retreat to Sylvia Beach's bookshop, Shakespeare and Company, and argue things out. If they failed to resolve an issue, such as the importance of not being inaccrochable in a story or who best used word rhythm and repetition, they would default to a discussion of who was the smartest writer—which never got resolved. Whoever had the best control of his ego had the trump card in any argument, according to Sylvia.

It was warm and bright in the large café. I sat down at a small round table and zipped open my leather case. The espresso machines were going strong and the coffee vapors they produced smelled good, but so did the rum and whiskey drinks. I could visualize Hemingway in his young argumentative days, sitting at such a table with his small notebooks and pencil stubs trying to write "true sentences." In his honor I ordered a rum St. James, specifying Martinique rum.

The tall waiter smiled when he brought it. I had diverted to work mode and was holding up and looking through 35mm slides of fermentation tanks, feeling good about what they showed. Hemingway was right: sweet rum warmed the soul better than coffee on a cold December day.

Postscript:

I have travelled to Paris sixteen different times. This story recounts aspects of four of those trips and probably not those that most tour guides would cite as typical. So, for those of you who have been to la Ville Lumiere, these remembrances will hopefully add some desire to return. And, for those who have never been there, to go now with expanded expectations. Vive le gai Paree!

Questions for Group Discussions

1. Which story was your favorite story in this book and why?

2. What did you find the most thought-provoking of the discussions within the stories?

3. Which adventure would you like to have had with Stanley and why?

4. Where do you picture yourself in the action most? How does it make you feel to be in the middle of that particular adventure?

5. If you had a free ticket to anywhere in the world, where would you go and what would you do?

6. What kinds of issues or perspectives on life came up for you in any one story in this book?

7. What is your personal perspective on the issue you chose?

8. How would you change any of the problems you read about?